EMPRESS EUGENIE
IN EXILE

TO

MY CHILDREN

THE

EMPRESS EUGENIE

IN EXILE

BY

AGNES CAREY

First Published in 1922
by Eveleigh Nash & Grayson Limited,
London

Republished in 2001 by Saint Michael's Abbey Press,
Saint Michael's Abbey, Farnborough,
Hampshire, GU14 7NQ

Second Edition: ISBN 0-907707-35-8

THE FARNBOROUGH ABBEY LOCAL HISTORY SERIES
is a project of the Benedictine monks of Saint Michael's
Abbey ensuring that books and pamphlets concerning
the history of Farnborough and its surroundings remain in
print, and that new titles relating to the area should be
encouraged, printed and published.

These editions are printed and hand-bound at the Abbey.

LIST OF ILLUSTRATIONS

PREFACE

During the ten months in 1886 that it was my good fortune to spend at Farnborough in the household of the Empress Eugénie (good fortune which I owe to an old family friend, who was intimate with the Empress), I kept up my life-long habit, when absent from home, of daily correspondence with my family. Hence these pages, culled from letters and diaries.

However disconnected and fragmentary the following account of the Empress may be, it has one merit, – truth to the fact. Anecdotes and an account of events were hastily scribbled at the close of each busy day. Realizing the value of spontaneity, I have purposely kept as much as possible to the wording of these notes, – written while the actual words the Empress spoke, and her impressive face and gestures, were fresh in my mind. Other incidents, since learned, might have inspired better stories, but would not be the words that came from her *own* lips. So I have preferred to give only what I positively *know* she said, merely adding a few words here and there for the sake of clarity.

Richard Watson Gilder was anxious to have me publish parts of this book many years ago, but during the life of the Empress I felt it would be an unpardonable breach of confidence, so I refused. Now that the end of her ninety-four eventful years has come, the "Empress in Exile" belongs to *history*.

AGNES CAREY.

CONTENTS

PART I

Farnborough Hill, an Empress's Home

PART I

"Meet the Empress at Wilton Crescent
tomorrow Wednesday at four.   ARCOS."

This telegram from Mme. De Arcos, an old friend of my aunt's, was the prelude to one of the most interesting periods of my life. Needless to say the message was speedily obeyed, and a few hours after its receipt, I was already whirling away in an express train toward London. It was the following afternoon, February 10, 1886, that I started for Mme. De Arcos's house in Belgravia, where after waiting for a few moments in the drawing-room with Mrs. Edmund Vaughan I was taken upstairs by her and her sister to see the Empress, who had come to London expressly for this interview.

Mme. De Arcos had already told me that I should find Her Imperial Majesty most gracious and I need not be in the least

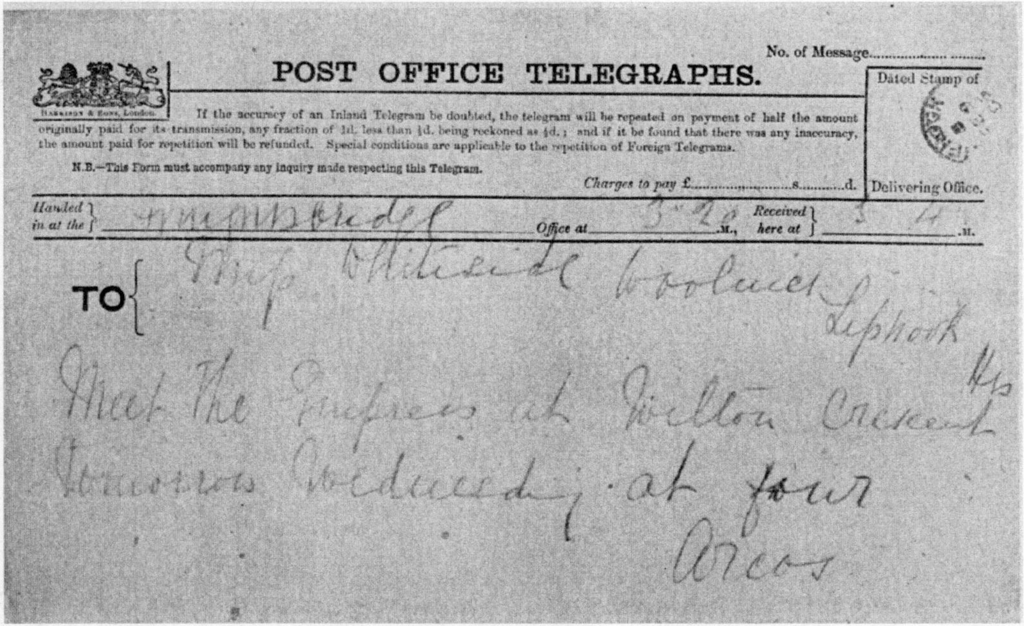

No. of Message..........................

POST OFFICE TELEGRAPHS.

Dated Stamp of

Delivering Office.

If the accuracy of an Inland Telegram be doubted, the telegram will be repeated on payment of half the amount originally paid for its transmission, any fraction of 1d. less than ½d. being reckoned as ½d.; and if it be found that there was any inaccuracy, the amount paid for repetition will be refunded. Special conditions are applicable to the repetition of Foreign Telegrams.

N.B.—This Form must accompany any inquiry made respecting this Telegram.

Charges to pay £..................s..........d.

Handed in at the Office at ....M., Received here at ....M.

TO Miss Whiteside Woolmer Liphook

Meet the Empress at Wilton Crescent tomorrow Wednesday at four

Arcos

"This telegram was a prelude to some of the most pleasant and interesting months of my life."

intimidated by her, but in spite of this reassuring assertion, my heartbeats quickened a little, just as I entered her presence and made my first low court courtesy. The Empress half rose from her seat, at the same time motioning me to a chair, and in the conversation which ensued praised my French unstintingly, put me so completely at my ease, and interested me so much as she sat there in her widow's weeds, in the dim light of a foggy winter's afternoon, – once the most beautiful woman of Europe, – that I quite forgot to lose my self-possession.

In less than half an hour I had made another deep courtesy and had taken leave of the Empress under Mme. de Arcos's wing, was complimented by her downstairs on my *tenue*, and had a few friendly hints given to me on court ways and the little difficulties I should be ready to encounter. Shortly after five o'clock, I was back again with my family, and able to give them the good news, – that the Empress had received me most kindly, that all was satisfactorily settled, and the details of my future life at Farnborough arranged; even to the hour of the train which was to carry me thither on the fifteenth.

From my diary:

It was quite dark when I reached Farnborough station about 6 p.m. on the appointed day, and I was glad to find a carriage waiting for me. On the platform stood a smart but most good-natured French footman, with a cockade on his hat and, five minutes later, I had driven through the lodge gates and had arrived at Farnborough Hill, where, through many circuitous passages, I was passed along by various pleasant men-servants, and finally shown up to my room.

While I was waiting there, not knowing what to do next, there was a knock at my door and a maid came to offer her services, which I declined. Then Mme. Le Breton walked in, accompanied by the Empress's two Spanish nieces, Maria and Antonia de Vejerano, whom she introduced as well as herself, and welcomed me most warmly to my new home, while apologizing for not having been at the entrance when I arrived. The coachman had brought me to a side entrance instead of the principal one, where Mme. Le Breton and the girls had long been vainly waiting for the carriage to drive up. At last they discovered the error, found that I was already in the house, and came up to me at once. Mme. Le Breton then rang for some tea, which was brought up on a dainty little silver tray. We talked a good deal about Chislehurst, and Mme. Le Breton was very much astonished when I told her that I knew her and the other inmates of the imperial household perfectly by sight, having constantly seen them all there on Sundays in the little Church of St. Mary's during 1879 and 1880. The nieces were rather shy and quiet, but very courteous and affectionate, and they appeared to my English eyes absolutely grown up, though only about sixteen and eighteen years old.

At seven-thirty my visitors left me to unpack the necessaries and dress hastily for dinner, M. and A. promising to return and fetch me, which they did at a few minutes to eight. They led me first through intricate passages, and then down a handsomely carved staircase into a splendid gallery, beautifully furnished, and filled with *objets d'art* and jardinieres of sweet-smelling flowers. Mme. Le Breton, carefully *gantée*, was already waiting there with M. le Duc de Bassano and M. Pietri, both of whom she introduced to me. Almost immediately afterward the Empress made her appearance, we ladies courtesying and the gentlemen bowing low.

Her Imperial Majesty welcomed me most kindly, hoped I had had a most pleasant journey and had left my grandmother well; and then, after a ceremonious bow from the *maître d'hôtel*, who announced, "Le diner de sa Majesté est servi," the Duc de Bassano offered the Empress his arm, M. Pietri took in Mme. Le Breton, and we three girls followed, passing into the dining-room at the end of the gallery.

It seemed strange to realize, a moment later, that I was

4

comfortably seated at the Empress's table, and stranger still, that I did not feel a little out of it, as I probably should have done anywhere else on a first evening, but I suppose the charm and perfect good-breeding of the Empress account for my ease in these new surroundings. H. I. M. was very much struck, when Mme. Le Breton told her about my *séjour* first at Chislehurst, and then in the house the imperial party had just vacated in London.

"Vous voyez, Mademoiselle," she said, "le sort voulait absolument que nous nous connussions [You see, Mademoiselle, Fate was determined we should meet]!"

She asked me many questions about Chislehurst, – one of them when it was I first went there to live. I tried, but vainly, to avoid answering, as it was the sad year (1879) of the Prince Imperial's death, and I saw tears gather in her eyes immediately I was forced into mentioning it.

After dinner, the two girls and I walked up and down the gallery for about half an hour with the Empress, who told us all sorts of interesting things about her past life. Then we went into the drawing-room and I was asked to play the piano; my pieces were apparently much liked and the Empress seemed pleased and anxious for more. After a little while, thinking I might perhaps be giving them a dose, I left off, but the Empress said with so much insistence, "Encore un petit morceau, Mademoiselle, si vous n'êtes pas fatiguée; vous nous faites tant de plaisir [Another piece please, Mademoiselle, if you are not too tired; you give us so much pleasure]," that I acceded to her wish. At ten o'clock the gentlemen came in from the billiard-room, and then, on a sign from the Empress, M. and A. got up, and kissed their aunt's hand (a custom in Spain). We three then shook hands with Mme. Le Breton and the gentlemen, courtesied to the Empress and retired.

Here follows the usual order of the day: At eight o'clock M., A. and I breakfasted in the dining-room at a little table laid for us in the bay-window. From eight-thirty to twelve we devoted ourselves to English and music. Then usually a tap at our door and a little visit from the Empress, with whom we nearly always went for our morning walk. At one o'clock luncheon all together; then another walk or drive – after which, at four-forty-five, rosary for the whole household in the chapel, the Empress herself saying all the prayers, both before and after. At five o'clock, afternoon tea all together in the *salon du matin* and after a more or less prolonged general conversation, the girls studied again till dressing-time at seven-thirty. At eight o'clock, dinner, after which our usual little walk up and down the gallery with the Empress, followed by needlework and conversation in the drawing-room, and bed at ten;– to begin again the same next day, till visitors or some unusual event occasioned some slight change of programme.

Farnborough Hill is a beautiful dwelling, much finer than Camden Place, the Empress's Chislehurst home for a good many years. Had it been possible for her to remain at Camden Place, she would never have made the move into Hampshire. Mr. Stroud, owner of Camden Place, would willingly have sold her his property, but the Empress could not succeed in getting possession of the adjoining land necessary for building the mausoleum for her husband and son which she had set her heart on. In telling us about her efforts, she spoke with much sadness and not a little bitterness: explaining how hard it had been for her to beg permission to buy a little land wherein to bury her husband and son, and to be refused it by a man who owned such broad acres as did Mr. E., a rich German toy-manufacturer, who seemed disinclined to sell an inch of land to the French Empress.

My letters, written at the time, give a most minute description of Farnborough Hill, and in the following pages I give some of the more important details, nearly always using the original words.

From a letter:

Farnborough Hill,
February 28, 1886.

The accompanying plan gives a little idea of how the reception rooms all open out on to the first central gallery, or hall, which is about 120 feet long by 20 feet broad, and filled with most artistic and lovely things. Grouped about the entrance to the *grand salon* are two lovely Louis XVI armchairs, some smaller chairs of the same period, two sofas, footstools to match, and four beautiful cabinets with splendid Sèvres plaques let in. These cabinets, even years ago, were each valued at 100,000 francs, according to Mme. Le Breton. They belonged formerly to Napoleon III's mother, Queen Hortense, daughter of Josephine Beauharnais (by a marriage previous to that with Napoleon Bonaparte) later the beautiful Creole Empress. At the lower extremity of the gallery are the Empress Eugénie's own private sitting-room and another called the "Prince Imperial's room"; beyond which, following along to the left, is a sweet little boudoir called *petit salon de l'Impératrice*; then come, beyond, the handsome old carved staircase, *le salon des dames* used as a study, and the large *salon du matin*. Further on, three enormous oriel windows, in front of which are tiled jardinieres, whose fragrant flowers perfume all the gallery, and so on to the dining-room door which ends the gallery. On the wall opposite each oriel window hang magnificent *Gobelins*,

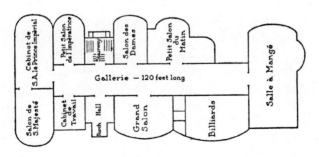

three of a series of six, which is completed in the dining-room. They represent different episodes in the life of the illustrious *Don Quixote*, and are always much admired by connoisseurs.

Next in sequence, on our return down the gallery, comes the billiard-room; then the *grand salon* and the entrance to the handsome vestibule, and back again to the Empress's apartments, whence we started on our travels.

From a letter:

Farnborough Hill,
February 28, 1886.

Scattered about among the Queen Hortense cabinets and other historic furniture, are palm trees, and a few good pieces of modern statuary by the best sculptors of the day, including a great number of busts. Napoleon I's immediate family has certainly not been neglected. They are all there: Charles Bonaparte, his father; Letitia, his mother, styled *Madame Mère*; his brothers – Joseph, King of Spain, Jerome, King of Westphalia, and Louis, father of Napoleon III, King of Holland; Caroline, who married Joachim Murat, King of Naples; and finally, Eliza and Lucien, these two being the only ones of the family who never wore a crown. Then, too, there is a bust of the great man himself, and many of Napoleon III; Queen Hortense; Princess Mathilde; and Prince Napoleon-Louis, brother of Louis Napoleon.

The walls of the gallery can boast some very fine paintings; a large, life-size portrait of the Empress and baby prince, by Winterhalter; a sweet one of the Duchess de Mouchy, the Princess Anna Murat, Her Imperial Majesty's niece; and the Duchesse d'Albe, the Empress's own sister, also by Winterhalter; also a wonderful *Sunset* on the steppes of Russia by Aivasovski; *An Eastern Woman*; a Madonna with the Infant Jesus and St. John by W. Bouguereau, and others more or less important.

In the outer vestibule, which opens into the gallery opposite the old staircase, are also some fine canvases, and one in particular, *The Empress and her Ladies*, painted by Winterhalter in 1855. It is a large picture about 10 by 18 feet, I should say, containing a life-size portrait of Eugénie seated in the midst of her ladies-in-waiting. When she showed me this picture one day, she gazed at it in a wistful way, while naming the different ladies and expatiating on the beauty of nearly all of them. She specially pointed out the Princesse d'Essling, her *grand maitresse* (Mistress of the Robes); the Duchesse de Bassano, her *dame d'honneur*; the Comtesse de Montebello; the Vicomtesse Aguado; the Marquise de Latour-Maubourg, and made interesting remarks about all of them. On either side of the handsomely carved fireplace hang life-size portraits of Prince Eugène de Beauharnais (adopted son of Napoleon I) and his sister Princesse de Beauharnais (Princesse en Bavière) both by Reisner. In front of these stands a bath chair, ornamented with gilding and pastel medallions, given by Queen Victoria to the Empress, when she, with the Emperor, came over to England as her guest to visit the first International Exhibition (1851).

Leaving the lower gallery and ascending the grand staircase, which halfway up branches off to right and left, we come upon a very striking portrait of Napoleon I during the Italian campaign. He is mounted on a white charger, full of life, clambering up a steep snow-covered ascent in the Alps. This is by David, and has been reproduced under the title of *Napoleon the Great Crossing Mount St. Bernard, May, 1800*. An enormous picture by Gérard, *Queen Hortense and her Two Boys*, and *Troops at Sunrise* by Protais, are other paintings on the staircase. By the time we have passed a few other smaller pictures on the way up, we find ourselves in a gallery the counterpart of the one below. In this upper gallery, besides more statues and paintings, there are several glass show cases filled with all sorts of interesting autograph letters, etc.

From a letter;

Farnborough Hill,
February 20, 1886.

After luncheon one Sunday, on returning from a little walk in the park with the Empress, she kindly showed me over the reception rooms, telling me the history of the beautiful things in the *vitrines*, and pointing out the best paintings, etc. I certainly could not have had a more interesting cicerone. First we went into the *grand salon*, which is a large room about 30 feet square with a deep bay-window, and the ceiling like the dining-room, painted to imitate sky and clouds; there is also a simulated balcony covered with creeping roses, the perspective of which is so good, that you think you need only climb upon it, to find yourself in the open air. Some of the furniture is modern, but most of it old – Louis XVI *meuble* – saved from the burning of the Tuileries, and covered with handsome *Gobelins*. In one corner of the room is the piano, in another the sofa, in front of which is the large oval table, around which we play cards or work of an evening. Here is where the Empress usually sits – bolt upright, but gracefully nevertheless and without stiffness, very rarely if ever leaning back. She has an inveterate hatred of modern sprawling.

On each side of the *grand salon* door are glass cabinets which contain interesting historical and other souvenirs, endless miniatures of the Empress Josephine, and a gold snuffbox, with a miniature of Napoleon I and his little son, *le Roi de Rome*. The Empress told me that Napoleon had this in his hand when he breathed his last at St. Helena. There is also a feather fan, brilliant with iridescent beetle-wings, the gold handle of which is set with large oriental pearls, given by the ladies of Algiers to the Empress during an official journey in 1860. In connection with it, she told me amusingly of her misery at a wedding in Algiers, in having constantly to swallow the jams and preserves made of violets and roses, which were presented at every minute. She remembered vividly also the

11

penetrating smell of attar-of-roses which permeated even the food and nauseated her. A beautiful gold tea service brought back for her from India by the Prince of Wales after his official trip in 1875; a shapely little marble hand (that of Princess Maud of Wales) and some splendid jewels, given the Empress by the different cities of France, when during her husband's absence in the Crimean and other wars, she was three different times (1859; 1865; 1870) proclaimed *Régente*. A sweet little Union Jack, too, in diamonds, rubies and sapphires, given by Queen Victoria, after the signing of some treaty between England and France, and numberless other fascinating things.

In this room are some of the best and most important pictures of the house, nearly all life-size and full length, by Gérard or David, which is praise enough. Eliza and her daughter by David; the Empress Jospehine; Louis, King of Holland, and his wife Hortense in their royal robes and insignia, all by Gérard. There are also two pastels, Princess Mathilde, the sister, and Princess Clotilde, the wife of Prince Napoleon (Plon-Plon), and two beautiful pictures, at least I call them that, a St. John and a copy of Raphael's *Vierge à la Chaise*, which are so marvelously executed that I had to be twice assured by the Empress before I could believe they really were mosaics. They had been sent for some far-away birthday, to the little Prince Imperial by Pope Pius IX, who was his godfather.

In the *petit salon de l'Impératrice* there is no modern furniture, all is Louis XVI, and the pictures themselves are mostly of that epoch. A painting of Marie Antoinette by the celebrated Mme. Vigée-Lebrun, who mentions the sittings for that very portrait in her *Memoirs*, which I have just been reading; several Wouvermans; two delightful heads by Greuze; a very sad looking head of poor little Louis XVII painted about the time of the Revolution, and several by Alexandre Couder and others.

12

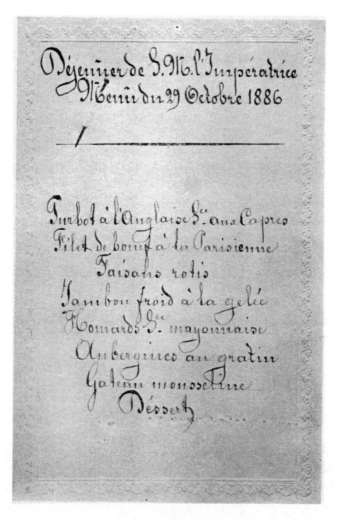

Déjeuner de S.M. l'Impératrice
Menu du 29 Octobre 1886

Turbot à l'Anglaise S^{ce} aux Câpres
Filet de boeuf à la Parisienne
Faisans rôtis
Jambon froid à la gelée
Homards S^{ce} mayonnaise
Aubergines au gratin
Gâteau mousseline
Dessert

A typical menu at Farnborough Hill

In a glass case lies the pocket-knife and a few relics of Louis XVI. The Empress told me she had formerly possessed quantities of other things belonging to him, but they were all burnt at the Tuileries during the Commune. In another carefully locked case, there are more miniatures of the different Napoleons, and one representing the Duc de Bassano's father, the first duke of that name and minister under Napoleon I; a simple but very lovely diamond and sapphire ring, Empress Josephine's engagement ring; the Empress Eugénie's own marriage prayer book of repoussé silver incrusted with diamonds; the Prince Imperial's *nœud de première communion* (a large white ribbon badge he wore French fashion around his arm First Communion day); magnificently jeweled *porte-bouquets* presented by different towns during her journey in Algeria; and so many other beautiful and interesting things that it is impossible to innumerate them all today.

From the *petit salon de l'Impératrice* I was taken one day by the Empress into the so-called *cabinet du Prince*. This was a great exception in my favour. It is a large room in which the Prince's things are arranged exactly as they were in the one he was occupying at Camden Place, Chislehurst, before leaving for Natal,– his writing materials and still unopened letters lying on the desk! She told me, poor Empress,– crying bitterly all the time,– that though she did not really expect such a terrible blow, she never could shake off a strong presentiment of danger, and as soon as ever her son had started for Zululand (having wrung an unwilling consent from her), she had all his belongings covered up carefully, the place of each marked with a piece of chalk, and the room locked, that nothing might be touched. She said that the night before she learned the news of his death, she wakened up suddenly, hearing her son's voice distinctly calling her. Of course, her extreme anxiety might easily account for this, but she herself quite believed it was no hallucination, but his real cry of distress,– Mère! Mère – which reached her; telepathy in fact.

The Empress showed me an album given her since that sad event by Queen Victoria. It contains sketches of the events of the Prince Imperial's entire English career, at Chislehurst and Woolwich, and during the fatal campaign in Natal. In this album is a water colour representing the *Last Bivouac*; the Prince is depicted sitting on a little mound making a sketch, while the savages crept up stealthily behind him. The Empress afterward showed me the Prince's own sketch. In looking through the Prince's private photograph-album with his mother that day, among those of his relations and college friends I came across the picture of E. S., one of three very beautiful sisters, cousins of mine, who lived at Chislehurst during the Prince's youthful years there. I had heard he was in love with E. S. and was told by Mme. Le Breton that he was often seen, when passing in and out of church, looking at her with admiring eyes. He gave her his photograph one evening, on returning from the opera while traveling down from London in the train. This was just before leaving for South Africa.

Nearly all round this *cabinet du Prince* are bookcases, containing his favourite books. On the mantelpiece stands an old clock formerly in Napoleon I's room at Longwood House, St. Helena; there is also a bronze bust of Napoleon III, and one of Abbé Duguerry, one time the Prince's tutor, shot during the Commune. Near one of the windows is a beautifully carved silver *bassinette*, swinging between two solid imperial eagles, and decorated with the Prince's arms and those of the *ville de Paris*, a gift from the city at the time of his birth.

There are several veiled pictures in this same room, representing the tragic moment of the Prince's death, pierced with Zulu assagais. These the Empress passed rapidly by. Here also are two glass cases, containing all the little personal treasures and souvenirs of his father and of his childhood; his first little uniform; presents given him by sovereigns, among others a beautiful little diamond-sheathed scimitar, from the Sultan of Turkey; all of the personal effects he had with him at the *Cape* – his sketch-books, plans, maps, check books, and note-books, and also the sword (originally his father's) with which he so bravely defended himself on that fateful day against the Zulus, until overpowered by numbers.

In the centre of one of these cases is a small ebony compartment. It contains the shirt stained with his blood and torn with assegais, together with the medal and gold chain his grandmother, Countess Montijo, put around his neck at his birth. This he retained to the last, the Zulus being afraid, when stripping him of everything else, to touch it, thinking it was a charm. Over this sad little sanctum is written in large letters: "Que votre volonté soit faite [Thy will be done]," and in front of it on a slab is a little white marble cross, on which Princess Beatrice has painted very prettily the word "*Fiat*" surrounded by violets.

The Empress, naturally, did not open this compartment for me, but silently passed it by with a lingering look of infinite sadness and a sigh. Her nieces tell me she has never yet had the courage to look on these sad relics, and Uhlmann, the Prince's faithful body-servant, keeps the key. Most of the above named things of the Prince's were obtained from the Zulu king, Cetewayo, by Queen Victoria, through the instrumentality of Sir Redyers Buller, or Sir Bartle Frere, the Empress said. Only one thing was never recovered; it was destroyed through the ignorant superstition of the Zulus – and that was the Prince's watch. An old warrior who was questioned concerning it by Dr. Scott, when accompanying the Empress on her journey to Zululand in 1880, said very innocently: "The little beast, you mean? – Oh, we were afraid of it, so we killed it." Having no notion about the nature of mechanism, they thought the ticking of the watch indicated a live creature, and so they stamped it out of existence.

From a letter:

The Empress next took me into the dining-room, through looking-glass doors with gilt framework, saved from the Tuileries, and which make the already long gallery look interminable. It is a very handsomely proportioned room, about 45 feet long, the ceiling like that of the *grand salon* imitating clouds and sky, and the walls covered with priceless *Gobelins* framed with carved oak. There are two huge bay-windows, in one of which as I have already told you, our little breakfast table is placed. The parquet floor is highly polished and in the centre, on a thick *Turkey* carpet, is the dining table. Though really large, it looks almost lost in that immense room.

Over the large marble fireplace, in which a glorious wood fire now nearly always sparkles and crackles, is a bust of the Empress Marie Louise; and on each side of the very valuable Louis XVI *dressoir* stand two large gilt candelabra, each about seven or eight feet high, supported by Sèvres figures. There, too, on one side, is a beautiful marble statue, *L'Innocence*, and on a console a clock from Toledo, given the Empress by King Alfonso and Queen Christina of Spain, the case of which is most elaborately worked in steel and gold, a curious but rich effect.

Now for the dining table itself. In the centre is a silver basket, well filled with growing ferns; salt-cellars and finger-bowls are placed around the table for everybody; and each person, too, has a toothpick,– to be used or not, according to indication. I do not patronize mine, but I am the exception – the other diners use them conscientiously, I assure you! I shall be perhaps less horrified by the thought, as time goes on.

The chef sends up good and varied dinners, but never too long. The carving is done at a side table, and the food handed around in silver dishes by the *maître d'hôtel*, old Schmidt. The plates, with the exception of a few Sèvres china ones used for dessert, are all plain silver, and have a large "N" and imperial crown engraved on the edge. This simple service, so-called, now in everyday use, belonged formerly to the Emperor's campaigning kit. The regular table silver used at the Tuileries was stolen, so the Empress told us, before the burning of the palace. At Farnborough for grand occasions, when, for instance the Queen dines here, there appears a lovely and very complete vermeille service, which once belonged to Queen Hortense, the Emperor's mother. I, for my part, do not enjoy using it, for unaccustomed as I am to eating off such precious metal, I never can quite get over the impression that it is brass my food is resting on instead of silver gilt.

All the men-servants except an English under-butler, have been soldiers in the French army and are *anciens serviteurs des Tuileries*. They look very trim standing behind the chairs,- soldierly, but less stiff and more human than the English flunky, and they serve so well! Every want is instantly noticed if not anticipated. Poor old Schmidt makes us all laugh sometimes, for as he hands around each dish his duty is to name it, and being very deaf and unable to control his voice very well, he often screams it out rather louder than necessary, to the surprise and amusement of every one. The menu is always headed thus:

"Diner (ou Déjeuner) de Sa
Majesté l'Impératrice."

The two meals are exactly alike, except that there is no soup at luncheon and the coffee is then served at table, whereas after dinner it is then brought into the gallery.

On Saturday the Empress is going to Windsor to stay a couple of days with the Queen, accompanied as usual on these occasions by Mme. de Arcos and the Duc de Bassano. I have just been sending off a telegram from the Empress to Princess Beatrice, asking what will be the most convenient time for

18

arrival at the castle. We shall be delighted when the Empress returns, for she and the Duke are the soul of the house.

M. and A. hardly ever speak at table unless addressed by their aunt, but alone with me they are most voluble and we have nice long talks about Spain, and especially Madrid, for which (in spite of all the Empress's care and kindness) they are sometimes a little homesick. So occasionally, when they have made some decided headway with their English conversation, I let them chatter away to me in Spanish, to our mutual satisfaction.

From a letter:

Farnborough Hill,
February 22, 1886.

The other day, as we were leaving our *salon d'études* and following the Empress upstairs to the chapel, she said to me, "Vous devez trouver, Mademoiselle, que c'est un peu la vie du couvent ici." To which I answered playfully: "Madame, je trouve que c'est un couvent fort beau et intéressant; si tous étaient aussi charmants, je n'hésiterais pas à me faire religieuse," * – and she laughed.

The rosary over, and before tea, the Empress having discovered that I had not yet seen the state bedrooms, went all through them with us for my benefit.

First, with the Duc de Bassano's permission, we visited his apartment, consisting of bedroom, dressing– and sitting-room, of which he did the honours most amiably, showing us among other treasured things, a painting of Empress Josephine, his godmother, a little pencil drawing of a white horse done by *le Roi de Rome*, Napoleon I's son, and also numberless photographs of his own children and grandchildren, of whom

---

* "You must find, Mademoiselle, that it is rather a convent life here." – "Madame, I find it a very beautiful and interesting convent; if all convents were as charming, I should not hesitate to become a nun."

he is passionately fond. The private passageway leading to the Duke's suite is full of engravings of European sovereigns and all the English princes and princesses, to which are attached their signatures. This smaller hallway in its turn leads back to the principal gallery, where, as I have told you before, in addition to the Empress's room, will be found that of Mme. Le Breton, a splendid room kept for the Duchesse de Mouchy, and others for the Duc d'Albe, Mme. de Arcos, Mlle. Corvisant and different friends and habitués.

With the exception of a splendid toilette table covered with gold fittings which she never by any chance uses – formerly the property of Queen Hortense – the Empress's bedroom is very simple compared with the rooms of most women of fashion. A large bed, two or three cane chairs, a priedieu over which hang a crucifix and rosary, a few sketches of the late Emperor's room done by herself, on the walls; a glass case with family souvenirs of an intimate kind, among others the Emperor's hat *criblé de trous*, worn the night of the Orsini *attentat*, a small table with a few books of devotion, and that is all.

None of my letters seem to speak of the Empress's dressing-room, so I supplement from memory. There was nothing particularly unique about this very plain room, which, however, contained all the toilet essentials. In one corner, a large table with a circular mirror at the back; on it absolutely nothing but an enormous flat wickerwork basket, lined with muslin; this was the basket given filled with flowers, by the *dames de la Halle* on her wedding day. In this, every morning and evening, her maid used to lay out a fresh set of underclothes. Simple, almost to shabbiness, as her plain outer garments were, her underclothes were very beautiful, daintily made and of the most exquisite materials, and she used to don her things with the most wonderful speed. Among her chemises, there were some which Mme. Pelletier told me were pet ones of hers, and which she wore only occasionally. They had belonged to Queen Hortense, and were of the most beautiful fine linen, cut out of a single piece and delicately embroidered by hand round the neck and sleeves.

The only other things of importance in the room, were a screen, which made a secluded spot for her to dress in; her porcelain bath tub, with curtains drawn around it; an upright wooden *portemanteau* on which her clothes were hung temporarily while dressing; and a large *armoire* à glace, partly filled with exquisite linen, and where, also in a compartment, amid delicious sachets, she kept stores of gloves made for her formerly in great quantities in Spain and Italy, and other personal things. Out of this *armoire* one evening she got some pairs of evening gloves for me, and at another time on our return from Osborne, when our trunks were belated, she very kindly presented me with a toothbrush from her supply. It was especially made for her and had Dr. Evans's name stamped on it.

She never went near her bedroom, except to dress or sleep, and kept none of her personal belongings there. She liked a rather hard bed, and used only a small hair pillow; always had her window open, kept the temperature very low and would allow no heat in the room at night, but in the depth of winter consented to a little fire in the morning to dress by. I never saw her in bed, but her nieces had done so several times, and told me she wore a very pretty, fluffy little nightcap. About ten o'clock was her usual time for coming downstairs of a morning, except for some special occasion, or on Sundays when we had to start early for church.

Close by was another room called *Les Atours*, after a similar one at the Tuileries. This contained cupboards with large sliding doors, where her dresses and outdoor things were put away, and materials and things for future use stored with the greatest order. She had two maids, Mme. Pelletier, a widow with several grown children living in Paris, and Elise,- both

excellent women. Mme. Le Breton also had a faithful and very
well-educated Swiss maid, and these three with another young
woman who used to come in and help them, could always be
found busily mending and sewing near the Empress's dressing-
room. They seemed devoted to their mistress, and when
she found something not up to standard and administered
a reproof, red eyes were the consequence. But a smile or
two from the Empress later on speedily cured their passing
sorrow.

From a letter:

Farnborough Hill,
November 22, 1886.

The turret chamber, called *chambre de l'Empereur*, was
shown me one day by Uhlmann at the Empress's behest. It
contains undisturbed many of his personal things and the
four-post bed he died in, covered now with artificial memorial
wreaths, from one of which Uhlmann gave me some roses,
white lilacs and violets. In this room it was that, talking about
father and son, Uhlmann told me those touching things about
the young Prince which I have recorded elsewhere.

From a letter:

Farnborough Hill.

Of the *salon du matin* and the billiard-room I will say
nothing but that they are simply and comfortably furnished,
thoroughly English, and contain some good pictures, among
others a Rousseau, eighteen feet long, from which ducks and
waterfowl attacked by an eagle seem positively to be flying out,
and one can almost hear their cries of distress. Another is
entitled *Stags and Dogs* by Mélin. In the *salon du matin* there is
a wonderful painting of a bunch of grapes by St. Jean; *Fruit*,
a composition by Rousseau; *Marguerite and Faust* by Merle;
a small portrait of Napoleon I on wood by Isabey; and a
charming portrait of the Prince Imperial at ten years old,

surrounded by hunting dogs, by Yvon.

The house chapel is very simple, just a large room with high roof and rafters showing, but it contains the most interesting of all the historical souvenirs in the house, an *antiquité* over one thousand years old, and the only thing personally saved by the Empress before leaving the Tuileries, after that eventful 4 *Septembre* which was her adieu to the throne of France. I will try to give its history as it was told to me.

In a Gothic, chiseled iron *châsse*, or shrine, about 12 by 20 inches (with niches wherein are tiny little saints), the whole ornamented with precious stones and pearls very much worn and discoloured by age, are three interior partitions. In that on the right hand is a tiny portion of a veil supposed to have belonged to the Blessed Virgin; in the left partition what is said to be a piece of the holy winding sheet of our Lord; and in the centre a curious old reliquary, about three inches in diameter and suspended by a short chain, having in the middle a pale green polished translucent stone, through which one can clearly distinguish the *relic* of the true cross beneath.

This *talisman* as it is called, belonged to the great Charlemagne, was prized and worn by him during the greater part of his life time, and was buried with him. Without explanation it hardly seems possible that these facts should be authentic, and that this priceless treasure should have found its way from Germany to France, and finally to a little English village. This is how it was brought about:

When Charlemagne died, he was buried in a vault beneath the Dom, or cathedral, of his favourite town of Achen (Aix-la-Chapelle). Curiosity as to the truth of a tradition stating that the Emperor was buried sitting in a chair with crown and scepter led Charles Quint to violate the tomb of his great ancestor. This much history tells us. The rest of the story is the Empress's version. The vault was opened, and for one instant the sitting figure was discernible – then it crumbled to dust. The talisman was taken out, with scepter, crown and

Farnborough Hill, Hampshire
from a drawing by B.B. Long

24

other non-destructible things, and deposited in the *treasure* of the cathedral, where they remained until Napoleon I, during some visit to Achen, intimated to the trembling custodian of the treasure that he wished the reliquary surrendered to him for the Empress Josephine. This was promptly done. At her death at Malmaison, she bequeathed it to her daughter, Queen Hortense, mother of Napoleon III, by whom in turn it was given to Eugénie.

When *4 Septembre* dawned and the Empress hurriedly left the Tuileries, she with her own hands took the talisman out of the shrine and confided it to the keeping of a faithful servant, whose home was in Paris, and who all through the dark days of the Commune kept it hidden in his kitchen cupboard, over which he had pasted a map of Paris. No one ever suspected this kitchen of containing anything so precious, and the talisman was saved.

Later on, under MacMahon, second President of the Republic, when affairs had calmed down, and a great deal of the Empress's private property was sent over to her in England, the talisman came too, and was put back in its châsse, which also happily had escaped the destruction. All this the Empress told us herself one evening, during our constitutional after dinner, and before going to bed I made ample notes of these interesting facts.

From a letter:
In the sacristy the Empress one day showed me some wonderful old Spanish vestments, and also the famous *rose d'or* that Pope Pius IX sent her at her son's baptism. She remarked that the *rose* seemed to have brought misfortune to all the sovereign women she knew who had been so specially honoured by the Pope: Empress Charlotte (Maximilian's wife), Princess Cloltilde, herself, etc. It is a rose delicately fashioned in gold, mounted on a conically shaped spray of golden

foliage which rises out of a vase of the same material; rather disappointing somehow, though of beautiful workmanship.

From a letter:

Farnborough Hill,
September 25, 1886.

If I wish my letters to go out by the three o'clock post, I must now always write before leaving my room, for at present there is no quiet nook downstairs. In the billiard-room there are usually some of the gentlemen; in the morning-room ladies, gentlemen, or both – always a noisy, chatty, somewhat boisterous party, who put all idea's out of one's head. Our late *salon d'étude* having been changed into a small drawing-room as formerly, it cannot now be used for writing. The drugget is up, showing the rich *Turkey* carpet beneath; the chairs and sofas have taken off their white pinafores and show their pretty pale-blue satin dresses again; the large useful table has disappeared, giving place to several antique pieces of furniture, on which *objets d'arts* are now tastefully scattered. In fact, the room is not recognisable, except for the beautiful pictures, which hang unchanged on the walls. There are several dainty Meissoniers among them.

By the way, tell H. that the large picture she admired so much – *Une Messe en Kabylie* – is the representation of a real scene which took place in Algiers. One day during his stay here, Prince Joachim Murat knocked at the door, and asked if we would give him hospitality for a few minutes and allow him to look at that particular picture of Horace Vernet. Of course we said "yes," and after he had gazed at it long and earnestly, he told us he always felt young again when he looked at it. Seeing our questioning astonishment, he explained that he himself was the young soldier-boy kneeling to the left of the altar, holding the bishop's crozier. Strange, that having as a child so often looked at an engraving of that picture, I should have the original constantly under my eyes and know one of

26

the personages represented! The officiating Dominican bishop the Empress also knows well; he it was who gave her the plain looking rosary she uses every afternoon at five o'clock. Talking of this during her tour in Algiers, and the startling impression that it made upon her when the men of the whole regiment rushed up the hill on which she stood and suddenly prostrated themselves before her.

From a letter:

Farnborough Hill,
October 2, 1886.

Mme. Le Breton, M. Pietri and I dined alone yesterday evening, as the Empress had a bad cold and did not leave her own sitting-room, and after dinner we joined her there instead of going to the drawing-room as usual. M. Pietri read aloud while we were working. The Empress, who is usually so industrious, could only listen, so over-powered was she with the grippe.

There is one important room I have not yet described, namely the *salon de travail de l'Impératrice*. Descriptions of other parts of the house I quoted from letters or from notes taken at the time, but this room was overlooked, and though now retaining a very vivid recollection of it as a whole, I cannot be sure of remembering all the things in it. I sat in that room for the last time in 1889, the day my husband and I lunched at Farnborough Hill on our wedding tour. One then entered the room from the gallery on the left. In the centre was a large library table, and the Empress generally sat at this when not using a low wicker chair on the right of the fireplace writing on a *buvard* resting on her knees, which was a favourite way with her. This central writing-table had on it all the necessary paraphernalia for the Empress's immense correspondence, besides several portraits – one of her son, and a miniature of her father, Don Cipriano, then Conde de Teba, and later

27

on Conde de Montijo. This miniature shows a very fine face, rather spoiled by having a large black patch covering one eye. Together with this eye he had lost also a leg in the battle of Salamanca, fighting for Napoleon I.

On other tables were numberless photographs of different royalties and friends. The English dynasty was well represented, and nearly all the portraits had autograph signatures.

Opposite was a mullioned window, which looked out over a terrace. All around the room were low book-shelves about breast-high, containing many of Her Imperial Majesty's favourite books, saved from the Tuileries. These volumes were very beautifully bound and many of them had the Empress's *chiffre* on them. On the top of the shelves were several bronzes and interesting ornaments. Turning one's back to the fireplace – on the right wall hung a life-size portrait of the Emperor in court dress, with his *légion d'honneur* ribbon. I think the painting is by Cabanel, and I have heard from friends who knew His Imperial Majesty intimately, that it was extremely like him. On the opposite wall were several modern pictures, one of which is particularly striking – a painting of an extremely graceful Eastern woman at a well. Next to it came a large bay-window with tiled jardinieres constantly replenished from the hothouses with exotic flowers, which gave forth a delicious perfume. Here were placed two or three wicker easy-chairs, in which the Empress used to be very fond of taking a sun bath, whenever the stingy English Sun-god permitted. Here also grew some pampas-grass brought by the Empress from Zululand, and which formed a kind of screen in front of the windows. The whole character of the room was one of luxurious comfort, joined with daintiness and good taste of arrangement. Beyond the bay was another door, which opened into the *cabinet de travail*, a sort of inner sanctuary, her workshop so to speak, where she kept her embroidery and silks, and the frame for her larger pieces of work. Here, too, were more books, principally for reference, and at one end of the room a large mirror, which hid the safe containing all the important documents referred to in one of my letters.

There was nothing else worthy of notice in this room, except a small picture, on the table, of Marie Antoinette at the age of fourteen. This portrait, I know the Empress valued highly. The first day she showed it to me, she drew my attention to the fact, that the little arch-duchess seemingly pointed to a thin red line around her neck, namely a narrow ribbon, in accordance with the fashion of those days. The Empress seemed to consider this almost prophetic. Moreover, in connection with Marie Antoinette, the Empress invariably drew a parallel between the ill-fated queen and herself. She told us one day about her visiting Marie Antoinette's prison cell, incognita, on a certain Palm Sunday during the Empire. To avoid crowds and recognition, she passed herself off with her ladies as a party of English tourists, she herself being thickly veiled. The Empress said she was about the same height as Marie Antoinette, and though she heard how the queen had knocked her head as she entered the low-ceiled prison, and the scornful "Baisse-toi fière Autrichienne!" from the jailer, in the painful interest of the moment she forgot, and on entering the cell met with the very same accident herself. This impressed the Empress very unpleasantly, and she was so overcome for a minute or two that the custodian who was showing the party over the prison noticed it and said to the other ladies, "Vraiment, cette dame est bien-émotionée [Truly, that lady is greatly moved]!" During the twenty years of her reign, she often had the presentiment that she would die by the guillotine. The more enthusiastic the people the more she expected sudden changes in the affections of the mercurial French.

From a letter:

Farnborough Hill,
October 2, 1886.

Her Majesty has been busy today planning a sort of museum she intends building near the coach-house for the reception of a number of beautiful things, far too many for the house proper, already well stocked – and these things are too interesting to be kept in obscurity.

There are some pictures by Gudin awaiting a suitable resting-place; these have never been unrolled since they came over from Paris.* Then, also, a grand piano most beautifully inlaid with ormolu work, a gift of the Emperor of Austria, and several glass cases filled to overflowing with precious souvenirs of all kinds. The gala carriages, at present in the coach-house, are also to be removed to the museum. These are really magnificent. So sorry H. did not see them when she was here, for I am certain she never has, nor will again have the opportunity to gaze on the like. There is the coach the Empress drove in to be married – lined most beautifully with white satin and large enough for six or eight people; another carriage built either for her coronation or the baptismal ceremonial of the little Prince Imperial, and which is much more splendid even than the first, both interiorly and exteriorly. The hangings of the coachman's seat (or hammercloth, as they are called I think) are of crimson velvet, most splendidly embroidered in solid gold and embossed with pearls and precious stones. The Bonaparte family arms and eagles represent a magnificent piece of work. This one carriage alone cost, I was told, over 4000 pounds.

The first time I visited the coach-house with M. and A. as guides, the head-coachman invited us to get into the wedding

---

* The Empress told us about some of her pictures which on arrival were found to be jabbed through and through by a bayonet or sharp knife – the work of some malevolent person.

coach and sit down in the Empress's place a moment, telling us we were the first and only persons who had entered that carriage since it had been in his keeping. I pictured to myself how the Empress's heart must have throbbed with excitement, satisfied ambition, and wondering doubts of the future, when she first took her place there! Besides these two gala carriages, there is the Emperor's favourite brougham (the landau, victoria and brougham in daily use here now also came from the Tuileries); a sweet little goat carriage sent to the Prince Imperial by the Sultan of Turkey and one other of his babyhood vehicles; a very pretty sleigh, given by the Empress of Russia; and the trappings of the horses on state occasions, – oh! how we pitied the eight poor beasts who had to carry all that weight! It was as much as we could do to lift one of the collar pieces with both hands. Hanging up in the coach-house were also the saddle and bridle of the little horse the Prince rode, as a boy of fifteen, at the battle of Sedan (his baptism of fire), a number of other saddles, riding whips and pistols, and a great many more things than I can enumerate, which were most interesting to see and handle as I did that day.

THE HOUSEHOLD AND ENTOURAGE

From my diary:

Mme. Poussin, or Marie, as the Empress used to call her, was the name of the housekeeper. Her husband was the Empress's favourite servant, and had been in the French army. He knew where everything of the Empress's was, and was constantly called upon to fetch things she wanted, and to do little errands. He was most devoted to his imperial mistress. Roulet was the name of another of the men, whom we used to find in the early morning sliding busily up and down the gallery, polishing the floor with the brushes strapped to his feet, and humming gaily to himself. A special man was kept for cleaning silver, and his office was no sinecure. The men-servants, as is usual in France, took entire care of all the sitting-rooms, the five housemaids officiating only on the bedroom floors.

In the kitchen there was a chef and one aide. They must have been wonderfully industrious men, for they had to prepare all the meals for both tables, and at one time we sat down daily as many as twenty for lunch and dinner, and there were twenty-five house-servants and visiting maids and valets to be fed besides. *

The kitchen was a marvel. Several times I went through it with Mme. Le Breton, when she was ordering dinner, and it hardly seemed possible to believe that work was going on in the place, all was in such perfect order. The numerous pots, for instance, all hanging in their respective places looking like burnished gold. One end of the huge central table was used as a chopping board, the other end covered with a spotless linen cloth, on which the many carving knives were arranged with exquisite neatness, like a surgeon's table.

All the practical working details of the establishment, management of servants, care of linen and furniture, etc., were attended to by Mme. Poussin, supervised by Mme. Le Breton. The latter, however, herself ordered all the dinners; at least, she went into the kitchen every morning to confer with the chef concerning the two menus, previously prepared.

I personally never heard the Empress, particular as she

---

* The two coachmen lived in picturesque little cottages on the estate or in the village of Farnborough; one, a burly and rather surly Englishman, the other a little wiry man who had been in a cavalry regiment and I think was the Prince's orderly in Zululand. Several grooms, gardeners and laundry people – quite a colony in all – occupied similar cottages. I often wondered how these two men could achieve all the work this implied, for they had little assistance.

was, find fault with anything but the chickens. She would say occasionally, regretfully comparing a Farnborough to some French chicken: "Oh, Mme. Le Breton, parlez donc au chef – çà sent le poulailleur [Oh, Mme. Le Breton do speak to the chef; this savors of the coop]!"

L'Office corresponded in some measure with the English still-room. Here of a morning the under-butler made delicate little cakes in paper cases, delicious *fondants*, *marrons-glacés* and crystallized fruits (fresh currants and other acid fruits dipped into boiling sugar), and prepared the butter in various ingenious shapes for the table. He had many other duties and was always cheerful and obliging. He took charge of the mail and telegrams. He also kept timetables, and looked up trains in brain-racking Bradshaws, which, together with his executive ability and very quiet composed manner, made him an invaluable servant to the Empress, especially when traveling.

The servants' hall was a large, pleasant room, opening with long French windows on to the entrance courtyard. It was simply and comfortably furnished. Here the special *valet de service* of the week and Poussin, who was always *de service*, held themselves in readiness to admit visitors or to be summoned by the Empress. There was a central table with books, newspapers and periodicals of the day; on the walls were several large paintings of the Emperor and Empress. There was a library for the servants containing a good selection of standard French and English books. Poussin or Uhlmann, I forget which, was the librarian.

The Empress with her usual executive good sense, never allowed her cooks and coachmen to be idle during her prolonged yearly absences from home. They were always given a good holiday first and then put on board wages; but their mistress insisted on their taking other places for the balance of her time abroad. She knew with accuracy in what houses the men took service, and saw to it that they remained there.

Schmidt, an Alsatian, the old *maître d'hôtel* at Farnborough, whose duties on account of infirmity and old age had become almost nominal, was a tall, fine old man, stooping slightly, and with his white hair and kindly beaming eye pleasant to look upon. He had been in the service of the Tuileries, and as soon as the Empress settled at Camden Place came at once, with several other of the domestics, to tender his services. When telling me about it one day, the Empress said how much this devotion touched her, in that hour of general abandonment and betrayal. She said these servants had nothing to gain by coming, offered to work for lower wages than they had been accustomed to, and several of them moreover had left their own families, besides the pleasanter life in France, to settle in an absolutely dull English village. Schmidt was tremendously attached to the imperial family. He could not control himself when he heard them spoken of without respect, with the consequence that he got into many scrapes in the old days.

In the last months of the Empire, when public feeling was very strong against the Emperor and Empress, this was a frequent occurrence. She told us of one particular episode, which all but proved fatal to this bravely pugnacious servant. He heard a man in the crowd running down the Emperor. Schmidt reasoned quietly with him but without avail, for he got more abusive and violent, and attacked Schmidt, who excitedly defended himself. The crowd then took up the quarrel, and went howling after Schmidt, apparently ready to take his life. He fled, bleeding and dazed, into the first house of which he found the door open, made his way upstairs, and suddenly appeared, breathless, in the bedroom of a lady. "Madame, hide me," was all he had time to say. With great presence of mind this lady took in the situation and pushed him into an *armoire à robes*. A minute later the crowd came surging in and demanded that he should be given up to them. The lady's feigned astonishment and ignorance, combined

The Prince Imperial

with her coolness and polite invitation to look for themselves, put the crowd off the scent and Schmidt's life was saved. He had already been very much knocked about though, was quite ill for a long time in consequence, and the Empress declared had never been the same again since that day.

Uhlmann, another Alsatian, filled the position of steward, paid all the wages, the tradespeople, and the farm bills, attended to repairs, etc. He was directly under the order of M. Pietri, who supervised his work, reports and accounts, before submitting them at stated times to the Empress. Uhlmann had been valet and body-servant to the Prince Imperial. He was a great big man, very serious, reliable, and invaluable in every way. I had several talks with him about the Prince, to whom he had been extremely devoted, and whose death was a blow – which he could not get over. Uhlmann had been with him nearly all his life, at Chislehurst and at Woolwich, where the Prince was following his military training. He also went out to Zululand, and was with his young master till the very eve of his death. He was a most excellent person for any young man to have near him – perfectly straightforward, sincere and earnest.

I never heard any one say a disparaging word of the Prince all the time I was at Farnborough, though Mme. Le Breton and M. Pietri could at times speak out very frankly about any one. He seems by common consensus of opinion to have been a wonderfully fine young fellow. Those who had only known him slightly were as loud in his praises, as those others who knew him more intimately. Uhlmann, who had had the greatest possible facilities for observation, spoke of him in glowing terms, and this means a good deal, for there are few exceptions, I believe, to the dicturn, that "no one is a hero to his valet." From all Uhlmann said, with what I had already gathered from others, and they had all been friends of his childhood, I could reach only one verdict about him – that he was deeply and truly good.* His chief characteristic seems to have been his wonderful truth of mind. He had a noble, straightforward nature, shunning pretense of all kind, and was deeply religious and spiritual-minded. He was beloved and looked up to by all his classmates at Woolwich, by all the servants, by everybody in fact who had ever known and come in contact with him. The English soldiers out in Zululand worshipped him, Uhlmann said, and no wonder, for besides his chivalrous and brave qualities, the Prince was always simple and generous, and shared everything with his comrades. When hampers of luxuries, in the shape of food and other things, reached him from his mother, he insisted on dividing up with the men, in spite of protest from those in authority, who thought *he* needed the extra food himself, as he was not very rugged.

Uhlmann also told me that one of his most striking characteristics was absolute fearless and unashamed recognition of his religion. Even in Woolwich days and camp life, and up to the very last night before starting on that fatal reconnaissance trip, he never missed saying his evening prayers aloud. He would call Uhlmann into his room and the two would kneel down together by the side of the bed, just as they had done always when the Prince was a little child. He never let anything interfere with his devotional duty.

A mortuary card, of which the following is a translation, was given by the Empress to her niece M., who made it over to me:

---

* I got the same impression from Monsignor Goddard of Chislehurst, and his friend the old Abbé Toursel of the "French Chapel" (the old historic Embassy Chapel) in London, the last outsider to see and talk with him before he sailed for Natal.

My last thought will be for my Country; for her I would gladly give my life. [Extract from his will].

NAPOLEON

Prince Imperial

Born at the Tuileries March 16, 1856.
Killed by the enemy in Zululand, June 1, 1879.

This Prince born to a throne, had a mind and heart even higher than his birth. The misfortunes of his house during his boyhood were unable to crush him, and from then on he showed much dignity, which owed nothing to good fortune. If he gained distinction from his rank he gained still more by his merit. [Bossuet – *Oraison Funèbre*.]

He acted courageously; fearing nothing, he did not fear the enemy. [II Pascal XXXII:7].

He died leaving to all an admirable example of faith and strength. [Adaptation II Maccabees VI:31].

Merciful Jesus, give him eternal rest!

Pray for the father and the son whom death has reunited.

On the back of the mortuary card is a prayer which, written out in his own handwriting, was found in his prayer book by the Empress after his death. It gives an insight into the deeply spiritual aspirations of the young soldier-prince. A translation follows:

My God, I give you my heart, but I beg You to give me Faith. Without faith there can be no ardent prayers, and prayer is a necessity of my soul.

I beg You not to remove the obstacles that traverse my life, but to permit me to overcome them. I beg of You – not that you may disarm my enemies but that you may help me to vanquish my own self. Deign, O God, to grant my prayers.

Preserve to my affection those who are dear to me. Grant them happy days. If You only wish to scatter over this world a certain measure of joy – take, O My God, the sum which would come to me, divide it up among the most worthy and may the most worthy be my friends.

If You wish to chastise mankind – strike me. Misfortune is turned into joy by the sweet thought that those we love are happy.

Joy is poisoned by the bitter thought: I myself rejoiced, while those whom I cherish a thousand times more than myself are suffering.

For me, O God, no more happiness. I fly from it – take it from my path. My only joy is to be found in forgetfulness of the past.

If I forget those who are no more, I shall be forgotten in my turn. How sad it is to think: Time effaces everything! The only comfort I seek is that which will last forever: that given by a peaceful conscience. O my God, show me ever plainly where my duty lies – give me the strength to carry it out on all occasions. When comes the end of my life I shall then be able to look back over the past without fear. My memories will have no remorse in them. Then I shall be truly happy.

O my God, make the conviction sink deep into my heart, that those I love and who are dead are the witnesses of all my actions. My life will then be worthy to be seen by them, and I will never need to blush at the most secret of my thoughts.

Maria and Antonia de Vejerano, though always called the Empress's nieces – but only so by courtesy because of the great disparity in ages – were in reality her cousins. I think they had a great grandmother (a Cabarus) in common. In any case, the girls and the Empress were all cousins of M. de Lesseps. They were pleasant, healthy-minded girls, affectionate and with nice dispositions, and accustomed to think of others first and themselves afterward.

Two years after their visit to the Empress, Maria married Paco de Ansaldo, and at their marriage her uncle gave her one of the numerous titles which he owned. They are now Count and Countess de San Enrique. Her husband occupies some position at the court of King Alfonso XIII, and she helps him in his literary work. She has now, I hear from her sister, several very beautiful children. Antonia a little later married Luis de Casanova. After a blissfully happy six months, he died, leaving her a widow at eighteen. She spent much time afterward at Farnborough and traveled with the Empress, who was very fond of her.

From my diary:

First and foremost among the few faithful adherents of the Empress, must be named the Duc de Bassano, Napoleon Hugues Joseph Maret, son of Hugues Bernard Maret, first duke of the name, whose title was created by Napoleon I. He inherited from his birth in 1804* traditions of devotion to the Bonaparte family, which were furthered by having Napoleon and the Empress Josephine for his godparents, and the little *Roi de Rome* for playmate; and these traditions were loyally maintained all his long life. The Empress had no truer friend than he in her hours of need. While others were leaving her to her fate he bravely spoke in her behalf before the Chambre des

---

* Many authorities say 1803; he himself gave the date as 1804. He died in Paris in 1898.

Députés, trying vainly to turn the torrent of anger away from her, or at least to obtain aid from the provisional government for her protection against the furious rabble. When her flight was *un fait accompli*, and she had landed penniless in England, without a single belonging but a few absolute necessaries hastily gathered together, and lent her by Mrs. Evans and Lady Burgoyne, the duke followed her almost immediately with only a carpet-bag (so the Empress told us), saying simply on arriving, "Madame me voici," and begging to be allowed to give her his services. She said he did it with so much cheerful grace, that she had not the heart to refuse his request, though she really had no means of maintaining a household.

When Napoleon III died in January 1873, the widowed Eugénie offered the duke his freedom to return to France and his family, from whom he had voluntarily separated himself in spite of his deepest affection for them. But he would not accept it and stayed on, unvaryingly cheerful, thoughtful and unselfish, with a quiet dignity that made you feel what a thorough gentleman he was. Again, after the Prince's death, the Empress gave him the chance of leaving her household, pointing out that conditions had changed and that there was no longer any reason for him to stay. But he again refused, and answered: "No, on the contrary Madame, now that you are entirely alone you need me all the more."

The Duke has left a delightful picture of himself in my memory as he was in 1886. A tall, handsome, dignified old man, with beautiful white hair; courteous to all, and with an especially chivalrous feeling toward women – the very type of the *grand seigneur* and *preux chevalier* of old, that one reads about but meets so rarely.

Mme. Le Breton was a widow of long standing, with several married sons and daughters, and was formerly one of the *lectrices* at the Tuileries; and, alone of all the women in

France, she did not abandon the Empress, but accompanied her bravely on that eventful journey on the fifth of September when they fled from Paris. With the exception of a few short periods of absence for little holidays, she never left her imperial mistress' side through all those years. She was a most faithful friend, tried patiently to help and comfort the Empress and to make everything run smoothly, and this when *Ma Souveraine*, as she playfully called the Empress in speaking of her, was in such a state of nerves that she was often irritable and difficult to please.

Mme. Le Breton was most capable and supervised the household wonderfully. Everything was the pink of perfection with nowhere visible any hurry or fuss. She did not at all relish it, therefore, when the Empress on rare occasions made some criticism. It used rather to upset her equanimity and the Empress often rallied her about her sensitiveness. In my peregrinations on some mornings through the kitchen with her, I noticed that she kept the household rather in awe of her. This was really necessary, for she felt herself, and was ultimately, held responsible. Her position was a delicate one, but, considering the difficulties, she acquitted herself well and remained unusually cheerful. Always kind-hearted, a warm, enthusiastic friend, she delighted to welcome anybody who would bring a little change into the Farnborough *milieu*, since life for its members, who knew all the interesting things by heart and had no further stimulus of curiosity, was often monotonous in the extreme. Though mentally bright, Mme. Le Breton cared not a pin for scientific talk, which fact often annoyed the Empress. What Mme. Le Breton loved was social chit-chat, and in consequence she thoroughly enjoyed her rare holidays, which put her in touch with her family and the old friends of the past, who flocked round her on her arrival in Paris, where she was a great favorite. Only, duty and true affection had kept her near her mistress through those long years of dullness, for society was the breath of life to her. *

Mme. de Arcos, who has been almost a lifelong friend of the Empress, was a Miss Vaughan. Her father had been an English consul in one of the southern towns of Spain, and she and the Empress made each other's acquaintance many, many years ago in rather a strange way. This is the story the Empress told us one evening, while walking up and down the gallery, leaning on my arm as she often did. Their two mothers, the Countess Montijo and Mrs. Vaughan, were on board ship going to England, where the Countess, who was ambitious for her beautiful daughter, was going to present her to Queen Victoria and bring her out in London society. Mrs. Vaughan was taking her daughter Christine to England also. It was very rough weather, and the two elder ladies were down below. The girls were on deck, but did not know each other then. It got more and more stormy, and Eugénie Montijo, violently sick, rushed to the side. The rail was quite low, and the seasick girl in such a state of indifference that she did not care whether she went overboard or not. Presently, she felt two arms put firmly around her waist with hands clasped in front, and she was dragged away. Struggling and indignant, she cried: "Leave me alone." Looking up, she saw a girl a good deal younger than herself, who spoke to her in English and told her that she was in a dangerous position, and helped her to a more comfortable place. The Countess Montijo, when she heard later how her daughter had been rescued from a rather perilous position, sought out Mrs. Vaughan, to thank her. Thus the parents became acquainted, and a lifelong friendship between the daughters resulted.

---

* She died at the age of eighty-two, very much regretted by the Empress and all her friends. In a letter received from M. Pietri, March 27, 1901, he gives me the details of her last illness, and thanks me *de la part de S. M. L'Impératrice* for the share that I take in sympathizing with her great loss.

Queen Victoria told the Empress on one of her visits to Windsor, that she well remembered her presentation that season as a young girl, and the impression made on her at the time. It was a semi-private audience, preceding a fancy ball at Buckingham Palace, and, the Queen told her friend she even recalled the costumes worn on the occasion. Eugénie Montijo was dressed as a Spanish Infanta, Queen Victoria as Queen Anne, and the Prince Consort as William of Orange.

Naturally when Eugénie, Condesa de Teba, became Empress, Mme. de Arcos always found a welcome at the Tuileries, – the friendship was further cemented, – and she, in her turn, remained faithful to Her Imperial Majesty all through the life of exile in England. She is the woman with whom the Empress has been most intimate, excepting, of course, Mme. Le Breton. It was Mme. de Arcos, an intimate friend of my aunt's, who suggested my name to the Empress, and was thus instrumental in my spending those interesting months at Farnborough. I shall always feel a debt of gratitude toward her for this alone.

One evening, walking up and down, the Empress talked of audiences and some of her difficulties when first confronted with her royal position and was saying how hard it had been to throw herself suddenly into this novel situation and how much she had had to learn. She then turned to me, laughing for a minute, and said: "Well, you know, Mademoiselle, you embarrassed me dreadfully that day I sent for you to come to London." I expressed my surprise. "Yes, you did indeed! I do not know when I felt so embarrassed, even in difficult situations at the Tuileries," she added, and explained that she had thought it encumbent on her to question me, and though she did not like to risk hurting my feelings, yet felt she must say something, for it would otherwise have seemed foolish to have requested an interview. She laughed again, and would not at first tell me why. "Never in your life could you guess the very first question I put to Mme. de Arcos about you. I said to her, 'Now, Zizi, before you tell me anything further about Miss W. in the first place – *louche t'elle?*'" Noticing Mme. de Arcos's hesitation and surprise, the Empress insisted: "'Well, Zizi, you must be perfectly sure about this matter, for if you cannot put my mind at rest on this crucial point, I won't have another word said about Miss W. coming here. Even were she an angel from heaven I would not, under the circumstances, have her cross my threshold.'"

The Empress added, sadly: "J'ai les personnes qui louchent en horreur. Je ne puis me défaire de l'idée que l'oeil qui louche, accompagne aussi un esprit qui louche, et le malheur m'est toujours venu quand j'ai été en relations avec une personne qui louchait."* She then mentioned Trochu and Bazaine, as squinting men, and expressed her special and intuitive dislike of Trochu, who behaved so shamefully before the fall of the Empire.

Mme. de Arcos's Belgravia house was always put at the Empress's entire disposal for any length of time she might wish, for either lunch or for resting, whenever she went up to town for shopping or for visits to the doctors.

Dr. Frederick B. Scott, a surgeon-major in the English army at Aldershot, was a constant visitor at Farnborough, and the Empress was very fond of him in a kind of grateful way. He was an excellent surgeon and a most conscientious man, but he was not brilliant, nor a good conversationalist. On any amiable pretext he could invent he came over to Farnborough – nearly every afternoon saw him walking or riding up the avenue. He had known and been devoted to the Prince Imperial, and accompanied him to Zululand, where he was supposed in an unofficial way, but more as a friend, to be in charge of the young man's health. He it was who went out

* "I have a horror of people who squint. I never can get rid of the idea that a squinting eye indicates also a spirit that is not straightforward. Misfortune has come to me every time I have had dealings with persons who squinted."

to search for and finally found the Prince's mutilated body the day after the boy had been killed, and later brought the corpse back to England in H. M. S. *Orontes*,[1] and took a prominent part in the funeral.[2] Since that event Dr. Scott has kept very much in touch with the Empress; and when she started for Zululand in 1880 accompanied her, going over the ground and showing her the places of sad interest in the pathetic drama.

Franceschini Pietri is a grandson of Paoli, the celebrated Corsican, and his mother was a Sebastiani, so that according to the Empress he is descended from Corsican patriots on both sides. He had been under-secretary to the Emperor and fought close beside him at the battle of Sedan, afterward sharing his imprisonment at Wilhelmshöhe. He is very intelligent, witty, has a great business capacity, and conceals a most excellent heart under somewhat brusque manners. "Il se laisserait volontiers tailler en morceaux pour nous [He would voluntarily let himself be cut to pieces for us]," the Empress has often said of him to me, and I am sure it is true – though his constant devotion did not prevent his seeing through his imperial mistress's little foibles. His attitude at such times was manifested by a characteristic gesture, an almost imperceptible smile and shrug of his shoulders while listening to her. He had lost all his worldly possessions when, in his absence at the front, the Tuileries Palace was burnt down. He was a man of sterling worth and one of the most reliable people about the Empress.

---

[1] At Spithead the coffin was transferred to Admiralty yacht *Enchantress*.

[2] In the party were also the Marquis de Bassano, Sir Evelyn and Lady Wood, and several other ladies who lost relatives in the Zulu War.

Mosignor Goddard

Francheschini Pietri

PART II

*Daily Events: Further Extracts
from Diary and Letters*

PART II

Thursday, February 18. This afternoon went with the Empress to see the Renaissance Memorial Church, which is a building on a neighboring hill in the midst of pine woods, a few minutes off from this house. The upper church is nearing completion; its crypt, which is really an architectural gem, is quite finished, and Napoleon III's polished, red granite sarcophagus (Queen Victoria's gift, transported from the Little Lady Chapel in St. Mary's Church at Chislehurst, with many wreaths and national private memorials) is in place to the right of a small altar. The sarcophagus of the Prince Imperial stands on the left, and a vacant place awaits the wife and mother in the center. The Empress told us of a rather strange coincidence. Without knowing it, she had selected haphazard out of a great many designs for the tessellated pavement, the very same one which is, at present in the "Invalides" in Paris (where Napoleon I is buried), and where her husband and son would have been laid to rest had not untoward events in France interfered.

From a letter:

Farnborough Hill,
February 20, 1886.

Yesterday morning we had a little taste of sport. Her Majesty allowed the gentlemen of the neighborhood to come into her grounds with the beagles for a hare hunt. The huntsmen assembled and started from the park gates, the Empress, Mme. Le Breton, M. Pietri, the girls and myself following, and keeping up with them for a little while. After losing sight of the sportsmen for some time in the heat of the chase, we found them again on the common near the Empress's woods in full tilt after the poor hare. We had a good deal of scrambling up and down to do, and were often ankle-deep in mud, as the roads were very heavy. Poor Mme. Le Breton was tired out and was obliged to turn back alone, but we went on in spite of all, over stiles and through gaps in the hedges; the Empress was delighted to find that she got on just as well as the younger ones – in fact better than M., whose rather heavy build and sedentary bringing up in Spain have not made her very athletic.

After luncheon we had some delightful music from Miss Smythe, who is quite a musical genius and spends most of her time in Germany studying for pleasure. One consolation, the Empress likes my simple playing quite as well as hers, and told us in the evening about a concert at the Conservatoire, given for Queen Victoria and Prince Albert, which lasted four mortal hours, and even sent the music-loving Prince Consort to sleep, to the disgust of all Paris. The Empress said that she herself, though she adores music, always passed for not liking it, for she really had not the courage and hypocrisy to follow the score, to beat time, to nod her head and appear *ravie* for whole hours. She owns frankly to neither liking nor understanding classical music. This latter assertion is, I am sure, strictly true. My *Pinson et Fauvette* is banal and superficial enough to be her favorite, and she is always asking for it and enjoys it. The conversation turned on Sir Arthur Sullivan (of Gilbert and Sullivan operatic fame), who has a little cottage in this neighborhood, where he retires from London when he wants to be quiet and work undisturbed. Sir Arthur told the Empress that just now he is writing to make money, but later on he is to bring out a serious opera he has on hand, which he hopes will add to his musical reputation.

After dinner, it being Saturday, the Empress allowed us girls to go to the billiard-room with the gentlemen for a game of *cochonnet*, a rather amusing French game played on a small billiard table. The *parti de cochonnet* over, we all joined the Empress in the *grand salon* and did not go up to our rooms till 11:30, but had quite sleep enough, for on Sunday mornings our breakfast is brought up to our rooms, as is that of the Empress and Mme. Le Breton, and we need only make our appearance at 9:30, at which time the various carriages are in readiness to take us to the soldiers' church at Aldershot. Called by courtesy a church, in reality it is nothing but a dreary, barnlike structure, perfectly gaunt and bare, and used in rotation by all the various denominations of North Camp. The commanding officer (a Catholic) and others were at the door to receive the Empress, and conduct her up the aisle to the seat reserved for her. Before mass, at which we had some very mediocre military music rendered exclusively by Catholic soldiers, morning prayers were said, and later we had a nice practical sermon from Rev. Father Corbett, the army chaplain. We returned home in the same order as we came, the Empress and Mme Le Breton in a brougham and pair, the two gentlemen, M., A., and myself in a closed wagonette, the guard turning out and saluting with bugles as we passed the barracks. Before and after luncheon a little walk in the park, and afterward the Empress took me herself into the drawing-room and the *salon de l'Impératrice*, showing me everything and telling me the history of the beautiful things there.

Now, dear, I must say good-by. This will probably be my first and last free time today, as it is just the rosary hour; then afternoon tea, and as a very extraordinary Spanish lady, the wife of General B., invariably comes to that little social gathering on Sundays, we shall have to sit indefinitely round the tea tray, listening to her very amusing stories in excruciatingly bad French. The Empress says she is as good as a play, and it distracts and amuses her to hear this visitor rattle on.

P. S. 11 p.m. – Bedtime. Yes, Mrs. B. is indeed as good as or better than the majority of plays – she kept us all in fits of laughter; the poor General does not seem to enjoy it though. He was as quiet as a mouse all tea time, and gave us plenty of occupation passing him cakes, and bread and butter, and refilling his cup. Instead of tea the Empress takes a small cup of boiling water with about a teaspoonful of milk in it, and no sugar. It must be a very horrid concoction, I think, but she finds it agrees with her better. I do not think you would like that brew, nor indeed any of the tea we drink here. What one gets of the flavor is delicious, but it is terribly weak. The Empress says that the Prince of Wales, when at home, has an urn and cups brought in every evening now at nine o'clock, and he also takes a hygienic cup of hot water, but perfectly plain. He does not even pretend it is tea.

Tomorrow Mme. de Arcos arrives on a visit; and soon the Empress and she, accompanied by the Duc de Bassano, are going to Windsor Castle. She has promised her nieces not to be long away – if possible only two days. We shall miss her dreadfully.

The Memorial Church, Farnborough Hill
from a drawing by B.B. Long

Monday, February 22. Mme. de Arcos arrived for luncheon. She was very gay, talked politics, and told us amusingly about the Queen's present dilemma. Each of the duchesses of the realm has offered excuses why she should decline being Mistress of the Robes, which is particularly awkward, as her English Majesty will have no one but a duchess.

Wednesday, February 24. Lady Jane Taylor, sister of the Duchess of Wellington, called with her daughter at afternoon tea time. After the rosary, the Empress showed me over her own bedroom, the Duc de Bassano's apartments, and other rooms.

This evening, during our after-dinner constitutional, the Empress gave us a most impressive and graphic account of her flight from Paris, a theme about which so much has been written, and so many false versions circulated even by well-meaning people, that it was doubly interesting to hear the details of it from her own lips.* She dwelt first a good deal upon the horrors of the war and its fearful anxieties. Appointed Regent in 1870, during the Emperor's absence, she was alone in Paris from July to September, and the strain of responsibility and anxiety was perfectly terrible. She never slept except with the aid of chloral, and often then had to be wakened up from her absolutely necessary though fitful slumber, to peruse telegrams arriving from the seat of war.

The people howled around the Tuileries all night, for they hated her for the share they supposed she took in causing the war. In telling us all this in French, the Empress said: "Oui, j'ai passé quelques moments terribles de Juillet à Septembre. Rien dans la nature – ni tempêtes, ni éléments courroucés – ne peut donner la moindre idée de l'horreur d'un peuple en fureur. A moins de le voir, personne ne peut se figurer ce qu'est toute

---

* On going up to my room within an hour of her recital, I made careful notes, from which this account, with very slight alterations mainly for the sake of clarity, has been written.

une populace hurlant contre vous – c'est atroce!"*[1]

She then told us how several times, when she was presiding at a council of war, malicious telegrams arrived announcing that the Emperor and her son were dead. She had to open these despatches, read them in public, and preserve her composure, while her mind was racked with uncertainty. When the signal defeats of the French army by the Prussians came about, similar false messages about husband and son were constantly arriving at the palace at night, and she was driven nearly out of her senses.

After common report asserted that the Empress had already left Paris, she stayed on one night longer, and left the capital the next day with Mme. Le Breton and Dr. Thomas W. Evans, an American – the court dentist. While foreign ambassadors and officials stood aloof fearing to implicate their governments, he came forward and put himself at her service in a most devoted and opportune way. Report said also that she was disguised, but she told us, and repeated it emphatically several times, that she never did and never would disguise herself. She refused absolutely to wear even a thicker veil than usual, and was dressed in her ordinary clothes – a simple black dress, hat and cloak, such as she wore every day in her private life at the Tuileries.*[2] The idea of disguising herself was hateful to her pride, though she was taking great risks in refusing to do so.

These three persons then left Paris on the fifth of September, in Dr. Evans's private carriage, driving down the

------

*[1] "Nothing in nature, neither storms nor the angry elements can give one the faintest idea of a people in violent anger. Without experiencing it, no one can imagine what it means to have a whole populace howling against you – it is horrible!"

*[2] This was her own description of herself to me and I wrote it down within an hour. Since then in reading over my notes I wondered at the plain black dress, but an account in a book by her intimate friend, Mme. Carette, tallies with mine.

rue de Rivoli in plain view of everybody. While so doing the Empress, who would not even consent to sit back out of sight as her companions implored her to do, was recognized by a little *patissier* boy, who began shouting excitedly: "The Empress!" Every one was on the qui vive, and, her life being eagerly sought by many, the situation at the outset of this eventful journey became critical in the extreme; but Dr. Evans, with great presence of mind, turned the tide of thought in another direction. Jumping out of the carriage, he caught the offending boy by his collar, shook him roughly, saying: "You little ragamuffin, how dare you cry, 'Long live the Empress'!" jumped back into the carriage with lightning speed and drove off, leaving the dazed boy neither time nor wits to even reason out how he had "put his foot into it." The *patissier* probably kept his impressions to himself after this, and as a crowd had had no time to gather, the incident fortunately caused no disastrous consequences.*

Once outside the gates of Paris (which only a thoughtfully prearranged scheme and much ready wit had enabled them to pass with impunity), Dr. Evans took the first opportunity to send his carriage back by another *barrière*, and the journey, on which they met with unheard of difficulties, began in dead earnest.

They proceeded slowly, sometimes walking so as to leave no trace of themselves, sometimes, when it seemed feasible, hiring a vehicle to get over the ground a little quicker. At one time it was raining hard, but there was nothing for it but to walk a long distance across open fields and then stand in the shelter of a barn door, while Dr. Evans reconnoitered and made further plans. They were of course anxious to

---

* One man, Her Imperial Majesty said, wrote openly to the papers, declaring he had gone to the Tuileries with the mob, prepared to kill her, and deplored the fact that she had left, and that he had arrived just five minutes too late. So the success or non-success of her flight was really an actual matter of life or death, and not only polite fiction.

avoid railroads as much as possible, as the Empress was being watched for everywhere and on the rail-roads in particular, as the most probable egress for her. Often, after much plodding over ploughed fields, Dr. Evans tried vainly to hire a vehicle for the two footsore women. At last he succeeded, and they drove for some distance, discussing eagerly the while about the next move. Dr. Evans thought it might be prudent to test the sentiments of the driver and see what kind of a man he was, before deciding anything further. Making a pretext of better seeing the country, he sat outside with the driver and began chatting with him.

"Eh bien, quelles nouvelles de Paris?" asked Dr. Evans.

"Ah," excitedly, "vous ne savez donc pas?"

"Non," answered the doctor.

"Ah! Elle nous a échappé!"

"Qui donc?" asked Dr. Evans, with as much ignorant indifference as he could feign.

"Mais – cette maudite femme – cette Impératrice! Ah! [with horribly abusive epithets and gestures suggestive of strangling] Si je la tenais... elle ne mourrait que de mes mains!" *

Dr. Evans tried to appear *pas au courant* and did not dare, of course, to defend the Empress, but he thought, that considering the would-be victim was within a few inches of this blood-thirsty individual, the cabriolet was decidedly an unsafe place. Quarreling about the fare accordingly, he dismissed the man and got his companions away as quickly as he could.

It proved impossible to find any other vehicle and they

_____

* "Well, what news from Paris?" asked Dr. Evans.

"Ah, you don't know, then?" excitedly.

"No!" answered the doctor.

"Ah, she has escaped us!"

"Who?" again asked Dr. Evans, with as much ignorant indifference as he could feign.

"Why, that cursed woman – the Empress! Ah, if I only got hold of her – she would die by my hands!"

had to walk on again across country, and strike out finally for the nearest railroad. Here they sat down nearly exhausted, on a bench in the little waiting-room of a small wayside station. Dr. Evans kept his ears diligently listening for reports, on which they might possibly shape their plans. At his wits' end how to conceal the well-known and strikingly beautiful woman from observation, he bought a newspaper, opened it out and pushed it into the Empress's hands as she sat there dazed and passive, saying, "Read that." Thus he forced her to keep this slight, temporary screen in front of her and hoped devoutly the peasants might not recognize her.

The fugitives waited what seemed to them an endless time for a train going in the direction they desired. Many market people sauntered in and out with their baskets on their arms, the Empress risking recognition every instant, and escaping in a seemingly miraculous way, till finally the train they were to take drew into the station.

The *chef de gare* then threw open the waiting-room doors and began to hustle the people out on to the platform. He seemed particularly to push the Empress, taking her by the arm and speaking very roughly. She told us that she could not help a first impulse to resent such a liberty, but of course had to control herself and submit. It was a tremendous transition from the treatment she had hitherto received, – even a few days before the utmost deference, and now rudely jostled with a crowd of peasants. She sadly reflected how quickly the change had been effected.

She got meekly into a third-class compartment with her two companions. Just as the train was moving off the rude station master jumped up on the steps, and, to her great surprise, touched his cap respectfully, reached his hand into the carriage while taking hers, and, bending over it, kissed it. He had recognized his sovereign, and his officious attitude with the people was evidently assumed to help her escape observation. This incident comforted her a little, and she told

Photo by Braun, Clement Co.

Duc de Bassano

Photo by F. Gutekunst

Dr. Thomas W. Evans

61

it to us with a break in her voice.

The next place they stopped was a common *auberge*, and here the Empress had to feign illness and go to bed, to avoid appearing in the public eating-room. During the several days it took to reach Deauville, all the food she tasted consisted of scraps that Mme Le Breton had been able to pocket surreptitiously. She never got a regular meal, nor had her clothes off her back all that time.

Finally they arrived at their destination, utterly worn out, and went at once to the hotel where Mrs. Evans was spending the season with her family; she had been notified beforehand of their probable arrival. The Empress was immediately taken up an unused staircase to Mrs. Evans's own bedroom, where she was locked in until midnight. Here her hostess paid her occasional stolen visits and smuggled up some food to her, but was not able even now to give her a properly served meal. Mrs. Evans could not do so without the servants' knowledge, and as they were strangers to her, and their character and sentiments unknown, it was felt that, with such a prize as the imperial head, the temptation to betrayal might possibly prove too strong. No one, therefore, was intrusted with the weighty secret.

The Empress's plan was to get to England, but of course traveling on the public steamers was out of the question, and Dr. Evans tried among the yachtsmen to find some one willing to take the fugitives across the Channel. Several refused point-blank, not liking the responsibility and complications that might arise out of such action. Sir John Burgoyne, when appealed to, gallantly declared he would be delighted and that he would risk anything to help; but added that his yacht was very small (only 40 tons) and with ladies aboard not really fit to cross the Channel in such a gale. However, he said, if the Empress was willing to risk a rough and dangerous passage, he would be only too glad to put the *Gazelle* at her disposal. Eugénie told us she would never to her dying day forget their tragic walk down to the quay in the darkness. Mme. Le Breton and Mrs. Evans walked ahead to see that all was safe, Dr. Evans and the Empress following. Everything was ominously still except the sea, which was lashed into a perfect fury.[*1]

In the early morning the *Gazelle* at last got under way, and the fugitives felt comparatively safe for the time being. Nothing, during the trip, could equal Lady Burgoyne's eager and tender, womanly kindness to the Empress, who told us that her sense of humor obliged her, even in the midst of all her own misery, fatigue and seasickness, to see the ludicrous and incongruous side of things and to laugh at intervals during this terrible voyage. Lady Burgoyne's principal idea of available help in the way of food was a crust of bread and champagne, which she was constantly pressing on her two guests, who lay wretchedly helpless and utterly exhausted in their tiny bunks.

Only after twenty-four weary hours did the yacht reach England, at Ryde, both passengers and crew having many times during the gale thought they would never see shore again. The Empress had no idea on landing where to look for her son – nothing but conflicting information as to his whereabouts greeted her. He was supposed, after the battle of Sedan, to have gone to Belgium and have since arrived somewhere in England, but there was also another report to the effect that he and Comte Clary, his tutor, had been killed. Neither could the Empress find her two Alva nieces,[*2] who had lived with her at the Tuileries since their mother's death in 1860. On account of possible danger they had been sent on to England, some time ahead. They were supposed to be at Brighton, but on reachinmg the hotel indicated they were reported gone, and had left no clue as to their whereabouts. Later on the

---

[*1] On that very night Sir John lost his nephew, Captain Sir Hugh Burgoyne, who was in command of one of the most powerful British men-of-war, which mysteriously disappeared at the mouth of the Channel.

[*2] One became Duquesa de Medina Celi and died after a year of marriage, much admired and beloved; the other became Duquesa de Tamames.

Camden House, Chislehurst
from a drawing by B.B. Long

whole party was discovered safely housed at Hastings, and the two Spanish girls had chosen that opportune time to indulge in measles. From Hastings the whole family soon after moved to Chislehurst, where Mr. Stroud very courteously put his residence, Camden Place, at their disposal.

When the Empress had finished telling us all these thrilling adventures, she continued walking for a few paces in silence and deep thought; then added, "Je ne sais pas comment je ne suis pas devenue folle, à bien des moments de ma vie! Aussi, on comprend l'état de mes nerfs à présent!"* She then went on and told us, that on March 20, 1871, after his release from imprisonment in Wilhelmshöhe, the Emperor arrived in Dover. She and her nieces went there to meet him, and many thousands of sympathetic English gave him an enthusiastic welcome. That day at the famous Dover hotel, the Lord Warden, the imperial party by a strange coincidence, came face to face in a narrow corridor with the Orleans family. They were about to reënter France after many years of exile in England. Napoleon III was leaving France and going into exile from which he was never to return. The contrast of the situation was sharp.

The two parties met, as I say, in a narrow passage. They eagerly scrutinized each other, this being their very first meeting. Then, on a sign from the Empress, she and her nieces, and attendants drew up against the wall, courtesying low to the Orleans family, as they passed along on their way toward home and country.

From a letter:

Farnborough Hill,
Saturday, February 27, 1886.

As M. Pietri is away, we now have one game of *cochonnet*

---

* "I do not know how I kept my sanity in many trying episodes of my life. My present state of nerves is easily understood."

every evening with the Duke, who otherwise would have no one to play billiards with, and who misses his one tame little bit of gaiety very much. He is such a dear old man, and wonderful for his age, and so kind, so courteous, and so dignified, and yet so amusing. He has been suffering lately from indigestion and heartburn, but he is so patient and nice about it. In answer to the Empress's daily inquiry, "Eh bien, mon cher Duc, comment cela va-t-il aujourd'hui?" he answers simply, "J'ai encore le fer chaud, Madame; que votre Majesté ne se préoccupe pas. Ca n'est rien – tout passe!"*

Yesterday being our staying-up-late evening, I was at the piano a good deal, each time the Empress asking for "More! – more!" The *Music Box* appeared to delight her, she found it such a close imitation of a real one.

Thursday, March 4. Mme. Le Breton spent the day in London. We three girls took a long walk with the Empress in the morning, and drove with the Duc de Bassano in the afternoon, when he spoke of many interesting things. He told us a good deal about the poor demented Empress Charlotte, sister of Leopold II of Belgium and widow of the Archduke Maximilian, made Emperor of Mexico in 1864 and shot in Quarétaro, June 19, 1867. The Duc de Bassano's daughter, Baroness d'Hoogworth, lady-in-waiting to the Queen of the Belgians, occasionally passes a day with the ex-empress at Laeken, near Brussels. For many previous years she used to spend her time in front of an easel, painting and repainting her husband's portrait, or writing pathetic letters, begging and imploring different sovereigns of Europe to give her soldiers and means to help her Maximilian (long since shot down by his rebellious subjects). Charlotte's latest craze, and she has had many and varied ones, the Duke says, is not to allow her

---

* "Well, my dear Duke, how are you today?" "I have the hot iron today. I beg your Majesty not to preoccupy yourself on my account – it is nothing – everything comes to an end."

ladies to eat anything at mealtimes. The Duke also said he remembered her as young and gay on her first visit to Vienna after her marriage. On her arrival it was discovered that all her baggage had been delayed on the road, and not having a court dress to appear in, she had to stay in her room during the official reception given in her honor.

From these matters we drifted into talking of audiences, for one of his duties as Grand Chamberlain was to interview the people who came to the Tuileries, asking for audiences, or who had petitions to present to the Emperor. The Duke told us many interesting incidents that happened in consequence.

One poor widow, who had lost her only son, her mainstay, had come to beg assistance of the always accessible sovereign. After seeing him she returned triumphantly to thank the Duc de Bassano for his good offices. In her gratitude she recounted the Emperor's kindness to her: "Ah, Monsieur," she said, "que l'Empereur est bon; il a bien voulu se mettre en redingote, parce-qu'il ne voulait pas trop m'impressioner."* The poor woman evidently thought that robes of state were always worn, and that the Emperor had only donned civilian clothes out of delicate regard for her feelings.

In the evening after dinner the subject of audiences again came up in conversation, and this time it was the Empress who told us her experiences.

She said how trying the hours of audiences were, as she was obliged to give them standing. If once she allowed people to sit down, she found from experience she never could get rid of them. Women were the hardest to deal with; they would stick pertinaciously to their request however ridiculous.

A country woman was ushered in one day and gave, with much excitement, the details of a great plot she said she had discovered - hidden bombs, etc., - and tried to intimidate

* "Ah, sir," she said, "how good the Emperor is - he very kindly wore plain clothes - so as not to overawe me!"

67

the Empress, who suspected the woman's sincerity and the truth of her narrative. She tested the woman by turning the tables on her, and in her turn frightening her. Feigning to believe her statements, the Empress told her that *she* would certainly be arrested for complicity in the plot. The terrified woman then threw herself on her knees and begged for mercy, confessed to her Empress that the whole story was pure invention, and that she had only taken this mysteriously threatening attitude for the sake of obtaining an audience; what she really wanted was only "U-ne pe-ti-te bas-til-le," which the Empress – mimicking her queer petitioner, – pronounced with a strong Marseillais accent, and which she told us meant merely, a little house.

Here is another audience our hostess told us about, which showed how constantly she had to keep her wits about her, not to be hoodwinked. A very saintly-looking Dominican monk one day early in her reign craved admittance to her presence in the Tuileries. It was neither the regular day nor hour for audiences, but as the monk said he had come from the celebrated Père Lacordaire, who was well known to the Empress and often sent her urgent cases for immediate relief, the Dominican was welcomed and listened to. He made a very thrilling appeal for his monastery. The Empress, who was much touched by his pathetic story of emergency regretfully admitted she had not at that moment in cash the sum required, but she would try to obtain it, and send it to his address before night. This he did not seem to relish; said he was very sorry but that arrangement, unfortunately, would be of no use, as urgent circumstances obliged him to leave Paris before evening! The Empress in her impulse to help, then bethought herself of the Emperor, who was busily working near by. She left the monk for a moment and went into the adjoining room to ask her husband for an addition to the sum she herself had in hand, which was 1500 francs. The Emperor questioned her about the case, disapproved of her giving in this offhand way, and though always so generous himself, absolutely refused for once to help. Doubts having been thus raised in her mind by the Emperor's firmness, something in the monk's attitude as she reëntered the room further aroused her suspicions of him. She noticed a certain discomfort in the way he walked; he entangled his legs as if not very much at home in his habit. As soon as the monk had left the palace, the Empress sent quickly for her *chef de police* and had the case investigated. No such Dominican was known to Père Lacordaire; the monk was just a dressed-up swindler. This was a lesson and made her less apt, she said, to act on sympathetic impulses without due inquiry first.

Friday, March 5. At dinner we talked about nuns, monks and religious vocations. The Empress said she thought, provided the vocation was real, that it was the happiest lot in life – with its absence of sordid care and anxiety, its peace, its quiet and regular work. She added, it was only steady occupation which made life bearable in her case. She asked a good deal about I. and F., and their respective convent and monastery, having evidently in mind to glean all possible information which might be useful for her own monastery adjoining the Memorial Church. She declared she would probably decide to have Benedictines there in charge.

Saturday, March 6. M. D'Antas, the Portuguese ambassador, came to pay his respects. The Empress started for Windsor later, and we went as usual to the gymnastic class at Aldershot.

Monday, March 8. Went up to London on the 12:45 train with M. and A. At Mme. de Arcos's house we met the Empress, who was returning from Windsor.

In the evening, owing to her return from Windsor, the Empress naturally told us a good deal about her visit, and the way she usually spends her time there; the kind of life they lead at the castle; some special visits in her private apartments;

and the routine of the day. She expressed her dislike to being dressed up – they change their costumes in the royal household four times daily, and to the quiet Empress it meant bustle and rush all day long.* She told us, too, of the fuss and commotion caused by the breaking of a drainpipe near her room, and how anxious the Queen was, – dreading typhoid, already so fatal in her family. The Empress's party had to move over into another wing of the castle in consequence.

She explained also, how frigid it always is at the castle, especially after dinner. The Queen's love of fresh air and cold is phenomenal, and a window is always open where she sits. This is hard on the ladies-in-waiting, who, in the evening of course, have to be décolletée in all seasons. The Empress told us an amusing little anecdote about Princess Beatrice, who, one particularly chilly evening, rather mischievously ran into the drawing-room ahead of her royal mother, quickly put the thermometer outside the window for a few moments and then hung it deftly back again in its accustomed place. The Queen, on entering the room, glanced mechanically at the thermometer, looked puzzled, and expressed her surprise at the low temperature registered. As soon as she had turned her back, the mercury naturally rose, but the Queen, once satisfied by her hasty glimpse at the instrument, sat down, perfectly unaware of the trick played upon her, and the ladies had a more comfortable evening in consequence.

Poor Princess Beatrice is nearly driven wild; she has so much given her to do and not half enough time to do it in. She is constantly at the Queen's beck and call and never even sits down to write a letter, so her imperial friend says, without

_____

* The Empress always (even in the heyday of her glory) put on early in the morning the dress she was going to wear all day, till she changed it for dinner. She expressed admiration for the English in this respect, as well as her dislike for the laziness of certain women of fashion, who spent half their waking hours at home in the negligées and tea gowns, which type of garment she thoroughly despised.

The Empress Eugenie and Napoleon III with the Prince Imperial

constantly being sent for by her mother. Her only real leisure is after a nine-fifteen dinner and the later social reunion of the royal household at ten o'clock (every one standing the while). She and her husband then go to their own suite of rooms at 11 p.m., and enjoy each other's society and their absolute freedom. The Queen then regularly settles down to several hours serious work, which does not prevent her from being up betimes; and it behooves her ladies not to be lagging either. If she makes others work hard, she at least sets them a good example. Every state document passes under her own eyes and is thoroughly mastered by her. She keeps well up in current English, French and German literature, and is an excellent linguist, as indeed are all the other members of the royal family.

Princess Beatrice in talking to the Empress about her husband, Prince Henry, and of Kaiser William's persistently unkind treatment of him, told her "auntie" that when her betrothed went to announce his prospective marriage at Berlin, the German Empress, in audience, kept him standing like a stranger the whole time. Moreover, when because of his betrothal to an English Princess he sent in his army demission to the Kaiser, Prince Henry waited and waited in vain for the document to be ratified, and apparently his communication was taken no notice of. In the meantime, the day fixed for the wedding was approaching rapidly; he could delay no longer, so he decided to start for England, _prêter serment à la Reine_ without the Kaiser's ratification, and shortly after the nuptial ceremony took place.

Kaiser William when he heard of it was perfectly furious, as his telegram in answer to the Queen's announcement of Beatrice's marriage, to the German court, shows. All he replied to his royal and imperial grandmother was: "Je viens d'apprendre l'étonnante nouvelle." *

---

* "I have just heard some astonishing news."

72

His wife says that if Prince Henry were now to return to Prussia he would be liable to five years' imprisonment as a deserter. Princess Beatrice further told the Empress that he feels intensely the rude and unkind treatment he has been subjected to, and is so extremely amiable and unassuming that it comes doubly hard on him. "If he were a criminal," she added, "they could hardly treat him more scornfully!" Princess Beatrice also spoke of her present anxiety about Prince Alexander of Bulgaria, Henry's brother. His relatives quite expect that he will be assassinated some day, and her husband has not the heart to open the telegrams, so she does it herself.

The Queen, in many ways so domestic and simple, is a great stickler for etiquette and precedent, and certain forms of deference are insisted upon in her presence. This must try her ladies in more ways than one, for possessing great physical strength she sees no reason, for instance, why they should not, well or ill, stand almost indefinitely in her presence. The Empress said it often made her own back ache sympathetically, thinking about the poor maids of honor as they stood up hour after hour behind the Queen's chair. They were expected, too, whatever the weather, to take long walks with their royal mistress.* The robust Queen was evidently unaware of the hardships these more delicate women underwent, for nobody could have been more usually considerate, kind or sympathetic, than she.

---

* The Queen while temporarily lame often drove in her private grounds, both at Windsor and at Osborne, in a bath chair drawn by a favorite donkey, and the Empress recalled many a time when she had walked by her side. One day in particular stands out. As the conversation between the two ladies waxed more and more interesting, the Queen unconsciously, if gradually, accelerated the speed of the donkey, till, getting no response to what she was saying, she turned in surprise to find even the quick-walking Empress speechless with lack of breath. The ladies-in-waiting cast a look of gratitude on the Empress, who, gasping for breath, explained the situation.

As an instance of her thoughtfulness, the Empress was much surprised, she told us, the first Friday she spent at Windsor, at finding a whole maigre dinner specially prepared for her. The service was so quietly and beautifully arranged that the many courses of the two dinners went on simultaneously, without any one noticing anything unusual but the one guest to whom the special dishes were presented. The table decoration on this particular day, the Empress recalled, consisted of blocks of ice in the center, surrounded by choice cut begonias.

Here is another anecdote lately told the Empress by the Queen, herself, in course of conversation, and which her imperial guest brought back to us. It shows the Queen's independence of character, willingness to abandon precedent when it suited her. Very fond of primroses, and finding none in the royal gardens, she sent word to have some planted. The gardeners, the Queen said, made many objections, and finding shortly afterward that her wishes had not yet been carried out she despatched a royal messenger to inquire the reason. "I suppose Queen Anne had none," she said to the Empress, "so they did not think it proper for *me* to have any; but I sent them word promptly that Queen Victoria would have some – and she *did*."

Tuesday, March 9. Today at lunch the Empress showed us how the Queen eats her orange, and advised us to imitate her, – cutting a small hole in the top, removing the central pith with a very sharp knife, and then scooping out the juicy pulp with a spoon, leaving the rind intact. Since the Queen cuts it thus, none of her ladies would dare depart from the conventional way, unless encouraged to do so by Her Majesty who, to their regret, does not so encourage them.

The girls and Mme. Le Breton went to a concert. I drove into Aldershot to make some inquiry for the Empress from Father Bellord,* one of the army chaplains. A long, cold drive

---

* Later on Bishop of Gibraltar, who has since died.

74

through the North and South camps and past all the barracks. After a warming cup of afternoon tea with the Empress, she took me into the *cabinet de travail*, where I had a long, interesting talk with her.

She told me another story apropos of Windsor, about an impromptu visit the Empress of Austria paid there some years ago. Empress Elizabeth arrived one Sunday unannounced, while all the Queen's household was attending service. Every one was in a state of excitement as to what should be done under these unusual circumstances. Divine service could not be interrupted, neither could the Austrian Empress be ignored. She had appeared suddenly on foot with a suite of fifteen persons, and remained walking about the grounds until the important members of the distracted court had collected their wits. After some cogitation the Queen left the chapel, went down alone to receive her inconsiderate and unceremonious guest and persuaded her to enter the castle. The Empress of Austria's large Newfoundland dog followed into the drawing-room and jumped up on the sofa beside the Queen, to the secret delight of the unconventional Austrian monarch and the intense discomfiture of the punctilious Queen of England. The animal, so Empress Eugénie said, snarled every time its mistress was spoken to, but Queen Victoria, who it appears dislikes large dogs in the house, had to submit to the discomfiture out of politeness. This story was told her by the Queen herself, and the Empress added: "This was the Empress of Austria's way of paying off old scores." What she meant exactly by this last remark I do not know.

A *la suite* of this, the Empress described to me an interesting ceremony she had witnessed years ago, and which took place either at the coronation, or as a New Year celebration, in which the Emperor of Austria, who is also King of Hungary, took the leading part. The Emperor, sword in hand, galloped up a small hill or mound, saluted the four quarters of the globe, and then rode down again. The cloak worn by him for this quaint ceremony had been in use many hundreds of years, and only Empresses are allowed to mend it; my Empress says it was shockingly cobbled and a disgrace to some of the imperial darners of bygone days.

Tuesday, March 16. Anniversary of Prince Imperial's birthday. He would have been thirty years old had he lived. Very sad day for the Empress. Loving hands have put quantities of violets, where generally one modest little bunch is to be seen, in front of his picture on the easel in the gallery. Passing by it, while going to and fro on our evening walk, the Empress told us about an illness of his at the same age as the Dauphin of France, and drew a kind of parallel between her son and the little *Fils de France*. "Mon pauvre petit garçon," she said, "était malade (tombé d'un trapèse et blessé à la hanche) au même âge, que le petit Louis XVII était aussi gravement malade. Marie Antoinette a fait tant de neuvaines et a tant fait prier, que lui a guéri, – mais pour son malheur; moi, je n'ai jamais une seule fois demandé à Dieu avec les autres que mon Louis guerisse! Je ne pouvais pas! – Une mère ne sait souvent pas ce qu'elle demande au Ciel. Mon fils a guéri, lui aussi, – cependant il aurait mieux valu pour lui qu'il mourût enfant, au lieu de guérir pour –"* Here she burst out into smothered sobs, and did not finish what we all knew she meant to say, – "live to meet a savage death among Zulus!" She told us also of her growing feeling, since her son's death, of devotion to the Guardian Angels, of her gratitude toward them, and the comfort it is to her, to feel that they at least were with her

---

* "My poor little boy was ill – he had fallen from a trapezium and had injured his hip, – at about the same age that the little Louis XVII had also had a dangerous illness. Marie Antoinette made so many novenas and had so many prayers offered up that he, Louis XVII, was cured – but for his own misfortune. I never once, with all the rest of the people, asked God to cure my Louis – I could not! A mother often does not know what she is asking of Heaven. My son recovered also – it would have been better for him, however, if he had died in childhood rather than recover to –"

The Prince Imperial
at the age of six

The Prince Imperial
at the age of twelve

boy when he was abandoned and dying. And, later on, talking of the Palace of the Tuileries, she said: "Je suis en somme contente que les Tuiléries aient brulé,*1 car tous les derniers enfants nés dans ce Palais ont été malheureux – le pauvre petit Louis XVII; Napoleon II (Roi de Rome);– mon fils."*2 She was not afraid of death, she explained, and she looked forward with joy to being reunited to those who had gone before her. "C'est la foi, qui donne le courage de mourir [It is faith which gives us the courage to die]." She was glad to feel her son had been a thoroughly good young man, that she had no doubt whatever of his being in heaven. "Si je pensais que mon fils ne fût pas au Ciel, – je ne désirerais pas y aller," – and noticing me draw in my breath in quiet horror, she added: "C'est peut-être terrible à dire, mais franchement ce ne serait alors pas le Ciel pour moi." *3

Wednesday, March 17. His Excellency the Marques de Casa la Iglesia, Spanish ex-ambassador, lunched here. The girls were delighted to hear and speak to a Spaniard again.

In the evening apropos of various health resorts the Empress and Mme. Le Breton told us their experiences in Holland with Dr. Metzger, to whom they had gone for treatment for rheumatism. World-renowned for his wonderful cures by massage, with more patients than he could personally attend to, and an autocrat by nature, he would not waste time

---

*1 In one of the vitrines the Empress showed me one day a small delicate porcelain statuette of the Prince Imperial, which used to be in her bedroom at the Tuileries, and which, in a wonderful way, had escaped the flames and the falling débris of the burning palace. Loving hands had found it in some nook protected by a fallen column, and restored it to its former owner.

*2 "I am after all glad that the Tuileries was burned down – for all the later children born in that palace were unfortunate, the poor little Louis XVII, Napoleon II (Roi de Rome) – and my own son!"

*3 "If I thought my son were not in Heaven, I should not wish to go there. – It is perhaps terrible to say so, but frankly, it would not then be Heaven for me."

going to the bedside of any sick person. High or low, therefore, journeyed thither to him, and at his hospital in Amsterdam he gathered a motley crowd – emperors, kings, breadwinners, beggars, were all treated alike by the doctor, who, though kindheartedness itself, handled them very roughly.

The Empress told us how the patients had to wait their turn in order of arrival, in a series of little cubicles open at the top, and how nervous it made her as she heard Metzger coming along from one compartment to another and getting nearer and nearer, his progress along the corridor being marked by the screams of the sufferers under his skilful but rough hand. At last, after a few days, she could stand it no longer and got worked up to such a pitch of nervous tension that she feared she would have to give up the treatment altogether. After several interviews, however, between the famous masseur, M. Pietri and Mme. Le Breton, and on account of exceptional circumstances, Metzger at last consented to a slight change, a wonderful and unusual concession. For the remainder of the course Her Imperial Majesty was allowed to take precedence over the other patients; she was always put into the first cubicle and was thus spared the misery of daily suspense.

Metzger charged one uniform fee and that a very modest one, to rich and poor alike. But he always welcomed, from those who could afford it, donations for his hospital and needy cases, and most of his patients in their gratitude gave generously.

Thursday, March 18. Sir Evelyn and Lady Wood, Major Parsons and the Marquise de la Valette, lunched here.* Dr. Scott came after lunch and accompanied us to the gymnasium. The Prince of Wales with his eldest son, Prince Albert Victor, called on the Empress in the afternoon.

---

* H. I. M. was agitated lest Sir Evelyn and Lord Wolsey should by some coincidence arrive on the same day; they were both expected about this time. They are rivals, if not open enemies, she says, and the meeting at her table would be awkward for all.

During our evening walk, mentioning the Prince of Wales's visit of the afternoon, Her Imperial Majesty spoke disapprovingly of his great severity toward his son, who is stationed at Aldershot. The other young officers of his regiment are allowed to go off shooting and have occasional days off, but nothing of the kind for Prince Albert. Never a single day away from his regiment, except to be made use of in opening some public institution, or doing some of those things the royal family get such a dose of. His mother fears that so much severity may make her boy hate the army, and have a bad influence on him.

Monday, March 22. General Lord and Lady Wolsey, Mme de Arcos, Mrs. Vaughan and her niece lunched here. We showed the latter all over the house and grounds. The Duc de Bassano left here at 10:19 for London en route to Paris, for a two months' leave of absence.

Wednesday, March 24. The Empress went up to London. She told us on her return about her crossing Hyde Park just as the Queen's procession happened to pass. A policeman, recognizing her, got a good place for her carriage to stand, saying, "I will arrange it all for your 'Ighness." He returned shortly after – having given the necessary orders – adding with much genuine unction, "I am so glad to see you, Madame."

Speaking of this little incident, brought out several reminiscences in our evening conversation. It would seem that it was often those to whose gratitude she had the most claim, who proved to be totally lacking in nice feeling; while on the contrary she often met with gratitude from unexpected quarters, as the following examples show.

In passing through Paris some years ago, the Empress told us she went over much of the same route she had taken during the eventful flight from the capital in 1870. Many of the officials recognized her; they looked carefully round first to see if they were observed, and when reassured, saluted her openly as of old. A woman at the railway station pressed up close to her one day, and in a touching way rapidly kissed the hem of her dress; then disappeared in the crowd without a word.

Another time in visiting incognita the chateau at Fontainebleau, she went about with the crowd, and was shown over the different apartments by the *gardien*. At last they came to some room very intimately connected with her son (probably his nursery, and turning away sadly, she gave a last wistful look back before having to leave it. The *gardien* let the other people ahead drift away, and gently pushing her back into the room closed the door, whispering to her: "Madame, je reviendrai tout à l'heure [Madame, I will return in a moment]." He had recognized the widowed, mother and delicately wanted to procure her a few undisturbed moments with her memories.

A man at the Galerie du Louvre came up to the Princess Mary of Cambridge one day, and said to her: "Etes-vous anglaise?" – "Oui." – "Eh bien, vous devez alors connaitre notre Impératrice. Dites lui que . . . [naming himself] se souvient d'elle." *

In connection with these anecdotes it might not be inappropriate to tell a somewhat similar experience of my own, when living in Paris at the end of 1886. It showed me once more how the memory of the Empress, and even more, that of the Emperor, lingers still undyingly in the minds of many of the French. Walking down the Champs Elysées one day with M. and J. de S., we stopped a few moments in front of a little toystall to buy some trifle. The choice made, I handed J. a one-franc piece, which he tendered to the very sunburnt and wrinkled *marchande*. She scrutinized the coin closely, turned it over several times in her hands, and just as I thought by

---

* "Are you English?" – "Yes." – Well, then you must know our Empress! Tell her that ... thinks of her still."

her behaviour she might be about to return it to me as bad currency, she put it to her lips and began kissing it vigorously, saying, "Ah, mon chèr Empereur! ma chère Impératrice! – Ah, qu'ils étaient bons – ah, hélas! comme tout a changé maintenant!"* The woman then rambled on volubly, making a great many comparisons between the Empire and the Republic; told us how the Emperor had often in the past stopped at her little stall to buy some toy for the Prince Imperial, and had always given her a gold piece in exchange for her wares. "Ah, – lui – il nous aimait bien, nous autres pauvres [Ah, he – he loved us well, we poor things]," she said, and much else in the same strain.

Having sufficiently drawn out her sentiments by listening interestedly to her, and recognizing her evident devotion, I could not resist the pleasure of telling her what I felt would please and agreeably surprise such an enthusiast, namely, that I, who casually stood before her, knew her Empress intimately, and that I had only a few weeks previously left the hospitable roof of Farnborough Hill. At this my *marchande* could not contain her astonishment and excitement, began kissing my hands, and to my utter surprise and discomfiture threw herself upon my neck and wept with joy, regardless of all the passers-by. After that her stall was never passed by us without a little friendly chat. I gave her a few violets from the Prince's and Emperor's tombs, which made her supremely happy and proud, and we were always sure of a warm welcome from the faithful and genuine old creature. The next visit I paid to Farnborough, I told this little story to the Empress, who seemed much touched by it.

Saturday, March 27. H. got here at 9:10 a.m. I went to meet her in the landau, which had just returned from fetching

---

* "Ah, my dear Emperor! my dear Empress! – Ah, how good they were! – Ah, alas! how all has changed now."

Mme. de Saulcy, who arrived on a visit by an earlier train.

Sunday, March 28. Mme. de Saulcy returned to Paris after a stay of two days only. She is an old friend of the Empress's, another of the coterie of devoted women – *femme si distinguée du spirituel membre de l'Institut*. She used to be a good deal at the Tuileries during the Empire.

From a letter:

Farnborough Hill.
April 2, 1886.

In spite of unpropitious weather, M. Destailleur, the Paris architect who is building the beautiful little Memorial Church, crossed the English Channel and managed to arrive here. All day, naturally, the conversation turned on plans for the adjoining monastery, which is to be commenced at once, and having a Benedictine brother, I was constantly appealed to by the Empress as to the necessities for a monastery! Next week Princess Beatrice and some other princesses are expected over from Windsor to see the Empress. If they come to luncheon we shall, of course, see them; if only for a call, perhaps we may not. However, time will reveal, and when I know more about the proposed visit, I will write you word.

Speaking of visits from royalty in general, the Empress said this evening that they are now too ceremonious for her to enjoy. She hates her daily routine being interfered with, and a royal visit involves so much fuss. The princesses are all extremely amiable and nice, but in her present state of nerves she would rather they stayed at home, excepting always, of course, Princess Beatrice, for "I am so fond of her," she said. Ordinary visitors, who come quietly and bring new ideas, are always welcome, and the Empress is as interested as ever in any new scientific theory or curious invention.

From a letter:

Farnborough Hill,
April 6, 1886.

My letters lately have been only hasty scribbles with little news in them, but this one will I hope be more interesting, as I have to tell you about the royal visit which took place yesterday. On Saturday we heard definitely that Princess Beatrice was coming. Sunday, telegrams kept arriving all day, first saying that the royal party would come by carriage from Windsor, – then by train, – and then again later the hour as well as the route were altered. After a good many changes of plan and much fuss in the house, – servants rushing about, putting the awnings up and the carpets down at the entrance, – Princess Beatrice with Prince Henry of Battenberg and his sister, the pretty Countess of Erbach, arrived by special saloon train, getting here about one o'clock. The first greetings over, the Empress went out with her guests on foot, taking them up to see the new Memorial Church, and returning about 2 p.m. for luncheon. We, poor things, who had breakfasted very lightly at 8 a.m., were dying with hunger, and while waiting for the royal visitors to take off their things, wickedly wished them back at Windsor, or even at Jericho. As they passed up the gallery, on their way to the dining-room, they made a slight pause, and the Empress presented each of us separately to the Princess, her husband and sister. We kissed Princess Beatrice's hand, and courtesied to her companions who were both very nice. The Countess is extremely *distinguée*, amiable and merry, and so is Prince Henry. I was sitting next but one to him at lunch, and he chatted away and laughed a good deal with M. and myself. Princess Beatrice was very quiet indeed, and seems dull and out of spirits, "suppressed," the Empress says, from the constant restraint of the Queen's presence. She was very simply dressed, shabbily I might even say, as her mauve woolen tailor-made dress was faded and had lost its first bloom of youth.

84

According to the Empress, Prince Henry keeps his wife (so well inured herself to all court etiquette) always on thorns, for he is unconventional and outspoken, and not in the very least awed by the Queen, as her own children appear to be on the surface. At the risk of offending his royal mother-in-law he gives his opinion frankly, whenever he finds an opportunity, and Princess Beatrice never knows what he may say or do next. During luncheon two telegrams came to Princess Beatrice from "Mamma" at Windsor – giving the latest account of the Duchess of Connaught's condition. The Duke, it appears, is in a great state of anxiety, as his wife is seriously ill. Her weakness is something appalling. Even lifting her head in bed makes her go off in a swoon, which lasts for hours, and her anxiety to get well so as to be able to start with her soldier-husband for India in June only throws her back.

The royal party left at 4:30, after having been shown the house and its treasures by the Empress herself. Again, before parting, we kissed Princess Beatrice's hand, which seemed to embarrass her, but as we had previously received our instructions the Princess had to fall in with the program as well as we. This time we shook hands with the others. A short drive took them to Farnborough Station, where a special train was waiting to convey them to Ascot, whence they were to go by carriage to Windsor.

Prince Henry was most amusing at lunch. Talking about his idea of London, he told us how deadly tired he was and how he hated going about continually opening this, that and the other institution, and presenting prizes day after day. He said that last week, driving in a barouche to go to Whitechapel, one of the horses slipped and fell, and during quite a long delay, while the men were getting the horse on to its legs again, there he was, surrounded by a highly aristocratic East End crowd! What made it most awkward was that some of the people looked very black at him indeed, and some few made faces, shook their fists and put out their tongues at him. He added, "It seemed hardly possible in decency to bow to them and take off my hat, in response to a tongue half a yard long," and still it had to be done. The Empress, in conversation about bowing to crowds and different incidents connected with this sort of salutation, urged its importance on the young people, ending with something like, "Enfants, c'est comme cela qu'on gagne les coeurs [Children, that is the way to win their hearts]." To which Prince Henry responded, smiling and thanking his hostess, and then addressing his wife: "Entends tu Beatrice? – Je te dis toujours que ne salues pas assez [Do you hear, Beatrice? – I am always telling you, you do not bow enough] !"

From my diary:

After dinner and during our evening walk with the Empress, talking over our guests, she began speaking about gatherings of people she had seen and been in, and dilated specially on the great mutability of a French crowd. She told me about a certain visit to Lyons, August, 1860, and the procession to the cathedral. The authorities begged H. I. M. not to go, as in the unsettled state of the town they had fears for her safety, but she scorned to change her plan. It proved a terrible drive, the horses walking all the way uphill in the midst of the menacing and gesticulating crowds. The Empress was alone in her open carriage with the little Prince Imperial, both smiling and bowing all the time, till her own charm and his baby friendliness finally conquered the sullen populace, and so completely, that before arriving at the cathedral it had gradually veered around and became sufficiently enthusiastic to take the horses out of the carriage, and to drag it proudly and exultingly themselves. In the evening the crowds were cheering so vociferously that they obliged her to leave the official dinner table and show herself on a balcony before they would be pacified.

A ball was given that night at the Hôtel de Ville, the courtyard of which was covered in with huge blocks of ice, and flowers in the center, as decorations. The heat was so intense that even one of the splendid, six foot Cent-gardes soldiers in his gorgeous uniform fainted, and a gentleman in full dress got into the fountain, hoping to revive himself. When the tired Empress at last was able to go to bed, she could not sleep for the noisy demonstration still keeping up outside. So she got up, took a lighted candle and appearing in flowing robes on the balcony, bowed to the assembled people, - and then blew out the candle. Their fancy was tickled at her dramatic manner of bidding them good night, and after one more rousing cheer, they took the hint and retired quietly to their homes.

By going out on the balcony, overheated, in response to the clamor of the people, the Empress told us she caught a fearful cold. Prince Napoleon suggested a remedy, - snuffing up water and opium. It was most efficacious, but a yellow nose all the rest of the journey was the unexpected result.

From a letter:

Farnborough Hill.

On Wednesday the seventh, I had a two hours' drive in the victoria alone with the Empress. She was so delightful, chatting the whole time about all sorts of interesting things. She inquired very particularly about you.

She gave me an account of how she eluded Bismarck's vigilance, and paid a visit to the Emperor in the castle at Wilhelmshöhe just after the war; she was halfway back to England before he got wind of the proceeding. Having first telegraphed to ask the Chancellor's permission to visit her husband, and being answered that if she did, she might be liable to arrest as a prisoner of war - she determined nevertheless to go at all hazards. She drove in greatest secrecy with her maid and the Comte Clary from Chislehurst to

London; there she dismissed carriage and attendant and went into the waiting-room alone, while Comte Clary bought the tickets. Reaching Cologne that night, they found they had missed the connecting train and had to remain in the waiting-room until the next morning. Finally they arrived at Wilhelmshöhe and presented themselves before the governor, who, misled by her matter-of-fact boldness, never doubted but that the Empress and her escort had permission to enter the fortress. He received the travelers very courteously, had rooms prepared for them, and the Empress was able to see her husband undisturbed for several hours, and to talk over all their affairs together with his faithful friends, Dr. Conneau, M. Pietri and others, who were sharing his captivity with him. Late in the afternoon she retired to her room *soi-disant* to rest, sending word to the governor that she would like a pass to leave the castle a little later on, to go into the town and buy a few necessaries before dinner. The polite and unsuspecting governor granted her request at once and she lost no time, but started off immediately with Comte Clary, having already quietly taken leave of her husband. The two made straight for the station. There they inquired eagerly, when the very first train was to depart and where, and were told – to Hanover, which seemed a long way around, considering London was their destination, but there was no help for it. They were hungry, not having had their dinner, but they did not dare delay or risk recognition by trying to buy food, or necessaries, though they had not so much as a hand bag or a traveling rug between them. The night set in bitterly cold. Regular traffic was suspended at the wayside stations, where they stopped often, and they had to walk up and down to keep warm, stepping as they did so over German soldiers, who were sleeping on the platforms while waiting for their trains.*

---

* They were being disbanded after the war.

Photos, W. and D. Downey

Prince and Princess Henry (Princess Beatrice) of Battenberg

89

In the railway carriage, she and the Count had much difficulty in hiding their identity from inquisitive and excited travelers, who insisted upon trying to draw them into conversation about the events of the day, fiercely criticizing the policy of the French Empire. Afraid to show their own knowledge of affairs, they neither dared to keep too much aloof, for fear of exciting suspicion. One man would not be silenced; he recommended hotels to the mysterious couple, and tried in every way to engage them in conversation, to put them off their guard, and to discover their names.

Several times they were taken for General and Mme. MacMahon, and at The Hague were placed in a most awkward dilemma about rooms. The hotelkeeper, taking them for husband and wife, which they did not dare deny even had they been able to make themselves understood in Dutch, and the hotel being overcrowded, insisted upon giving them one room together. At the last gasp they barely got out of the difficulty by Comte Clary's explanation, in halting language eked out by many gesticulations, that they were brother and sister.

They walked about the streets for some time next morning. The Empress was very anxious to have speech with her great friend, Queen Sophie of Holland,* but the husband, Wilhelm III, was such an irascible man that H. I. M. feared to get the Queen into trouble by an open visit, and so the travelers began casting about for some way of making their presence privately known to the Queen.

Comte Clary no less than his companion looked so travel-stained and shabby that he was refused admittance to the castle, when he inquired for one of the ladies-in-waiting, known to him and of whom he meant to ask aid in his scheme. They were dejectedly turning away wondering what they had

---

* First wife of Wilhelm III, formerly Princess of Wurtemberg and first cousin to Plon-Plon and Princesse Mathilde through Catherine of Wurtemberg, wife of King Jerome (brother of Napoleon I).

better do, when luckily the Queen's carriage drove past and although she had not the slightest knowledge of the Empress's visit to The Hague, she had with one swift glance recognized her stately form. She drove on, however, seemingly oblivious of everything. But she had seen her, and on arriving home made it known that strangers were to be expected, for when the shabby couple presented themselves a second time at the castle, they were admitted immediately, although the halberdier evidently did not like their looks. They were taken up a small back staircase to the private apartments of the Queen, where the Empress had a comforting talk with her friend. Soon the Empress heard steps approaching, and she noticed that the Queen, always in deadly fear of her tyrannical husband, began to be very uneasy and restless. The Empress said she herself was not in an over-comfortable situation, when King Wilhelm suddenly walked in, and intensely surprised both ladies by his great and unexpected amiability toward both his wife and her visitor. The call passed off most pleasantly, and when it came to an end the King himself gave the Empress his arm and conducted her ceremoniously down the grand staircase, at the bottom of which he gave her the royal salute – a kiss on both cheeks – in sight of the bewildered halberdier.

The Empress told me she never should forget that guard's face on seeing the shabby woman whom he had so recently and scornfully repulsed, kissed by the King, by which token he knew immediately that she must be a sovereign. His expression of dismay was so fear-laden and so ludicrous that the Empress burst out laughing in spite of all her anxieties.

Comte Clary and she got back to London safely from this trip, and reached Chislehurst just eight days after leaving it, having been to bed only two nights out of the eight, nearly all the time without sufficient food. The Empress said she had managed the whole so quickly that Bismarck with all his keenness had no time to suspect, or frustrate her plans.

Before the end of our drive we drifted into talking of second sight and kindred subjects, and the Empress told me about Malvina, the old negress who had come over from the Island of Martinique with Josephine de Beauharnais, wife of Napoleon I, and lived afterward with Queen Hortense at Arenenberg in Switzerland, and who was a clairvoyant. In a trance one day during Prince Louis Napoleon's absence from home (supposedly on a hunting trip), Malvina became very much excited and called out suddenly to her mistress: "Oh, je vois le Prince, – il se trouve dans une ville! Je vois de grandes maisons! . . . Il est entouré de soldats! Ah, mon Dieu! on le prend!"[1] This all turned out to be true. As soon as there was time for the ill news to travel, Hortense heard that her son's supposed hunting trip was only a blind in order to get off unhindered – a subterfuge to save her anxiety of suspense. In reality he had hastily gathered a few faithful friends about him, had attempted the coup d'état of Strassburg which failed so signally, and was at that moment a prisoner.

This was on October 30, 1836. Louis Napoleon was condemned by the French government to exile and banished to the United States. After some delay he was taken to Lorient, and there embarked on the frigate *Andromeda*, which sailed November 21, 1836. After a long tour via Rio de Janeiro by order of the government, he was put ashore at Norfolk and was there set at liberty March 30, 1837, after which he made his way up to New York, where he lived some time.

The Empress told me also the most amusing story about the escape of Louis Napoleon later on, from the fortress of Ham,[2] where he had spent several years. Without tremendous

---

[1] "Oh, I see the Prince – he is in a town! – I see tall houses! He is surrounded by soldiers! Ah, God, they have seized him!"

[2] He had been imprisoned there after the second coup d'état, which failed like the first. It was called L'affaire du Boulogne, August 6, 1840, and brought much ridicule on all concerned.

audacity, coolness, and that feeling of strong belief in "his star" that all would end rightly, he could never have dreamed of such a madly rash attempt, nor have succeeded in getting out safely in spite of all the jailers and sentries guarding him.

The following story of a strange coincidence I heard at Farnborough, but not from the Empress's own lips. It touched on the chance which gave her one day (November 12, 1836), as a young girl, her first glimpse of her future husband. Taking her dancing lesson with the daughter of the Prefet de Police of Paris, M. Delessert, the children were allowed to go to the window to look out and see, – crossing the courtyard of the *prefecture*, – a prisoner just brought in for interrogation. It was Louis Napoleon, under arrest after the Strassburg affair.

From a letter:

Farnborough Hill.

On Tuesday, I think I told you, we had some Parisians to lunch, Count and Countess and Mlle. de Pourtales. The mother used to be a renowned beauty *sous l'Empire*, and is still very fascinating, so at least the Empress thinks, but we three girls talking it over afterward all agreed that the Empress herself was far more charming. All visitors who are not royal are generally shown over the house by us three, so I am beginning to be a regular walking catalogue of the different historical curios in the glass cases, the paintings, etc.

M. says her aunt told her today she was going up to see Dr. Chepmell next week, so if I accompany them and the Empress should take the girls sight-seeing somewhere, I shall avail myself of the chance of paying you a visit. At any rate Easter is so near at hand now, that I suppose we shall meet soon. Young Prince Napoleon Murat* is coming from his

---

* Louis Napoleon Charles Achille Murat, born 1870, son of Prince Achille Murat (grandson of the King of Naples).

Jesuit college at Canterbury, to spend his holidays, and I may be needed here, but the Empress with her usual kindness and thoughtfulness will manage, I am sure, to let me spend at least a few days with you in London.

The other day the Empress lent me a most interesting book to read. It is one the Queen sent her lately, on the title page of which Her Majesty has written, in her usual clear, bold writing, the following words:

> *Pour ma chère Soeur,*
> *l'Impératrice Eugénie,*
> *de la part de son amie devouée,*
> *Victoria, R. I.*

The volume is very prettily bound in blue morocco, and contains the account (taken from the Queen's diary) of the Emperor and Empress's visit to Windsor in April, 1855, and the subsequent return visit of Queen Victoria and Prince Albert, – "Vicky and Bertie" as she calls them always – with a huge suite to Paris, the following year. I cannot tell you how much it has interested me, knowing personally so many of the people mentioned, besides being acquainted with a great many others by name, hearing them so constantly referred to here. I don't think much of the Queen's style, it is decidedly simple and commonplace, but she has said some very pretty and true things about the Empress, of whom she repeats over and over again that she finds her most charming – and with whom, she evidently was quite fascinated from the first, in spite of preconceived prejudices to which she owns quite frankly.

In offering me the Queen's journal to read, and speaking of it and the visits themselves, the Empress told me incidentally, that things were done on a much more lavish scale for England's sovereigns in France, than for the Emperor and

Empress in England. One ball alone given at Versailles for Queen Victoria cost 300,000 francs.

The Empress also told me, at the same time, about another fancy ball at the Tuileries, in which all the gods of Olympus were represented. François de Noailles, son of the Duc and Duchesse de Mouchy, who was only a very little boy at the time, represented Cupid. In the middle of the entertainment the poor child got so tired and sleepy that he cried and refused to personate the love-god any more, and had to be sent off to bed.

From a letter:

Farnborough Hill,
April 11, 1886.

Just a few words with some violets, which we have been picking in the walled-in garden near the greenhouse since tea, which Major and Mrs. Scott, and General and Mrs. Byrne took with us. We made a bouquet for the Empress, one for Mme. Le Breton, a buttonhole for M. Pietri, and a large bunch each for ourselves. I am sending you mine.

After picking the violets, we also took a few cuttings from some historic willow trees. These trees as small cuttings were brought back witb great care by the Empress, when on her journey to Zululand in 1880, she stopped at St. Helena. She cut them with her own hand from the famous willow tree under which Napoleon I used frequently to sit and meditate – and they have now grown into quite large trees. A peach slip brought from the Cape at the same time, has also reached mature growth, but a peculiarity about it is that it insists upon keeping to its original African blooming time (about midwinter here).

In seeing the willows and speaking of them, the Empress gave her personal reminiscences of St. Helena. She told us her ship *The German* touched there for a few days on the way out from England to Zululand.*¹ She described to us her reception on the island, and remarked how strange it was that she should be the *first* and only Bonaparte to visit St. Helena since Napoleon I's captivity there. On reaching the port the Empress was met by an old lady*² who presented her with a bunch of violets, telling her that as a little girl she had done the same thing for Napoleon I when he arrived at The Briars, where he stayed as a guest while "Longwood" was being made habitable for him by the British government. The old lady gave the Empress many interesting details about the royal prisoner, whom she had seen a great deal of, and remembered well.

The Empress said that portions of the island are lovely, but Longwood House and its environs dull and uninteresting. The only part in which the Emperor was allowed to roam freely was a bare arid space like the bed of a crater, which it probably had been, and shut in on all sides. In front of his dwelling Napoleon, who was passionately fond of flowers, had planted a field full of pink geraniums, which he cultivated himself. He was given permission to ride, but finding himself always closely watched and followed, he gave up availing himself of the privilege, such as it was. Sir Hudson Lowe refused him the use of the Plantation House, wishing to

---

*¹ The Prince Imperial's funeral had taken place on July 12, 1879, a short time before my arrival at Chislehurst. I remember the impression made upon me one morning after mass, the following spring in the little Chislehurst church, at seeing suddenly a white hand coming out of the darkness and grasping the open iron-work door of the Prince's mortuary chapel, where his leaden coffin was resting covered with wreaths. It was the Empress Eugénie. She was inside making a farewell visit to her son's grave, and praying there, before embarking for the Cape, where she was going to visit the scene of his death, and find out all she could about his last moments.

*² Evidently Mrs. Elizabeth Balcombe Abell, for, the account she gives in her book, *Recollections of Napoleon at St. Helena* (1844), which I have lately read, corresponds almost exactly with every detail the Empress told me that old lady had given her in 1880.

occupy it himself. Longwood House, the Empress said, was a low wooden building, very much like the officers' camp-huts at Aldershot, and wretchedly furnished. The Government House on the contrary was splendid, surrounded by luxuriantly fertile land. When Napoleon became seriously ill, the French asked that he might be removed to the better dwelling of the two, but this was again refused. The Empress confided to me several times how keenly she felt England's ungenerous attitude toward a fallen foe.

The climate of St. Helena the Empress found delightful, and, according to the old lady, storms were almost unknown. Never in her recollection, so she told the Empress, had there been a violent storm, until the day of Napoleon's death. Napoleon's favorite walk was by a little stream, the water of which he drank and thought it benefited him. It ran through a grove, the willows near which he was buried two days after his death, and where his body remained till removed to France and entombed on the banks of the Seine, – that river which, in his own words, he "loved so well." When death released Napoleon I from his captivity on May 5, 1821, Longwood House was shut up and dismantled. At the time of the Empress's visit, there remained in the death chamber only a railing around the place where the great man's bed had been, and a bust in the center with many wreaths surrounding it.

From a letter:

Tuesday.

On Saturday we had a Mr. and Mrs. Russell to lunch. He used to write for the *Times*, and the Empress says he was merciless toward herself and her husband in 1870. He has a charming little wife, an Italian, daughter of the Countess Malvezzi, who used formerly to be invited to the Tuileries and the house parties at Compiègne. Mr. Russell is a most intelligent man, and entertained us mightily the whole of lunch. He it was who wrote those interesting descriptive articles on Ischia at the time of the disaster there some years ago. He had a narrow escape himself, leaving the island only a few hours before the occurrence of the earthquake, which swallowed up all his friends.

Wednesday, April 14. Lunch at 11:30. The Empress went to London on business with M. Pietri, and we girls took a drive to Aldershot where we saw two races; the horse which was just winning, stumbled in leaping the last hurdles, threw its rider, and fell on him. Dr. Scott, who was with us, ran off at once to offer his assistance.

Thursday, April 15. Before returning home on Wednesday from London, the Empress went to Marshall and Snellgrove's and chose some very pretty white dinner dresses for the girls, and yesterday after dinner she was telling us about all the pretty things she had seen. While I was dressing this morning there came a knock at my door and in walked Mme. Pelletier, saying Her Majesty had sent her to take my measurements, that she might also choose me a pretty dinner dress at *Marshall's*, and wanted to know what color I preferred. The Empress meant to give this as a surprise Easter egg, but Mme. Pelletier was obliged to tell me beforehand because of the needed measurements.

From a letter:
Farnborough Hill,
April 16, 1886.
The week has gone so quickly, that here is Friday evening and I have not written you in time; I fear you will be anxious. The dinner gong has sounded already and we are all waiting, but fortunately for me the Empress has been busy with M. Pietri, who starts for Paris tomorrow morning, and she has only this minute gone up to dress. I shall just have time to scribble this and send it off as it is, without any further news though, as H. I. M. positively dresses in five minutes (we have more than once timed her) – helas, here she comes!

From a letter:

Farnborough Hill,
Sunday, May 2, 1886.

It is now a quarter past four and as yet I have not had a minute to write to you, for after church this morning we went out into the woods till lunch; immediately after which the Empress asked me to trace out some plans of houses from a book she has for her architect in Paris. I have only just this minute finished, and must hurry that this may leave tonight. I thought so much of you, dear G., during the return journey, and wondered yesterday how you were getting on. Mr. Wilmot's book about South Africa and the Zulu war, which was given me to read in the train on starting, is most interesting. I read the chapters about the Prince Imperial's tragic death and the subsequent court-martial of Captain Carey.

Arrived here safely about six o'clock, and found every one glad to see me back. The Empress I did not meet till dinner, and then she inquired very kindly after you, and wanted to know all the London gossip, etc. She said, in fun, that it was shameful of me not to bring back a large stock of news from the capital to "nous autres pauvres campagnards [to us poor country folk]." They are rather dull down here and much in need of new faces on the scene, and a change of ideas. Visitors will be hailed with delight by all and several are expected soon, I hear. In telling how deadly monotonous the country could be, the Empress remarked that she thoroughly realized now the truth of the saying, which some old aunt of hers used frequently to repeat in her childhood, that anybody who lived buried deep in the country, away from all communication with town and the intellectual life going on there, after a time became *bête, sale et gourmand*. They would first stagnate mentally, then become careless in their clothes and habits, and finally greedy, looking forward to meals as events of undue importance in the monotony of the day.

Wednesday, May 5. The Empress was born sixty years ago today. No reference to the anniversary was made, as birthdays are not in favor here. One evening, however, some time ago, the Empress in speaking of her chequered career, had already told us about her coming into the world in the midst of an earthquake, exactly five years after Napoleon I had closed his eyes on the world she was entering. "La nature même semblait vouloir dès le commencement rendre ma vie orageuse!" was her comment.*

From a letter:

Farnborough Hill,
May 5, 1886.

It is after tea time and they are all gone out for a drive in the various carriages, but not having had a minute to myself for ever so long and wanting to answer your two letters, I have remained behind, and am now sitting outside enjoying the fine weather and the lovely view. We simply live out of doors in a tent. It is one of those the Empress took with her, and lived and slept in, during her up-country journey from the Cape to Zululand in 1880. The wicker chairs also, and lounges, are the same she used during the months of her stay in South Africa. We are most comfortably installed, have a table and all our books, and it is for the time being a regular sitting room, and a very pleasant one.

Little Prince Napoleon Murat is still here. He is a nice, simple schoolboy, and very bright and amusing when alone with us, but rather subdued with the Empress. He returns to his college on Saturday morning. The day before yesterday we had a long drive of two and a half hours with him. We formed quite a procession of carriages, the Empress and Mme. Le Breton in the victoria; M. and A. driving with a groom

---

* "Even Nature herself seemed to wish from the beginning to conspire in making my life a stormy one."

Catholic Church at Chislehurst

Interior of Catholic Church at Chislehurst

101

in one dogcart; Prince Napoleon and myself, with another groom behind, in a second dogcart, the Prince and I driving alternately and he giving me many points. We drove Umgeni, a small saddle horse the Empress brought from Zulu-land and which she prizes highly. Glad H. saw the procession of the Queen at the opening of the Colonial Exhibition. I have not had a minute to look at a paper, but hear it all went off very well, and it appears the Queen was much pleased with the reception given her. She wrote herself to the Empress this morning to tell her so.

From a letter:

Farnborough Hill,
May 9, 1886.

Lack of time again, helas! In the morning it was decided that the Empress would go to town to see her doctor, taking Mme. Le Breton and M. with her. Just as we were leaving our tent for a very early luncheon, at 11:30, on the Empress's account, Mme. Le Breton came to ask me to change my dress quickly as I was to go in her place, since I was better equipped than she for a shopping expedition. At 12:30 we started from here, accompanied by Mouron, the footman, who always goes up to town. A private carriage was waiting for us at Waterloo Station. We only returned by the 5:45 train, dividing all that time between Dr. Chepmell and some of the leading shops, choosing all sorts of pretty things for the girls. I was pilot, interpreter and bursar of the expedition. Hoping to preserve her incognito, and thereby save herself from extortion, she insisted on speaking English to me on these occasions, till I gently suggested that our usual language would perhaps attract less attention. The Empress must have been quite tired out, for even we active young people had had all we could stand, and were delighted to get home again. We had traveled up in the morning with General Fielding.

The girls had asked their uncle to send me some Spanish music from Madrid as a little gift for the seventh, but no one else knew of my birthday, – they are not *à la mode* here. Even A.'s the other day, though known to all, was paid no attention to.

We take our morning walk now directly after breakfast from 8:30 to 9:30, it being too hot at noon. Then we go to our tent and work till lunch at one o'clock, after which we again retire to our open air study-room till a quarter to five and then come the "month of May devotions" in the chapel. After tea at about a quarter before six, the Empress, if well, goes out for a good brisk walk, taking any one of us who cares to join her. Dressing for dinner follows, which is at eight, and the usual evening all together. This is our present program, modified to suit the warm weather, so you can follow us through the day if you wish.

On Thursday the five ladies and Prince Murat drove to a very pretty winding canal near here, called the Basingstoke Canal, where we hired two boats of which there are numbers. The Prince and M. went in one, A. and myself in another, the Empress and Mme. Le Breton walking abreast of us along the bank, bewildering us with conflicting directions, and the carriages following a short distance behind. M. and her companion got on famously, for he is a good oarsman, but A. not being able to row, all was left to my exertions, and my own very slight knowledge of the art. In consequence we soon got behind, so Mouron was put into our boat to help, and before the hour and a half was over we were far ahead of our rivals. It was lovely on the water, – the officers' canoes gliding about, the pretty surroundings, and the setting sun made a charming picture.

Tuesday, May 11. M. de Varu, military attaché to the French Embassy, lunched here today.

Thursday, May 13. M. and A. were away at a concert. I remained at home alone with the Empress and had a long and interesting tête-à-tête with her at tea time.

She began by talking over the news of the day and her fears of a war between England and France. She gave as her opinion, that war is certain if England does not evacuate Egypt; that everything points to a rupture. France with over a million soldiers does not fear to engage a small number of troops, she said, but will not quarrel with Germany.

She seemed very much excited over the French newspaper she had been reading and said:[1] "Nous touchons à un temps terrible, à un boule-versement-complet de la société. Tout est usé – il n'y a pas moyen que cela continue à marcher comme cela en Europe; il faut un changement absolu. Tant qu'on avait de la religion on était résigné et on souffrait en espérant le Ciel, mais maintenant le nombre des mécontents s'augmente de jour en jour, et bientôt ils auront le dessus, Si je vis quelques années encore, je suis sûre que nous en reviendrons à *dig, dig, dig!*[2] Il faut une révolution complete, et c'est maintenant qu'il faudrait un génie pour arranger les choses car si la reforme vient d'en haut, ce sera bien, mais si elle vient d'en bas (du peuple), nous verrons une époque terrible, mais elle sera courte et alors l'équilibre se rétablira. Pour le moment, il n'y a, à mon avis, que l'émigration. Si j'étais libre, je dirais adieu pour toujours à cette vieille Europe dégénérée, pour trouver une nouvelle vie dans les pays non-civilisés." [3]

Then we drifted somehow into talking of the unpleasant treatment the Empress had met with from Belgium and

---

* This seemed so interesting to me at the time, that I wrote down the words as nearly verbatim as I could remember.

* Here she made a vigorous gesture as if digging, implying that European affairs had reached such a pitch of social tangle, that we should have to go back to primitive methods again before things could properly readjust themselves.

the kindness of some other nationalities. Belgium, she said, was the *only* country where she met with rudeness after her troubles. On one journey from Dover to Ostend on board one of the government steamers, commanded by retired Naval officers, she had engaged a private cabin – the captain's. On her being recognized, the officials refused to let her have it, on the pretext that they had no right to assign it to her. It remained unoccupied the entire voyage, and the Empress stayed on deck all night without shelter, not choosing to go below to the one common saloon. This was, she said, only one of many discourtesies offered her by this nation. Leopold II was the only sovereign who did not go into mourning with his court at the Emperor's death. He absolutely refused to do so. She spoke very frankly of her personal dislike and *mépris* of the private character of Leopold II. He was narrow and mercenary. She knew him well, for he spent a whole month with his suite at the Elysée Palace in Paris at the Emperor's expense. "Il est si mielleux s'il veut quelque chose de vous; et puis il ose si peu moralement,"*4 she said finally.

She told me what she thought might be the origin of Leopold's marked hatred of France. The then French

---

*3 "We are verging on a terrible time, a complete upsetting of society. All is worn out, – it is not possible for things to continue going on as they are now in Europe; there must be an absolute change. As long as people had faith to count on, they were resigned, and they suffered and hoped for Heaven – but now the number of malcontents is increasing from day to day and soon they will get the upper hand. And if I live a few years more I am sure we shall come back to dig-dig-dig! There must be a complete revolution – it is now that the advent of a genius would be welcome to read-just matters, for if reform come from above, it will be all right, but if it come from below (from the populace), we shall see a terrible epoch – but it will be a short one – and then the world's equilibrium will be re-established. If I were free, I should say goodby forever to this old degenerate Europe, to find a new life in non-civilized countries."

*4 He is so fair-spoken if he wants something from you; and then, he has so little moral courage."

ambassador and Bismarck met some where at a dinner; after the meal they sat talking in a friendly way about the affairs of Europe, and jokingly named what each would like to "gobble up" for his country. When the Iron Chancellor had finished enumerating the slices of Europe he coveted, the French ambassador gave his list, naming Belgium among others. Bismarck feigned not to understand clearly, and pushing pen and ink toward the Frenchman, asked him to draw a little map, so as to explain his meaning better. The ambassador fell into the trap and made a little rough drawing, which the crafty Chancellor immediately pocketed. This little sketch Bismarck unscrupulously showed to several people, and the affair ultimately got to Leopold's ears. He never forgave the offense.

The Empress then went on to tell of the kindness of other nationalities, from whom she had less reason to expect it – of the great deference and courtesy shown her everywhere while traveling through Germany, and the very cordial visit paid her there, at great personal inconvenience to themselves, by the Crown Prince and Princess. She mentioned also the Czar of Russia's friendly visit to her at Chislehurst, and his trip afterwards to Woolwich to see the Prince Imperial, who was pursuing his course of military training there.

From a letter:

Farnborough Hill,
May 13, 1886.

Well, I have not yet told you that M. was allowed by her aunt to go to a grand ball given by the officers last week, so now that it is known she goes out a little, there will be plenty of invitations, this being the very gayest season here. The other day five tickets came from Sir Howard Elphinstone for a play at the Royal Engineers' Theatre. Mme. Le Breton did not wish to go, it being in English; A. also refused for the same reason, but M. was delighted, and when the Empress asked me if I would care to go, I accepted with pleasure. General and Mrs. Byrne dined here at seven, and at eight they, M. and myself started for Aldershot. The acting was exceptionally good and the music too (the Engineers' band from Chatham). It was a nice little theater, very well arranged and managed entirely by Sir Howard. The combination of the officers' uniforms and ladies evening dresses was very pretty. We had some of the best seats in the front row, and quite near us sat Prince Albert Victor of Wales in his hussar uniform. He came in with Lady Elphinstone. Tomorrow there is to be a review, and I think there will be several carriages going from here, so we shall all go. It will be a novel and interesting sight. The Empress and I will have the *Mois de Marie* to ourselves today, and tea also, as M. and A. have gone out with Mme. Le Breton. Tomorrow she will be left quite alone.

Later: I broke off in the midst of describing last night's performance, and never told you how much M. and I enjoyed the play. At 11:45 p.m. we left Aldershot, and at 12:30 were home; the whole household was in bed when we were safely deposited in the hall. All late comers are let in by the night watchman, an officially appointed policeman, who perambulates through the house all night. The Empress has had the same man ever since she arrived in England, now sixteen years ago. When the Imperial household moved from Chislehurst here, the Queen allowed him to follow. He has now been transferred exclusively to the service of the Empress. During tea the Empress and I had a long tête-à-tête and she told me many interesting things, mostly about Spain and Italy. One old Spanish custom she spoke of was most probably a very useful one: *The Vicaire* of the parish church always goes the day before a wedding and interviews the girl who is going to be married, asking her in private if she is really taking the step of her own free will. If she says "yes" it is all right, and the ceremony takes place, but if she says "no" he conducts her to a convent till the appointed day is past, and the disappointed and unprincipled relatives have regained their equanimity and good humor.

Then talking of the present rage for dressing children in sailor and Highland costumes, the Empress said that at one time the fashionable way for boys to dress in Spain was like monks; and in her youth during a revolution the fashion was changed to *Guardias civiles*.

On Maundy Thursday, in honor of Our Lord's washing the feet of the Twelve Apostles, the feet of twelve poor men are washed and afterward a dinner is given to them in the royal palace. Each man brings with him a large basket, into which he is allowed to put everything that is presented to him in the way of food, and even the dishes, plates and spoons that go with it. The men do not attempt to eat the meal, but being permitted to take it away, find it more profitable to carry it off and to sell it. The money received will buy them many ordinary dinners. It is a custom among people of good family, who wish to eat a dinner from the royal kitchen, to buy these baskets and their contents; and servants in livery may be seen waiting in line outside the palace gate for this purpose. It is also the Spanish queen's prerogative on that one day of the year to pardon a criminal sentenced to death.

The Empress then went on to speak of Italians, and to draw a parallel between their characteristics and those of the Spaniards. The Italians, she feels, are the greatest natural diplomats in the world, and are the most pleasant people to mix with socially, much more so than the French – "mais, je ne leur confierais ni ma femme, ni ma fille, ni mon argent."* The Spaniards even of the lower classes (Castilians), on the contrary, have the greatest natural sense of honor and loyalty. Business matters of the greatest importance are transacted only by word of mouth and a clasp of the hands. This is

---

* "But I would not confide to their care my wife, my daughter, nor my money."

considered sufficient guarantee. You can also, she says, reach them by politeness and make them do heroic and difficult things by simply appealing to their honor. As an example, the Empress told me the story of some official she knew of as a girl, who had charge of a great sum of money in gold. His house was surrounded and attacked by a revolutionary mob. Completely at their mercy, and not being able to defend his trust single-handed, he bethought himself of some way to save it. He asked speech with the chief of the band. Addressing him and his followers politely as *caballeros*, he handed the keys of his house to the ringleader, saying that he "trusted to their honor" not to touch or hurt anything. This worked like a charm. They went away proudly, never having touched a single thing.

Education in Spain, the Empress says, is making rapid progress now, but the nation at large still remains very ignorant, though they often make up for their educational deficiency by an astonishingly great amount of natural wit. "The Marquesa-, my father's sister, who lived to a very advanced age, was most ignorant scholastically,- knew nothing, and did not want to learn, - but still she was able to fascinate and hold the attention of young and old by her witty conversation, and had a most interesting salon." With some malice the Empress also told me that there is a very appropriate portrait of her aunt by the celebrated painter, Goya. She is depicted holding a closed book. Once on hearing Napoleon I mentioned as a great general, she showed her utter and astounding ignorance of Spanish history and its heroes, with whom even the peasants are familiar, by evidently mixing him up with *el Gran Capitan*,[*] and saying with some astonishment: "But Napoleon must be *very* old!"

This same Marquesa speaking of her father-in-law, who lived on and on to a great and apparently interminable old

_____

[*] Gonsalvo de Cordova, 1453-1515.

age, said, wittily, if not very reverently: "Je savais bien qu'il y avait un Père Eternel; mais je ne savais pas qu'il y eut un beau-père eternel!" [1]

That same evening after our long talk at tea time, the Empress resumed the subject of Spain and told us about her very earliest recollections. One of the first things she remembers is the cholera in Madrid, and the terrible fear everyone had of it. She called to mind perfectly the dead cart coming around morning and evening to carry away its gruesome load. An association of gentlemen, of whom the Count de Montijo, her father, was one, was formed to assist in burying the numerous dead. Ignorance made the wrought up populace distrust everyone who went near a fountain of poisoning it, and the perplexed government found it convenient, so as to allay their fears, to allow the unprotected monks to be suspected and massacred by the enraged mob for three days unhindered. From the windows of her house Eugénie Montijo one day saw a monk fleeing from an assassin, caught by his hood and stabbed. The awful picture of the spouting stream of blood haunted her for all the years of her childhood; it recurred in every bad dream and even nowadays, she said, the sight of a friar always instantaneously brings back to her mind that horrible scene.

She remembered, also, during a revolution, a journey *en diligence* to Barcelona[2] for safety, with her sister, mother and little brother Paco, protected by *torreros*; and told us how the Jesuits and others had all escaped being killed, through the power the ringleader of the mob possessed over it. En route the Montijos took refuge in a monastery one night, and after their departure the next day, they heard that their late hosts,

---

[1] "I knew well there was an Eternal Father – but I did not know there was an eternal father-in-law."

[2] This flight of the Montijo family from Spain must have been that of July 29, 1834.

the monks, were all murdered. The family next stopped at a *lazaretto*. They had a *sauf conduit* to go on further, but this did not apply to the *torreros* or other fugitives who accompanied the party, and these were held. A riot ensued among the bullfight-loving people there, to have at least the favorite *torreros* released, but these favorites gallantly said it was no use releasing them alone, as they would positively give no bullfights unless all of them were set free, so to obtain their favorite sport, even in the midst of a riot, all were let go and escaped in that way.

Here is one more anecdote the Empress told about herself as a young girl, showing the effect of youth and womanhood on the chivalric, romantic Spanish people. This is how Eugénie swayed the feelings of the crowd in favor of Queen Isabella. It was at a time when the revolutionary feeling was again rife and people made menacing gestures while the Queen was passing. Eugénie Montijo, driving at the time with her cousins in an open carriage, sensed the situation, waved her handkerchief with particular emphasis as the Queen passed, while the latter continued bowing to the scowling crowd. Eugénie, indignant at their disrespectful attitude, called out, rather peremptorily, to some men near her own carriage: "Take off your hats!" They looked up at her for a moment astonished, and then said smilingly, "Como podriamos rehusar algo à esa chica [How could we refuse anything to this girl]?" and dropped their sullen way as by a charm. The Empress added in telling us this, "L'Espagne est le pays de tout autre, où la femme est reine, pourvu qu'elle soit jeune et jolie!"*

Monday, May 17. At 4:30 during tea time, a telegram came from the Queen of Spain, announcing the birth of a son. Later on another telegram from Queen Victoria, repeating the

---

* "Spain is the country of all others where woman is queen – provided she is young and pretty."

same news. These are copies of the answers sent by me at the Empress's request, one of which went to Ex-Queen Isabella, grandmother to the new-born infant:

> A la Reine Isabelle d'Espagne,
>   Hôtel de Castille, Paris.
> Je felicite Votre Majesté de la naissance du roi.
> J'espére que cet heureux evénement adoucira la douleur
> Votre Majesté. *
>   Comtesse de Pierrefonds.

> To the Queen,
>   Windsor.
> Thank you kindly for sending the welcome news
> from Spain. It has given me great pleasure.
>   Comtesse de Pierrefonds.

From a letter:

> Farnborough Hill,
> May 18, 1886.

I suppose the birth of Queen Christina's little son is in all the papers today. The poor little fatherless king, who succeeds to the throne, was born at 12:30, and at 4:30 we knew of the event here.

The arrival of the telegram started the Empress telling us many things about Queen Christina. She spoke sympathetically about her lonely position as queen, widow and mother; of what a responsible task she has before her as regent in governing wisely a restless country, where an Austrian archduchess would not naturally be liked; how fine and intelligent a woman she is, how well she has brought up her daughters, and with what

---

* I felicitate Your Majesty on the birth of the King. I hope that this happy event will soften Your Majesty's grief.

The Empress Eugénie
from a Sèvres miniature

tact she is winning her way gradually with the people of her adoption. The chivalry of the nation is appealed to by her fine, dignified way of meeting the situation and its difficuities.

Then the conversation turned upon the mother-in-law, ex-Queen Isabella, who now lives in Paris – her former great popularity, and how she has not the slightest particle of *rancune* against anybody. "It was left out of her nature. She still has *très grand air*." Her irrepressible unconventionality was shown by her meeting with Don Amadeus* in a Paris salon. She waved her hand and called out to him across the room, "Hola compadero, que tal (Hello comrade – how goes it)!"

The following story about Queen Isabella and the Infanta Eulalia, was meant to illustrate the former's courage and thoughtfulness of her subjects. She and her daughter were driving, the Empress said, during some disturbed period of her reign when her popularity was on the wane. There were constant menaces from the crowd, who even pelted the carriage, but the two ladies continued bowing, apparently unconcerned. Isabella might very reasonably just then have been thinking of her own safety and her daughter's, but standing up and with real anxiety in her voice, she called out to the coachman, who had to force his way through the gathering crowds: "Take care, go slowly, do not crush anyone!" In a few minutes this act of courage changed the menace into enthusiasm. Some one in the crowd called out, "Que valiente es esa! Vive la reina [How courageous she is! Long live the queen]." Isabella returned home to the palace, not in the least frightened nor ruffled by the episode.

The Empress remarked that Isabella had much natural nobility of mind and heart; spoke of her ignorance and lack of political education, – in her absolute naïveté she was made to do all sorts of harm as the tool of unscrupulous people. When

---

* Amadeus, Duke of Aosta, elected King of Spain in 1870; resigned 1873. Then came Alfonso XII.

dethroned and expelled from Spain,* she arrived at Biarritz, with her son Alfonso. The Empress and Prince Imperial went to meet them, and the two boys, wholly alive to the situation and white as sheets, embraced and cried in each other's arms, while Isabella remained perfectly cheerful and insouciant, as if no distressing event had taken place.

Isabella's generosity, and independence of public opinion were also touched upon. In 1870, when Napoleon III was a prisoner in Wilhelmshöhe, Queen Isabella dared to telegraph openly to him in his prison: "Tous mes bijoux sont à votre disposition si vous en avez besoin [All my jewels are at your disposal, if you need them]," and she meant it, the Empress added. In spite of her utter failure politically as a sovereign, she had many fine qualities as a woman, was the warmest of friends, and would willingly have been as good as her word and have sold every jewel she possessed to come to the assistance of the Emperor. The Duchesse de Montpensier (the Infanta) is so different from her mother, with a nature so bitter against everybody. The Empress told us about the Infanta's rudeness to her at a fancy fair some years ago.

From a letter:

> Farnborough Hill,
> May 18, 1886.

Now about Friday last. I have already told H. that we enjoyed the field day very much, that it was most interesting, and gives one a very tolerable idea of what a terrible thing a battle must be. Thursday night a letter came from General Fielding saying that the Duchess of Connaught and the Grand Duchess of Oldenburg would drive over from Bagshot Park and would start again from Farnborough station at 10 a.m., that we must follow the royal carriage everywhere to the places

---

* Flight to France, September, 1868. Deposition declared September 29. She abdicated in favor of her son Alfonso, June 25, 1870.

reserved for us, so that we might see to the best advantage. Every one was punctual, and the scene a most animated one; the road filled with soldiers of all sorts, infantry, cavalry, and artillery with all their heavy guns and ammunition carriages. Some of the horses were beautiful animals. All along the road there was a mounted escort for the Duchess, and when we arrived at what is called Long Valley, six miles from here, we found the scene a very busy one indeed – officers dashing past like the wind, regiments appearing and disappearing behind the huts and into the woods, and the booming of cannon in the distance. General Fielding commanded the South Force, and Major General Sir Drury Lowe, the attacking force, supposed to have marched on Aldershot from London. The great feature of the day was the taking of the pontoon bridge over the Basingstoke Canal, and the firing was very heavy there. From a hill overlooking the valley and surrounding country, where our carriages were stationed, we saw splendidly. While we were standing with all the other people, who had alighted from their vehicles and were chatting in groups, Lady Burgoyne introduced me to Mrs. and Miss St. Quentin. Sir Howard Elphinstone and Surgeon-Major Scott rode up and spoke to us. The noise even in the distance was very great, but nothing to what it was later when the supposed enemy came to capture our hill, and soldiers were swarming up the steep heather covered sides like ants. There were hundreds of them and we had to get out of the way as best we could, but there was no danger, as they used, of course, only blank cartridges in their rifles. The noise was deafening when the artillery pulled their guns to the top of our hill and thundered at our makebelieve enemies below, and there was great excitement, as the vibration from the cannon was so great that it made every one jump. Some ladies were very much startled, especially when a few horses who did not understand the fun, began to rear and plunge and try to get away. The Empress's horses never moved a muscle, but those of the

116

Duchess of Connaught, considering everything, were not so well behaved. One brougham, which had been stupidly placed just behind the artillery had its windows smashed in at the first discharge. Fortunately, its occupants were on foot at the time, as was indeed everyone else, and so no one was hurt.

At one o'clock "cease firing" was sounded, the fight was supposed to be over, and the carriages proceeded down into the valley to see the troops march past. We were in an enclosure quite near the royal carriages all the time, and as the union jack was planted there, and the spot became a center for all the bands, too, it was very animated. The saluting of the officers as they passed was very pretty. The Duke of Connaught and the Grand Duke of Oldenburg in his light blue uniform, with several generals, remained on horseback throughout. The Duchess bowed to us and the Duke rode up and spoke to us. We were not home till 2:30, and the poor Empress and Mme. Le Breton, who had remained behind, were famished. The former had thoughtfully sent us word by a mounted groom not to hurry home, which was very kind of her, but even had we wished to try it, we could not have made our way through the dense throng of troops. There were in all nearly seventy thousand soldiers out that day, and with the beautiful horses of the artillery and the bright uniforms of the regiments, it was an impressive sight, which I shall never forget. The royal party and staff officers went to lunch with Sir Archibald Alison, commander-in-chief.

Since Saturday we have not seen a soul, and as the young French lady, who is to come with her aunt, is ill, we shall have no one till about the seventh of June. What a terrible tornado they have had in Madrid and the neighborhood. Several relatives of our girls had a narrow escape for their lives, and the Empress heard today that a chateau she owns at Carabanchel, near Madrid, is an almost complete ruin. Pleasant news! especially as another place of hers, near Granada, was swallowed up by an earthquake last year, and some of the vineyards have become useless on account of the phylloxera, which has destroyed the vines. This has caused a serious monetary loss – about 4000 pounds out of her income of 25,000 pounds. The Empress is quite depressed, and said the other day, with tears in her eyes, in connection with this accumulation of bad news, "Tout ce qui m'appartient parait voué à la destruction [All that belongs to me seems doomed to destruction]." It certainly does seem true.

From a letter:

Farnborough Hill,
May 21, 1886.

I was delighted to receive your welcome letter this morning, and to see that my description of the field day interested you so much. I did not expect to have anything new to tell you about today, but yesterday at 5:30, after tea, we went out for a very long drive, – the Empress, Mme. Le Breton, M. and myself in the landau, with A. driving in a pony cart behind. We went by quite a new route, past Wellington College, and just as we thought we were turning toward home, the Empress told the coachman to drive in at some handsome gates, which were right before us, – and we found ourselves in some beautiful grounds in front of Broadmoor Asylum. We asked for the governor, who is personally known to the Empress, and she immediately got permission for us to see the grounds inside the huge walls. Presently the governor appeared, seemed delighted at the Empress's arrival, and not only showed us the grounds, but the whole establishment, which is admirably kept and managed. All the inmates have committed murder or have at least tried to kill some one; only escaping the death penalty because found insane. There are 140 women and 450 men, and everything is done for their comfort and cure, but they are, unknown to themselves, closely guarded and well watched, in case of alarming symptoms or attempts to escape. The two head doctors and four or five uniformed keepers went with us everywhere, though the precaution seemed quite unnecessary. The prisoners or patients, for they are both, without exception looked wonderfully quiet and happy, walking about or reading, working and chatting. Some of them are perfectly sane in everything, except for their one savage inclination.

In one of the private bedrooms, busily painting, we found a certain Miss E., who, you may remember, some years ago in Brighton poisoned a number of children with sweetmeats, which she had maliciously tampered with and then returned to the shop, pretending they were not what she wanted. She exchanged them for others, which she also poisoned and returned to the shop with disastrous results. Her mania was only discovered after her deadly scheme had been put in operation several times, and thirty little innocent children had died. Miss E. has handsome features, is well dressed, skilfully rouged and with her hair dyed, so that though the doctor said she was fifty-eight years old, she hardly looks thirty.

My companions passed on to other rooms. I was so much interested in looking at Miss E.'s very artistic sketches, that I did not notice she had gently closed the door behind me, till one of the doctors, who missed me from the rest of the party, came back rather hurriedly and got me out with what seemed rather over-zealous haste. Once outside in the corridor he explained that Miss E.'s killing mania was not over, that she had several times lured people into her room, closed the door on them and then sprung at their throats. I was grateful to the doctor and after that kept close to his side notwithstanding the innocent looks of the patients.

Among the men, who were walking about freely out of doors, and cultivating their little gardens, we saw a madman who tried to shoot the Queen two years ago, – and many other notorious persons.

We did not get home till eight o'clock, and as the household knew nothing of our visit to Broadmoor, they could

119

not make out why we were so exceptionally late in returning from our drive.

Saturday, May 22. The little King of Spain was baptized today, and was christened Alfonso.

Monday, May 24. The Marquise de la Valette came to lunch with her niece, Lady Emily Fitzmaurice, who is to be married on June second.

Tuesday, May 25. Great excitement about the possible expulsion of all princes from France; if all, and not only *prétendants* to the throne are expelled, and their property confiscated, it will make the greatest possible difference to the Empress and mean a great monetary loss, as she owns a good deal of house property in Paris. She also owns a good deal in New York and London.

Wednesday, May 26. Mme. Pelletier started for Paris on her usual little visit to her family, and also to lay in a stock of small necessaries of clothing for the Empress, buying among other things, quantities of long, buttonless gloves, called *gants belges* at the Bon Marché. England's Queen, who one day at Windsor much admired the practical comfort of the Empress's gloves, has ever since got all hers there also, though few know it, bought for her by Mme. Pelletier during this yearly shopping trip for her own mistress.

From a letter:

Farnborough Hill,
May 26, 1886.

Last Saturday, Major and Mrs. Bigg came to lunch, and afterwards all went for a drive, the objective point of which was the North Camp, Aldershot, to see a polo match between the 11th Hussars and a club called the Freebooters. The latter won the game, much to the disgust of Prince Albert Victor, who was present, and saw his own regiment beaten. Just as the game was over up came the Duke of Connaught's four-in-hand, he himself driving, and sitting beside him the Duchess of Connaught, with the Grand-Duke and Grand-Duchess of Oldenburg behind.

The polo game was a very pretty sight, the players in white, mounted on lovely little ponies as swift as the wind. Today his Excellency M. D'Antas, Portuguese minister, has been lunching here, and has been conversing with the Empress in her *salon de travail*. She is very *agitée* about the law concerning the expulsion of princes, for if it goes through it will bear heavily upon her too. She will lose, in that event, all her private house property in Paris, though she is innocent of any cause for uneasiness on the part of the French government. We shall probably get a telegram this afternoon, saying whether or not the bill has passed.

May 28. Mme. de Arcos came to lunch on her return from Paris.

From a letter:

Farnborough Hill,
May 30, 1886.

Last Sunday, the twenty-third, a number of people came for tea, which we had out of doors on the terrace. We were about seventeen in all. Among others: General and Mrs. Byrne, Miss Montague, Mr. and Mrs. Freeman, Major and Mrs. Scott and their niece Flora Dunolly, and Captain Blake, formerly stationed at Dover, who knows my cousin very well. After tea we showed them the entire house and its treasures. Yesterday Dr. Tyler, who is governor I think of the Agra (India) prison, and in charge of the Hindoos at the Colonial Exhibition, came to look at the rug which his prisoners had been working on for the last two years, and which has some little defect they are going to try to remedy. He brought one native with him and in a few days two others are coming to help. It was a most amusing visit. Dr. Tyler asked me very politely where the gentleman was he had been corresponding with, during M. Pietri's absence, and was much surprised to find that I was "A. Whiteside, Esq., Private Secretary to the Empress" as he had addressed the envelope to me. I enjoyed the joke. After luncheon and much talk over the rug business, the Empress sent us driving with Dr. Tyler and the Hindoo, to show them the neighborhood. During the drive the doctor told us very many interesting things about his political prisoners, several of whom are princes. He seems a very able man, and wants us very much to go to the Exhibition, where he is all-powerful, and would much enjoy showing us the inner working of everything. But just now the Empress is too wrapped up in the outcome of the pending law in France to think of pleasures for this household.

The young Indian prince (he is a political prisoner) who came yesterday, is of a very high caste, and would not for the world have touched anything cooked by Christians, nor sit at the table with us; neither would he eat what to him was orthodox food if a Christian's shadow had been cast across it. He however accepted some fruit and bread, which the girls and I gave him. Dr. Tyler told us that his "boy," as he called him, could take these from us as a gift, if given with our own hands.

Sunday, May 30. The officers who receive the Empress at the church door on Sunday morning and escort her up the church, are nearly always invited by the Empress, on entering her carriage afterwards, to come and have tea with us in the afternoon. Captains Galton and Bolton thus came today, and we showed them afterwards about the house until 7:30.

From a letter:

Farnborough Hill,
Wednesday, June 2.

I am writing you this from the tent, where since this morning we have taken up our abode afresh. Yesterday early

The Empress Eugénie, about 1860

we had a real deluge, but the afternoon was lovely, and before dinner we three had a good long walk to Sandhurst and back, – about eight miles I should think. It was great fun, as there were numbers of stiles and five-barred gates, and now, as a result of the gymnastic lessons at Aldershot, M. and A. are much more agile, and they find barriers a pleasure instead of an annoyance. Since Saturday last a good deal has happened that will interest you.

Dr. Tyler came again, bringing with him four Hindoos to arrange the wonderful rug made by the prisoners at Agra. It is from 80 to 100 feet long, a perfect beauty, whose only defect is that it does not lie flat. Dr. Tyler said it would be a very easy matter to remedy, though to us it seemed almost an impossibility. It was very interesting to see the prisoners working over the rug. They never touched it with their hands, but did everything with their feet, and after three of them had labored over it for an hour or two, their little bare feet always scuffling and shuffling over it from the center toward the border, it came out as absolutely flat as if it had been rolled by some heavy machine. The Empress was as much pleased with the change in it as she had been disappointed when it was first put down.

Their greeting to the Empress was very picturesque and touching. She came forward to shake hands with them, but they gave her no opportunity of so doing. After removing their sandals they bowed low to the ground, touching their foreheads to her foot and kissing it, and making a great many obeisances. Dr. Tyler told them in Bengalese a few words about the Empress, and translated her questions and their answers. Their costumes were brilliant and picturesque, and we took some photographs of them. This delighted the "boys," and they enjoyed roaming about the park after they had finished their task.

I think I told you about the tea the Empress gave Saturday afternoon (in honor of the Queen's birthday) to 180 poor children from Farnborough village and Aldershot Camp. The Empress herself went down to the school to greet her little guests, and we, with some ladies of the parish and their clergyman, served the children who had wonderful appetites. Just before our dinner hour, when the little ones had played about and enjoyed themselves to the full, they were marshaled into the Farnborough grounds and marched past the Empress, who stood near the house to see them. They cheered her lustily, and also the Queen and the royal family, and then went home very much pleased, I think, that the Queen had attained another year and given them the opportunity of enjoying such a delightful birthday feast.

On Sunday evening at about 10 o'clock, M. Pietri arrived from Paris, having crossed the Channel with old Prince Lucien Bonaparte. M. Pietri brought with him a nice elderly gentleman, M. Rambeaux,* who formerly held a high appointment, *l'ecuyer de l'Empereur*, in the Imperial household of Napoleon III. Also a young soldier of the French army, Captain Bizot, playfellow of the Prince Imperial and son of General Bizot, whose widow was made governess to the Prince Imperial at his birth; and finally M. Urbain Chevreau, son of the last minister chosen by the Empress. All are very gay and merry, and the house is quite animated now.

On Monday, the eve of the seventh anniversary of the Prince's death, the Empress with Mme. Le Breton went privately and quietly to Chislehurst to pray at her son's tomb, as she said she did not care to show her sorrow to the curious, who would probably be there in crowds next day. The next morning, the first of June, we ladies went to a requiem mass at the camp church, where we all received holy communion. The day was naturally a sad one, and we were very glad when the Duke, M. Pietri and the three French gentlemen, who

---

* Mentioned elsewhere in connection with the attempted assassination of the Czar.

attended the more solemn requiem at Chislehurst, returned, as then there was a little animation, and the Empress was obliged to put her own sorrow aside for her guests' sake.

Wednesday in the morning, M. Rambeaux, who is a splendid amateur photographer, took advantage of the sunshine to take some views of the house and grounds. For one of these photographs we were fetched from our tent, for a group with the gentlemen of the party. I do not know what the result will be, but I suppose time will reveal. I hope M. Rambeaux will give me some prints when they are finished, as they will be a nice souvenir of Farnborough.

Young M. Bizot left in the evening for Paris, and tomorrow M. Chevreau returns to France, too, so the party here soon grows and diminishes again.

In the evening, apropos of foreign deputations, which had come over in years gone by to greet the Emperor and his son on different occasions, H. I. M. told us the following funny anecdotes:

One was about a Corsican, who forming part of a deputation to the Prince Imperial on his legal majority (18 years) in 1874, got as far as London en route for Chislehurst. It was his first journey to England. He went to bed, knowing nothing about London black fogs. When he had slept himself out he got up, but finding it still dark went back to bed. This manoeuver he went through several times, always with the same result. At last, wondering why he felt so wide awake and thinking his watch must have played him false, he rang the bell, for he heard people moving about the hotel. He made some inquiries, and found it was the late afternoon; he had been waiting all these hours for daylight, which never came. His astonishment was great when the situation was explained to him.

Another anecdote was about a member of the deputation to congratulate Alfonso XII, the late King of Spain, on his twenty-first birthday, when, as an exile, he was undergoing his military training at Sandhurst College. This Spaniard left London at six in the morning and only arrived at his destination at five in the afternoon, his cravate blanche rather the worse for so many hours passed in the underground railway. When he got to the necessary underground station, instead of changing as he should have done, he continued on quietly going round and round the "Circle" underground, wondering whether he would ever get to the terminus. Finally, well on in the afternoon, he inquired of some one who understood French, and was put on the right track and really started on his journey. Arriving finally at Sandhurst he expressed his astonishment, saying naïvely: "Mais on me disait que c'était tous près de Londres [But they told me it was near London]."

From a letter:

Farnborough Hill,
June 6, 1886.

Our first lesson in tennis, given us by Dr. Scott, who spent the day with us. I wish we were going to the Exhibition. We and others here have given as many delicate hints as possible, and Dr. Tyler has written "by desire of the Prince of Wales," with whom he dined the other evening, to say that all could be arranged comfortably for the Empress if she liked to visit the Exhibition. Nothing has as yet been decided. I suppose we shall get there some day, and at any rate we must not grumble, as we have had a good many pleasures lately, and having such pleasant visitors in the house is an agreeable change from the daily monotony.

This afternoon while I am writing, M. Rambeaux is taking photographs again in different parts of the grounds, and we are being called and grouped constantly. I wish the Empress would allow herself to be taken, but that, unfortunately, she will not consent to. She has an almost morbid horror of having her portrait taken now.

© Chas. Taylor

Tomb of Emperor Napoleon III at Chislehurst
Afterward removed to Farnborough Hill

© Hills & Saunders

Tomb of the Prince Imperial
At Farnborough Hill

I told you, I think, that on Thursday we all went with Sir Howard and Lady Elphinstone by special permission, to see the Duke of Connaught's place, Bagshot Park, the family being away at the time. We had a delightful drive in the four-in-hand, and when the opportunity presented itself in the conversation, I inquired of Sir Howard if he had seen Sir William Anderson lately. He said, no, but spoke very highly of the dear old man, and said he was much pleased to meet a niece of his. After they had shown us all over the Duke of Connaught's house, which is just an ordinary, large, comfortable dwelling, but nothing more, we had tea. Lady Elphinstone had ordered it beforehand, and did the honors very charmingly. Then we went out to the grounds and through the hothouses, which are really very fine. Sir Howard picked each of us a flower as a souvenir of our visit. Mine was a piece of stephanotis.

On Friday nothing happened outside the usual routine, but yesterday afternoon we three girls went in the landau to Sandhurst Military College grounds, to see the cadets' athletic sports. Part of the grounds were inclosed for the officers, their families and friends, and we met a good many people there we knew, and had great fun. The most ludicrous thing of the whole affair occured just after tea and before the giving of the prizes (by Lady Jane Taylor, the governor's wife). It was a donkey race. Imagine about thirty-five donkeys with their riders dressed in the most absurd costumes possible. An organgrinder's monkey; a gigantic youth dressed as a baby in long clothes, and urging his donkey on with his feeding bottle; Gladstone with a mask and his huge collar – he was hissed and knocked about unmercifully; an old market woman; an élégante with parasol, veil, etc.; several chefs in their white caps, one of whom won the race; a barrister with wig and gown; the "Private Secretary" with all his innumerable parcels and bundles; and a Japanese, who was afterward introduced to us, and turns out to be young Hussey Walsh. It was great fun;

everyone was in fits of laughter at the efforts to make the donkeys go on, and the tumbles and struggles to mount again incidental to the petticoats of some of the gallantly mounted cadets, added not a little to the mirth. There are a good many more coming events on the horizon, and I am selfish enough to hope there will not be too many visitors here when they come off, as I should be obliged sometimes then to relinquish my place to the strangers.

Thursday, June 8. After tea, lawn tennis with Dr. Scott and M. Rambeaux. Mme. Le Breton told me that the Empress, accompanied by her nieces, is soon going to the Exhibition by invitation of the Prince of Wales.

From a letter:

Farnborough Hill,
June 11, 1886.

M. and A. were delighted with their visit to the Exhibition, and well they might be, for they saw everything under the best auspices. The Empress was received in style by the authorities, and a magnificent carpet was laid down for her to walk over. They were shown everything, and at twelve Princess Louise and the Marquis of Lorne joined the party, and there was a great crowd, it appears, to watch the royal and imperial ladies meet and embrace each other.

The lunch given by the Prince of Wales in his own pavilion was magnificent, and during it a band of the Guards serenaded them. Several very pretty little souvenirs were ordered by the Prince for the Empress and the girls, and each of the ladies had a beautiful white and mauve bouquet given to her. The whole thing was royally done, and the Empress it appears was delighted, though she says had she known how formal the reception was to be she would have refused to go, as she had never, since the Prince Irnperial's death, consented to appear in public.

From a letter:

Farnborough Hill,
June 16, 1886.

Without anything special having occurred, what with studies, walks, perpetual scrambling to be ready for meals, going to bed late and getting up early, I have not had a minute during the last few days to write to you.

Nearly every day there has been some one for lunch; on Sunday, Sir Algernon and Lady Bothwick, and their little boy, who is at school near here at Mr. Morton's. On Monday, M. le Comte Minszech, a very amusing Austrian and a great friend of the Empress. M. Rainbeaux left on that day, so we shall have no more photographs taken now. Yesterday Mme. de Arcos came to lunch, bringing with her Father Antrobus of the Oratory. Today we shall, I think, be only our own home party, but tomorrow the new Spanish minister, Leon y Castillo, and an attaché from the embassy, Señor Osma, are expected, so we shall come in contact with plenty of new people. This makes a little change for us, as with the exception of seeing lunch visitors, our everyday routine is at present unbroken. We had so hoped to go to Ascot for the races, and several friends had offered to take us, but it did not come off. The Empress likes arranging surprises herself, and I fear the affair failed by its having been too much spoken of beforehand.

Mme. Lefèvre, the French lady who is still staying here, is very friendly, bright and pleasant. We shall be sorry when she goes back to Paris. Her husband was *préfet* (or *sous-préfet*) under the Empire, and very devoted to the Bonapartes. She herself, an intelligent partisan, worked very pluckily in the Empress's favor against public prejudice. She was absolutely fearless, and when everybody turned on the Empress, she showed the metal she was made of.

From a letter:

Farnborough Hill,
June 19, 1886.

Our everyday routine, which I told you we had quite resumed, was broken, and very much broken, yesterday. The day previous the Empress had arranged for us to go to Windsor, as she wished Mme. Lefèvre, who was leaving this morning, to see the castle first. Accordingly, we left here, – Mme. Le Breton, Mme. Lefèvre, M. Pietri and ourselves, at ten, and after a good many changes of train, arrived at Windsor. We went at once to the castle, where we saw the state apartments, and enjoyed them very much. I need not tell you anything about them, because you are familiar with them, and besides I must hurry, so as to get on to the telling of the end of our day.

After lunching at a restaurant, we drove from Windsor through the beautiful park to Virginia Water, where we again took the train and were back at Farnborough about seven. We were glad to find some tea waiting for us, as it was a very warm day and we were tired out. We quite appreciated the Empress's kind thought.

Now, before I go on, I must tell you that M. had been invited to a ball that night. Yesterday morning she heard that General and Mrs. Byrne could not take her, which was, of course, a great disappointment, but she had philosophically made up her mind to give it up. After dinner, just as we were going into the drawing-room about nine o'clock, the Empress called me aside and said, how sorry she was for M.'s disappointment, and asked me if I would be willing to take Mrs. Byrne's place and go with her. Of course I was willing, so the Ernpress announced to M. that I would chaperon her and she might go after all, ordered the carriage, and sent us off upstairs to dress. She herself went up to her own room to choose me some pairs of evening gloves frorn her store, besides getting with her own hands some flowers, as I had neither proper gloves nor flowers on hand at the time. An hour later we two were starting off together in the large carriage, M. in a pretty white tulle dress and I in my new pink (the Empress's Easter gift), which came in most appropriately and looked very handsome. The ball was at Sandhurst Military College, and given by the cadets and officers in charge.

Lady Jane Taylor, who received, was very gracious and introduced numbers of dancers to M. and myself. She danced the whole night and I could have done the same, but I thought best to refuse during the early part of the evening, not knowing exactly what was expected of me as M.'s chaperon. Several ladies, however, who knew us well and who often come here, pressed me very much to dance too, and as I saw M. enjoying herself, I accepted the partners found for me and started in. By that time it was a mere pretense of dancing, for there was such a terrible crush that one only got trodden on and had great difficulty in getting around the room. You will readily believe this when I tell you that there were nearly 800 people present in all, – cadets, officers, and their friends. The scarlet and Highland uniforms with the ladies' dresses, which were mostly white, looked very effective indeed. The supper and refreshments were served in a marquee adjoining the ball room.

At two o'clock we returned home, as we had promised to be in early, but I do not suppose the ball was over till four o'clock at least. I was not in bed until daylight, for having been away all day in Windsor, and dressed and redressed several times in much violent haste, I got everything topsy-turvey in my room to such a degree, that it was a long time before I could disentangle and straighten them out sufficiently to get into bed.

June 22. Mme. Bartolini, an old friend of the Empress's, another of the small coterie of fearless women who upheld the Empress in French society when vast numbers were against her, arrived from Paris for a few days' visit.

The Garden Front at Farnborough Hill
Maria M. Chevreau, Antonia, the author, Captain Bizot

From a letter:

Farnborough Hill,
June 23, 1886.

Yesterday, Mr. and Mrs. Ayliff from the Cape of Good Hope, and who are traveling in England, lunched here, bringing with them a whole bazaarful of curiosities from South Africa for the Empress. They had been very kind and had entertained her on the Cape in 1880. They are simple genuine people, and enjoyed their visit here very much. They know Mr. Wilmot out there, it seems. A Captain Pemberton of the Royal Engineers (on leave from Malta, a friend of Captain Auld) arrived and lunched here too, and we all, at three o'clock, drove over to Aldershot to see some athletic sports given by the officers of the regiments quartered there. It was much the same as at Sandhurst lately, but on a grander scale.

Dr. Scott remained with us all the afternoon, and we only got home at 6:30. M. went afterwards to a ball at the Officers' Club with General and Mrs. Byrne.

From a letter:

Farnborough Hill,
June 24, 1886.

I think there is just a possibility of our going up to London soon, as on July 2 there is to be a grand review at Aldershot, and according to present plans the Queen and royal family are to be present, and will stay at the Queen's pavilion for two or three days. Queen Victoria, the Empress says, is sure one day to invite herself over to lunch, and as she hates making new acquaintances, and as the girls were despatched off to London the last time she came, we might all be sent off on this occasion.

Wednesday, June 30. the Marquise de la Valette and Earl Sidney came to lunch. Talking of his coming visit, the Empress spoke so nicely of the latter and his wife, and said, "J'aime toujours tant à voir les Sidneys ensemble, ils sont comme au premier jour de leur mariage – il ne se quittent jamais. C'est rafraichissant de voir comme ils s'aiment."*

At five Mme. Juliette Conneau and her daughter arrived on a visit from Paris. She was the widow of Dr. Conneau who had been for many years the Emperor's faithful physician, bequeathed to him so to speak by his mother, of whom he had taken much devoted care in her last illness. He was one of the Emperor's most faithful friends, and had been in prison with him for six years in the fortress of Ham, in 1840, and helped him escape later on; and again at Wilhelmshöhe after being made prisoner with his Imperial master at the battle of Sedan, 1870. The story the Empress told us of Mme. Conneau's marriage was a romantic one. Both families lived at that time in Corsica, and the doctor was an intimate friend of Juliette's father when she was quite a littie girl. Conneau often talked to her and told her stories, and used sometimes jestingly in his daily visits to the house, to call her "his little wife." This went on for years, and everyone had grown so accustomed to the appellation that no one attached any meaning to it whatever. The doctor, however, who had been steadily growing fonder of his little friend, went one day to her father and said, "What I have been calling your daughter in jest for years, I wish could come true – I wish you would let me marry her." The father was much astonished and protested that Conneau was much too old, for though only thirty he was more than double her age. He agreed, however, when he saw that Conneau was in earnest. "You are my best friend and I could wish no better husband for my daughter. So, if she is willing, I consent to the match, but it must be of her own free will – there must be no pressure brought to bear on her."

---

* "I do so like to see the Sidneys together – they are exactly as in the first days of their married life – they are inseparable. It is refreshing to see how they love each other."

Juliette was then just fourteen. The doctor went to her at once, told her that he was really serious, and asked her what she thought about the project, and whether she would like to marry him. There and then she answered, "Oh certainly, I like you very much. I should be glad to be your wife, but on one condition. You must do one thing for me – take me where I can have singing lessons." Of course he said "yes," and so very joyfully, and in a very childlike way she accepted the doctor. They were married before her fifteenth birthday, having first obtained special license from the Emperor, as she was under the legal marriageable age. The Emperor was delighted that his friend should marry out of love, and the union turned out a remarkably happy one, in spite of the disparity of their years.

Louis, the son, who once came on a visit to Farnborough, was barely sixteen years younger than herself, and, mother and son were the greatest friends, almost playmates. Mme. Conneau, once married, got her heart's desire, – singing lessons by the best masters, – and was found to have a most beautiful voice. Dr. Conneau being the Emperor's physician, the family always lived within reach of one of the royal residences, either Fontainebleau or Compiègne where the Imperial family came at stated times of the year. Louis Conneau was a constant playfellow of the Prince Imperial's. Mme. Conneau, in talking over those days to me, told me how anxious she used to be during many hours daily, because these two boys were so daring. They kept her in a state of perpetual anxiety, until it was time for *Monseigneur* to go home, and she felt that she could conscientiously have her mind at rest until his next visit the following day. The Empress told her not to interfere with or protect him, and let him have absolute freedom to do whatever he wanted. So, these two venturesome boys spent most of the time climbing chimneys, jumping from roof to roof, and doing all sorts of dangerous things, which she was powerless to prevent, but for which she felt nevertheless she would have been held morally responsible if any accident had happened. Small wonder then her relief when the Prince went home safely in the evening.

When, after her busband's death, she was left with little money to live upon and educate her children, she turned her talent to account, became a professional singer, and this very charming woman was soon extremely popular in Paris.

From a letter:

Farnborough Hill,
July 1, 1886.

Today on coming up to my bedroom I found a quantity of pretty flowered sateen on my bed, and on inquiry found that the Empress had sent it me as a little surprise gift. She had been getting a number of pretty dresses for her nieces and wanted me to have the same. It was nice of her to think of me.

Tomorrow will be the review. Earl Sidney, who lunched here yesterday, told us that the Queen's plans are all changed; instead of remaining three days, she is to arrive at 4:30 p.m. for the review only. It will commence at five, be over about nine, and then her Majesty will return at once to Windsor, and according to this plan, she will not of course come to Farnborough at all. I hope we shall all go to the review, but I doubt it, as we are such a large party now, and I do not think the Empress will care to have her several pairs of horses out for so many hours at a stretch.

From a letter:

Farnborough Hill,
July 4, 1886.

They are in the midst of hay-making just now. The Park looks very picturesque with the harvesters and the haycocks.

Mme. de Arcos and Mrs. Vaughan were here for the review and were going to Brighton the next day to see my aunt and give her news of me. She will be much pleased. I need not tell you anything about the review itself; the papers gave a better account of it than I could. We went a party of twelve. We saw everything; we were in one of the enclosures and quite close to the royal carriages, whose occupants we readily recognized. There were present the Queen, with Princess Beatrice and Prince Henry of Battenberg; Princess Louise of Lorne; the Princess of Wales with her three daughters; the Prince of Wales and Prince Albert Victor; the old Duke of Cambridge; the Duke and Duchess of Connaught; and the Duke and Duchess of Teck with Princess Victoria, or *Princess May*, as she is generally called. The march past was a grand sight, and had it not been for the blinding dust, would have been perfect. To our delight, we found in the carriage delicious sandwiches, fruits, soda water and champagne, so we refreshed ourselves. We left the review ground at 7:30, as soon as the Queen left, and returned home to dine a party of fourteen.

Monday, July 9. Dr. Scott called in the afternoon to play tennis, while the girls and Mme. Le Breton were at a garden party; we two were alone with the Empress.

Over our cups of tea, we talked of her very early days in England. The Empress told us that she "failli prendre la maison à Berkeley Square [had been on the point of taking the house at Berkeley Square]," celebrated for its terrible ghost stories, which have kept it uninhabited during several decades. She actually went over the building with the Prince, with a view to hiring it, but on coming out was warned by a strange gentleman who saw they were unknowing strangers.[*] Also about a visit to Huntley and Palmer's enormous biscuit factory; her sensations in going up *en ascenseur* for the first time; and how very many biscuits she had to *croquer* before she left the large building with its 4000 workmen. At each different section of the many rooms she visited, she had to

---

[*] It has since been pulled down as unprofitable property.

accept and eat samples pressed upon her by the hands, who wanted to do her the honor of presenting her with their own special brand.

Talking of Camden Hill and a tame monkey of hers, the Empress told us how angry he became with the Duchesse de Mouchy for laughing at him one day. It was at afternoon tea, and the little creature came up to the tea tray gibbering, made a dash at the cups and saucers, and viciously smashed the valuable Sèvres service all to bits before he could be stopped. She told us also of her mingled horror and embarrassment once, when this same monkey jumped onto the head of a solemn diplomat who was calling on her, and made off with the wig he wore. The monkey had for some unknown reason taken a special dislike to him. After this escapade the monkey had to be relegated to a menagerie.

From a letter:

Farnborough Hill,
July 7, 1886.

We have had several people here lately. Old Prince Lucien Bonaparte dined with us on Monday. He is the son of Lucien, brother of Napoleon I, and there is no mistaking his kinship. The likeness is the more striking, as he even has the trick of sticking his left hand into the front of his buttoned-up coat in exactly the same way the *Petit Corporal* did. He is quite poor; lives in a small house in Bayswater, and devotes his entire life to scientific research. He is a great chemist and naturalist.

Yesterday M. D'Antas, the Portuguese Minister, and his wife dined here, and today Countess Clary has arrived for a visit of a day or two.

Thursday, July 8. The Dowager-Marchioness of Ely came to lunch and stayed till 4:45. She was for many years Mistress of the Robes and intimate friend of Queen Victoria. Mme. Conneau sang several songs for us after luncheon. She has a

Prince Jerome Bonaparte

Prince Lucien Bonaparte

141

lovely voice and we all enjoyed listening to her very much. A little song by Augusta Holmès called *Noël* especially took our fancy.

Tuesday, July 13. I returned to Farnborough after a few days' absence at Downside. I had the same nice welcome, which has always awaited me on my various homecomings. Found the Marquise de la Valette here on a visit.

We heard definitely this evening that we are going Saturday next to Osborne, on a visit to the Queen.

Thursday, July 15. The Père Pollin came to see the Empress. After much cogitation all is finally settled now; the Premonstratensians* are coming to take charge of the Empress's Memorial Church and the monastery adjoining, as soon as completed.

Friday, July 16. Mrs. Byrne and Mrs. Scott came to take leave of the Empress.

* Members of a religious order founded at Prémontré, France, in 1119.

PART III

The Empress visits Queen Victoria

PART III

From a letter:

Osborne Cottage,
East Cowes, Isle of Wight,
11:30 p.m., July 17, 1886.

It is late as you see, but I cannot go to bed without at least commencing a few lines to tell you all about this day, which has been tiring though a very pleasant one. My note written this morning must have reached you tonight, and told you that we left Farnborough at 1:50 p.m.; the horses, carriages and most of the servants having gone ahead yesterday to be in readiness for us here today. We reached Southampton at 3:30 p.m., and went down to the docks accompanied by the station-master and part of the crew, numbers of people lining the way, for they had seen the royal yacht getting up steam, and were curious to know who the distinguished travelers might be. The pretty little *Alberta* was put at our disposal. Its white and gold fittings, bright awnings, and the scarlet drugget on the gangway, looked very gay and made a good groundwork for the uniforms of the naval officers and the crew, drawn up to receive the Empress. We went all over the yacht before she weighed anchor, and then sat on the upper deck enjoying the fine weather and the pretty view of the harbor. The short journey to the Isle of Wight was over only too soon, and at 4:30 we came ashore at Trinity Pier, the Queen's private landing, with much formality, and found our own carriages waiting for us. By 6:15 we had reached Osborne Cottage, enjoyed the first peep at our rooms, and were drinking some delicious tea all together. We thoroughly appreciated it after an hour's blow on the sea.* Directly afterward the Empress, M., A. and I started out for a walk. The Empress wished to show us the little old town of West Cowes, of which she is very fond, and she is obliged to make hay while the sun shines, for on Tuesday the Queen arrives, and she would be horrified, and would positively veto for the Empress a trip on foot through the long, narrow, straggling street which constitutes the town. *En chemin* we met Lady Burgoyne, who was delighted to see the Empress and took us off to the Royal Yacht Squadron Club, where her husband, Sir John, joined us and did the honors of the place. We returned at 8 p.m., just in time to go to table (we do not dress for dinner here). After dinner we sat in the drawing-room a while and came upstairs rather early. I have since un-packed all my belongings and written this, and now I must really pop into bed, for I am quite tired out. I shall

---

* On our arrival we telegraphed our absent hostess: "To the Queen, Windsor. Just arrived, splendid passage. Osborne looks quite beautiful. – Comtesse de Pierrefonds."

add more to my letter tomorrow, but think it prudent to get at least so far done, in case of unforeseen hindrances later. Good night.

From a letter:

Osborne Cottage, July 20, 1886.

This is a cottage in name only* – in reality it is a pretty little country house, with a large veranda running around it. There is a central staircase, and all the bedrooms open out into a gallery overlooking the hall. The whole is daintily and simply decorated, the furniture very plain, old-fashioned, and stiff, – but it is impressed upon us many times a day that we must nevertheless be very careful of everything, as the Queen is most particular. She will notice the least damage done to anything, when, at the end of our visit, following her usual plan, she may come in person as the Empress has known her to do, and look over the empty cottage with a housekeeper.

There being only the one little sitting-room, we are not supposed to leave any of our personal things about. The chairs must remain during our stay arranged exactly as we found them, also the books on the central table; anything that is moved must be put back on the same spot. It is the only place into which the Queen or the Princesses can be shown, and as they are likely to come in at any moment, it is kept more or less sacred to Her Majesty, and we therefore commonly use the dining-room or our own rooms. One royal housemaid belongs permanently in the house as caretaker, but the Empress has had to provide all the other servants, carriages, horses and silver. Gifts of most delicious French bread, though, are brought us every morning from the royal bakers, and fruit from the Queen's hot-houses.

---

* The castle being too small for guests after the accommodation of the large royal household, the Queen was in the habit of offering Osborne Cottage and others, built on her own grounds, to members of her family or distinguished visitors.

Since the first day's walk we have not seen much of Cowes, as the girls have been busy, and when there has been leisure after tea, torrents of rain have come down regularly to drive us immediately home; but I think we are soon going for a little trip on the coach, which passes this door daily on its way to Carisbrooke Castle, and perhaps other expeditions may be proposed.

You were very much in my thoughts on Sunday. Mme. Le Breton and the two girls sat in what you have described to me as your old pew in the quaint little Catholic church. (I pictured you and my aunt as little girls kneeling there with your mother.) I knelt just behind them with the Duc de Bassano. The Empress had a priedieu in the sanctuary. I wish I could identify the house you used to live in, and which you describe. Lady Burgoyne knows our friend Captain Thelluson very well. The *Boadicea* she tells me has been sold and belongs to an elderly maiden lady, who has rechristened it the *Ariadne*. Mr. and Mrs. Peter Thelluson are coming down here for the regatta. They have only a tiny yacht. Lady Burgoyne is going to find out all she can about their plans and let me know.

On Sunday, as our royal hostess had not yet arrived, the Empress, with whom we went for a very long walk in Cowes, took the opportunity of showing us over every nook and corner of the grounds of Osborne Castle (it is known officially as Osborne House), a modern building erected by Queen Victoria. She told us the while many interestings things about it all. The park is magnificent, and the view of the sea through the foliage is beautiful. We went down and picked up shells on the sand, while the Empress rested part of the time. We saw Princess Beatrice's bathing place and walked along the lovely terrace-wall, which, shaded with trees and overhanging rocks, skirts the sea for miles. How the good breeze there would have refreshed you, dear G., if our long, steady tramp of two and a half hours had not first killed you.

In front of the castle there are some trees planted many years ago by the Emperor and Empress, and quite a few others put there by celebrated personages. The names of most of the sovereigns and princes of Europe are inscribed on the little metal plates which record the date of planting. This afternoon at 1:30 amid great clatter of horses and carriages, Highland regiments and bagpipes, the Queen arrived, and everything is bustle and brightness in the land now. A mounted messenger has already come up to the cottage to announce the first royal visit, and another followed a few minutes later bearing notice of postponement and change of plans, which will keep us constantly on the qui vive. Her Majesty is expected any minute now, and everyone has retired to his or her room, so as not to be in the way. It is not etiquette for anyone to be seen, except those whom the Queen has specially asked for, and it is still worse form to be seen hurrying away. To avoid the dilemma, therefore, there is nothing for us to do in this tiny house but to remain closely secluded.

The Empress has just sent up word to the girls that if the Queen asks for them, they will be fetched, if not, they are to remain out of sight. I have been showing them how to improve their low courtesy, as I am supposed by the Empress to be an adept. Mme. de Arcos arrived here yesterday to stay some time.

I should answer H., but I have not a moment. It is only thanks to the Queen's presence that we are at this moment comfortably installed in our rooms and have ink. So far we have had to stay in the garden with our books a good part of the day, and are not allowed even to take an inkstand about with us, for fear of spilling it. This is one of the privileges (?) of living in a house belonging to Queen Victoria.

It seems so funny to have everything in the house marked with the Queen's familiar monogram "V. R.," and the arms of England, – even the hot water cans, towels, sheets, and books.

Osborne Cottage, East Cowes, Isle of Wight

It is also strange to see nothing on the walls but portraits and engravings of the different members of the royal family. Over the piano is an engraving after Winterhalter, representing the Prince Consort, the Queen and three or four of her children; and a Landseer, *Prince Consort and Dogs*, is another one. Goodby for the present.

From a letter:

Osborne Cottage,
July 22, 1886.

I said I should only write to you after the naval review tomorrow, but as I have a little time today, while M. and A. are writing home to their uncle, and as I may possibly not have a minute later, it is best to begin while I can. Yesterday morning we went for a walk with the Empress and Mme. de Arcos. We missed our way and got lost. An unknown lady we met showed us the right road, and invited us to her house, where we sat and rested on her veranda, and admired her lovely sea view. Mrs. Firman, as her name turned out to be, was delighted at the opportunity of thus unexpectedly giving hospitality to the Empress, and begged us to come again.

After lunch at three, the Empress, the Duke, and Mme. Le Breton returned the Queen's official visit of the day before. We three girls started for a drive, but the blue sky was suddenly obscured, and such torrents of rain fell we were obliged to turn back immediately. This morning, for the first time, A. took a sea bath. I accompanied her, but did not care to go into the water, as the beach here is covered with rough shingle, and as it is necessary to hold a rope on account of dangerous undercurrents the bath would have seemed too stupid after the delightful freedom of Ostend. A. found it a great scramble, as we had driven to the bathing place (quite the other side of West Cowes) with the Empress, who got out and walked with Mme. de Arcos while we were down at the water's edge, and of course we could not keep her waiting too long. Tomorrow will be the naval review, and unless plans are changed between this time and then, we are going with Mme. de Arcos to see it, on board the man-of-war *Northampton*, which is commanded by Captain Fane, a cousin of hers.

Princess Beatrice says she does not know whether the Queen will be present. Her Majesty thinks herself it would be well for her to do so, but she so hates and dreads the sea, and it makes her so ill and nervous, that her daughter has not the courage to "persuade mamma" to go. It seems she told Prince Henry, who was urging the Queen to go, that if he knew the state her mother would be in, he would never again press her to do so. The yacht *Alberta* and the other larger royal yacht, *Victoria and Albert*, are lying in readiness, in case they are needed by the castle. I think the Empress is going to dine with the Queen this evening, but alone, without any lady or gentleman to accompany her, as Her Majesty finds it too hot for large parties just now, the Empress says.

M. and A. have not been presented yet. Tiresome, after our long wait of two and a half hours the other day, closely imprisoned in our rooms, without being able even to go out and to get a book, – and with no work, or anything on earth to do. It was exasperating, but it will be the last time, I hope, that this will happen, as that was the Queen's official visit. From now on, Her Majesty's daily calls will be quite private and informal. She comes down now through her grounds from Osborne Castle alone, and across the road which separates our place from hers, passing through a small wicket gate just opposite my window. At any hour in the morning now we are apt to hear the key turn in the lock, and see her appear through the gate and walk into the cottage unannounced, with possibly one of her little grandchildren or her collie dog for sole companion. Then I am always supposed to give the alarm quickly: "The Queen," which promptly sends the rest of the household, Mmes. Le Breton and de Arcos, the Duc de Bassano and others, scrambling to their various rooms to leave the coast clear.

If the morning visit fails, Her Majesty sends a messenger in the afternoon to name the hour she will come for afternoon tea, and many changes of plans are gone through again, before that little social affair is finally *un fait accompli*. Her Majesty, and the princes and princesses who may accompany her, always have tea alone with the Empress, while the ladies-in-waiting and other lesser visiting mortals drink tea with us.

Wednesday evening. Instead of keeping this letter to finish until after the naval review, I think it will give you more pleasure if I send what is written tonight. The Queen's private messenger carries the royal despatches, and also takes our letters twice a day to the mainland (Southampton), so you will get this some time before evening, I hope.

From a letter:

Osborne Cottage,
July 24, 1886.

At eleven o'clock M., A., Mrs. Vaughan and myself drove to West Cowes. There we took the steamer *Carisbrooke* for Ryde, where we were joined by Colonel Vaughan, Mme. de Arcos's brother, with about twenty other people, prospective guests of Captain Fane of the ironclad *Northampton*. After waiting on the pier a little while and signaling to the man-of-war, we went aboard the *Argus*, a small Admiralty steamer doing omnibus duty, which dropped the invited guests at their respective ships. Then we were transferred to rowboats and boarded the *Northampton* about two o'clock, finding in the mess-room on the main deck a delicious lunch laid out, which was done great justice to by all, as each one of the thirty guests seemed ravenous.

The lunch over, Captain Fane and six of his officers took us all over the ship, and showed us everything in detail. It was most interesting. The crew numbers 600 men, and the *Northampton* is a ship of 12,000 tons. The guns are terrible looking things, and the noise between decks, while firing

R.Y.S. Clubhouse
West Cowes, Isle of Wight

Osborne House
The Isle of Wight, home of Queen Victoria

salutes, is something dreadful. A. and several other ladies fired some off. The guns are so perfected now that they can be worked by simply pressing an electric button some distance off.

You have no doubt read all about the review in the papers, so I will not waste time telling you what you already know. All I will say is, that it was extremely interesting, and when the *Alberta* steamed through the fleet, we were surprised as it passed close alongside to see our Empress sitting composedly on deck with the Queen, and to recognize Mme. de Arcos, the Duke and Mme. Le Breton with the royal suite, on the *Victoria and Albert*, which followed. We had left the rest of our party in the morning all quietly at home, not expecting to go to the review at all, – hence our astonishment. No sooner had we started off, it appears, than a royal invitation came for all of us. We were delighted to have escaped it, and probably enjoyed our day on the *Northampton* very much more than we should have done amid the honors and restrictions of the royal yacht.

Tea, ices, etc., were served at 6:30 p.m. before starting home, and we arrived at Osborne Cottage only at 9 p.m., very tired and wet. Had it only been fine overhead instead of raining cats and dogs without ceasing, it would have been one of the most delightful days I have ever spent and full of most interesting and novel experiences.

From a letter:

Osborne Cottage,
July 26, 1886.

Yesterday morning we were suddenly interrupted by the Empress, who brought a letter inviting us all to visit the *Victoria and Albert*. Nothing loth, we three soon had our things on and with the Empress crossed over to the Queen's landing place, where the royal yacht Alberta was lying. While waiting for Mme. de Arcos to pick up a few friends of hers in Cowes we got into the Queen's barge, a small steam launch, and young

Lieutenant Carr took us for a short cruise around several vessels anchored in the bay. When our entire party had been rounded up we were received on board the *Victoria and Albert* by a whole legion of officers in uniform, who showed us all over the magnificent yacht. She is immense and has a crew of 180 men, which is sufficient to give you some idea of her size.

Queen Victoria's bedroom and sitting-rooms are exactly like those of a small country house, decorated in white and gold, and though simply furnished, contain everything one could possibly want in one's home. The cabins of the princes and princesses are smaller, but roomy and pretty, and the suite, too, is comfortably provided for, as are also the servants. These latter, I think, are almost better off than the officers, for though lodged below the main deck, they have plenty of light, air and space. The engine room is simply a picture, so beautifully kept, all as bright as silver and no smell whatever, and the kitchen with its huge fires and the many white-capped chefs superintending the roasting of large joints for the crew, would make one quite forget one was anywhere but in an ordinary town kitchen.

I wish the Queen would offer us the *Victoria and Albert* for a cruise around the island, such as Mme. de Arcos and Colonel Vaughan made last year with the Prince of Wales. The small steam pinnace has been put at the Empress's disposal for our entire visit on the Isle of Wight, but that trip is so long and time is flying.

M. and A. have been in suspense all week, for according to etiquette the Empress could not present them to the Queen till the latter expressly asked for them, which she only did this afternoon. The Queen, Princess Beatrice and Prince Henry came to afternoon tea at 4:30. They joined the Empress in the little drawing-room and the rest of us, as usual on these occasions, entertained the Queen's lady-in-waiting in the dining-room. A few minutes before Her Majesty's departure the girls were hastily summoned, and went to make their courtesies and kiss her hand. Literally in two minutes they were back, having found Her Majesty very simple, gracious and kind.

The contrast of her small stature and great dignity surprised them very much. It seems strange that a woman of her build, verging on extreme old age, bereft of many former physical attractions and unbecomingly dressed, should have such a dignified bearing, and be able to impress everyone who comes in contact with her by her queenly personality and charm. Her delightfully modulated voice and sweet, genuine smile, have, I think, much to do with it; and her strong sterling qualities of mind and heart make themselves felt in spite of the somewhat plain exterior. The Queen's memory for names and faces is something marvelous. Like the Empress she also takes a great though impersonal interest in people, whom she has never seen, and probably never will see; makes inquiries into incidents of their lives; and, years after, surprises her hearers by her remembrance of the details which have been given her.

So far the Empress has only dined once with her hostess, as the Queen is busily occupied just now with a change of ministers. The Empress looked lovely the evening she went to the castle. I do not wonder people raved about her when she was younger, for she is still so charming and withal so majestic.

And now I am going to answer all your numerous questions about the castle and Cowes. First of all, I have looked about everywhere and cannot see your old house, Ivy Cottage, nor do I know where Lord Henry Seymour's place was, unless it could have been Norris Castle, just across the water adjoining Osborne. It is an old thirteenth-century chateau-fort, with lovely grounds, and stately peacocks strutting about and perching on every available piece of stonework, while showing off their gorgeous tails and uttering ear-splitting screeches. The place has now been bought by the Duke of Bedford and made a present to his wife. The Empress was telling us the other day during our walk in Norris Castle grounds that the Queen, who is so fond of Osborne Castle, spent a good part of her girlhood in the vicinity. After her father's death, the Princess Victoria and the Duchess of Kent, it appears, lived here in this very Norris Castle and the details of her life as they came direct from her own lips to the Empress and repeated to us, were most interesting.

H. I. M. told us a great deal about the Queen's young days and of the help which Leopold I of Belgium, her maternal uncle, had given her in those times of quasi-poverty. Without him her mother could not have afforded the many professors and masters called in to give the young Victoria the thorough education which helped so materially to make her in after days a good and useful queen. In the gardens we saw a small pavilion, where the little Princess took most of her lessons in fine weather.

Her Majesty's early training made her thrifty, but, in spite of her saving, she did not accumulate the large fortune which most people attribute to her, as there have always been many private outlets for her wealth. She herself said, that she had been gradually paying off the enormous debts left by her father, and not until 1880 had she finally succeeded. Princess Beatrice, she said, had long before (as a measure of precaution) been provided for, because should she marry after the Queen's death, she could not obtain the marriage portion granted to the daughter of a king, but not granted to the sister of a king, as she would then be.

These things seem to me to reveal the character of Queen Victoria, always a strong, vigorous, earnest woman, who took her life's responsibilities seriously and strenuously, and who proved herself a true and loyal friend to those who had the honor of close intimacy.

From a letter:

Osborne Cottage,
Monday, July 26, 1886.

Today we were just going out for a walk with the Empress on our way to the baths, when on passing the pier where the *Alberta* is moored, we saw that preparations had been made for the reception of some one. The officers were *en grande tenue*. We passed by, not thinking the gala clothes were for us. When we were almost out of sight the captain came running after us to say he had received orders from the castle, and the steam launch was waiting the other side of the *Alberta* to convey us to the turret ship, *Colossus*, the great feature of the review the other day. It was then 12:15 and the whole crew had been since 11:30 on tiptoe in expectation of the Empress's visit on board the man-of-war, so we lost no time in starting off, and soon came alongside. The crew was drawn up on the main deck as was also a detachment of marines, and as soon as the captain handed the Empress up from the gangway to the deck, they presented arms, the bugle sounded, and one of the sailors piped a sort of mournful whistle, which is supposed to be a mark of great honor. We were shown everything. The Armstrong guns are marvelous, and to see whole turrets of iron and steel with monstrous guns turning around and moving to the requisite position, by just the slightest pressure on a small spring, makes one shudder to think how the mind of man can invent, perfect, and be focused on such instruments of destruction. The whole battle can be fought, the ship managed, and orders given to the men below, by three officers placed in a turret called the conning-tower, the walls of which are sixteen inches thick, with ingeniously arranged slits through which the enemy can be seen. There are mathematical instruments of every sort, a whole battery of electric buttons, and speaking tubes which go down to the very depths of the ship. The officer in control can fire guns, give his orders, slack

161

or accelerate the speed of the ship, without moving an inch away from his post. It is simply astounding!

We only got home at two o'clock and found Osborne Cottage quite anxious at the Empress's non-appearance, as they knew nothing of our expedition. By some mistake, the Queen's mounted messenger bearing the letter of invitation with particulars had never reached the cottage till five o'clock in the afternoon.

The Empress's servants were to accompany those of the Queen's sight-seeing at 3 p.m., which they did, and as luck would have it a number of people came to write their names in the Visitors' Book during their absence. A German prince, Augustus of Saxony, arrived in one of the royal carriages to call, and after him came the Duke and Duchess of Connaught, who reached Cowes only today. It amused the Empress very much, as there was no one available but the Duc de Bassano to open the door.

I must finish now abruptly, or I shall miss the post, and tomorrow I shall be unable to write, as the Empress has accepted an invitation to cruise, and we shall be away all day.

P. S. Yes, the ferry joining East- and West-Cowes still exists, as it did in your youthful days. We all wish there was a bridge instead, as it is such a tiresome, slow business getting horses and carriages over each time we drive out from here.

From a letter:

Osborne Cottage,
July 28, 1886.

Now, I daresay, you would like to hear a little about our yachting trip of yesterday, – but there is not much to tell you, except that we enjoyed the yacht itself very much, for as we were suddenly becalmed we never got to Alum Bay and The Needles at all. We saw nothing of the contour of the island, and remained perfectly motionless for hours between Yarmouth on the island and Lymington on the mainland. It was a great pity, as it is our only chance for a sail at present, the *Modwena* having been lent to Sir John and Lady Burgoyne for the Empress's use on that one day only. The owner, a Mr. Gretton, was away, and had put his yacht at their disposal with a splendid luncheon and every comfort possible, besides a substantial tea at five o'clock. The schooner is not so large as I remember Captain Thelluson's *Guinevere* to have been. The *Modwena* is pretty fast and very comfortable, and has just returned from a long cruise around Norway and Sweden.

We landed at 6:30 p.m., having been taken out each time and brought back to shore by the Queen's steam launch. It is not true, as the papers state, that Osborne Cottage has been offered us for a month longer, but the Empress is going to stay on for another week anyway, and we shall most probably only return to Farnborough Saturday week, and shall therefore I am glad to say be here for the regatta.

From a letter:

Osborne Cottage,
July 30, 1886.

There is not very much news just now, but still the time passes quickly, and on the whole, in spite of many annoying restrictions, I shall be very sorry when we have to leave. I told you about our afternoon on board the *Modwena* on Tuesday. Well, M. and I have not done anything very special since then, but A., who is a better sailor than her sister and enjoys the water, went yesterday for a little cruise with the Empress and Mme. de Arcos in the steam pinnace. The party returned to tea at five, bringing with them the young officer in command, Admiral Phillimore's son. Today M. too, is to venture out on the sea. They are going with the Empress for a sail in the Duke of Connaught's yacht. This morning as we were coming home from the town, after A.'s sea bath, we met the Duke and Duchess of Connaught, and further on, this side of the Medina River, we got a very cordial bow from Princess

163

Beatrice, who with her husband was driving down to board their tiny yacht, *Leander*.

Wednesday was quite a royalty day. At 11 o'clock the Queen came to see the Empress, bringing with her two of her little grandchildrcn, the Connaughts, and accompanied by Princess Beatrice, who remained with the Empress after the Queen's departure till past one o'clock, when she, too, returned to the castle through the little wicket gate opposite my window. A Mrs. Everett lunched with us. In the afternoon the Empress went to return the call of the Duke and Duchess of Connaught, who are staying at Kent House, one of the Queen's guest cottages. The Empress then drove to the castle, where the Queen was waiting with Princess Beatrice, to take their imperial friend for a drive.

The members of the royal family, though so exceedingly domestic and affectionate, have developed – true also of the people connected with the court – a strange surface dread of meeting the Queen, which is perfectly incomprehensible to outsiders. It is quite genuine on the part of her children, and is probably the result of their rather stern bringing up. As little things they were much loved, but also subjected to much discipline. The efforts they now make to vanish into thin air, when the Queen comes upon them unawares, are most ludicrous. from the members of the family the entourage has caught this same spirit, which often leads to amusing incidents. Here is one which happened yesterday:

The girls and I had been in the afternoon for a quiet walk to look at Whippingham Church, designed and built by Prince Albert, and where Princess Beatrice was married last year. Returning home, we came suddenly upon a party, which turned out to be Mme. de Arcos and the Duke, who having met Prince Henry aud the Duke of Connaught with their aids-de-camp, were walking leisurely home toward Osborne Cottage with them. Naturally, we slackened our pace, when to our dismay we saw looming in the distance certain white ponies and outriders. Caught between two fires, we paused a moment, took in the situation, and quickly decided that we had just time to scramble to safety before the Queen's carriage could draw up at the door. Seeing that the advance party had already turned into the ivy-covered porch, we gave wings to our heels and bolted in, and came upon them saying goodby to one another, nearly knocking them over in our mad haste. What followed was most amusing. Prince Henry and the Duke of Connaught, seeing our breathless condition and hearing at the same time horses' hoofs quickly approaching, sensed the impending danger and left their conversation unfinished, having in common with us only one idea, – that of getting out of the Queen's sight at once. Prince Henry, who knew his way about the cottage, waited for no one and dashed off through our small private gate; but the Duke of Connaught, less versed in the topography of the place, turned appealingly to me, asking piteously to be shown some way out. A few seconds later I had hastily guided him through our hall and dining-room and out by the long French window, and he was madly careering down our garden, leaving the aids-de-camp, Majors Bigg and Edgerton, to get away as best they could.

The Empress was much amused at hearing the story at dinner, and told us she had seen over the garden hedge, as she drove by with the Queen, the two gentlemen running away and wondered what it meant. She says she has often seen even the Prince of Wales, in years gone by, hiding behind bushes in the grounds of Osborne Castle, when he thought his royal mother was coming along.

Poor people or perfect strangers the Queen never minds seeing at all. It is only those whom she knows something about, that she does not care to encounter, as it would put her in the awkward position of either being discourteous and passing them by, or being forced to talk to them when she feels disinclined to do so. Hence out of deference to the Queen's feelings there is a tacit understanding that one must never be seen on her path. This has grown into a stereotyped rule.

Friday, July 30. Went with A. on foot to the baths. Coming back, met the Duke and Duchess of Connaught in Cowes, and at the ferry Sir John and Lady Burgoyne, who invited the girls and me to take tea with them on Sunday.

From a letter:

Osborne Cottage,
July 31, 1886.

M. and A. enjoyed their little trip on board the Prince of Wales's yacht, lent to the Duke of Connaught for that particular occasion. The *Aline*, you remember, was Captain Thelluson's first yacht, which he brought to Ostend during several summers, and on which we spent such pleasant days when I was a child. Later on, after building the *Guinevere*, he sold the *Aline* to the Prince of Wales. They had tea on board with the Duke and Duchess, and returned home about 7:30.

The Empress, Mme. de Arcos and the Duke are expected for dinner at the castle at 9:15. The Duke looked unusually handsome and dignified in his court dress, the very picture of an old courtier; Mme. de Arcos, resplendent with diamonds; and the Empress so *distinguée*, her soft gray hair so prettily dressed, and her whole person so graceful and so wonderfully young looking. Her youthfulness was accentuated by her simple black dress with only a suggestion of jet trimming, her short sleeves and low bodice showing to perfection her still beautiful arms and shoulders. The Queen has always allowed her friend while in mourning for her son, as a great exception to the cast-iron low-neck rule, to wear in its place only an open bodice, and adopted the same for herself. The other evening, however, as the Queen had lately resumed the regulation low bodice and short sleeves, the Empress in spite of the permission granted her did not like again to be the only exception, so with a great effort she went in full dress, and for the first time since the Prince Imperial's death in 1879.

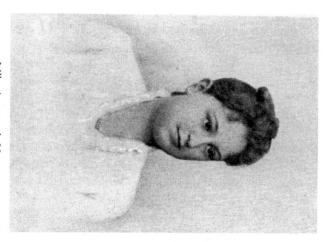

Mlle. Antonia de Vejerano

Mlle. Maria de Vejerano

On returning from dining at Osborne the Empress told us some stories about Prince Henry's free and easy ways, and how he stopped the carillon one day, so that his accidental unpunctuality might not be noticed. Also, a tale concerning him when unable once to get back in time for dinner. He was out sailing, and being becalmed the time slipped away, and he saw with terror the sacred dinner hour approaching. At last, after much manoeuvering and by rowing his little sailboat part of the way, he was able to reach land several miles from Osborne, and secured some kind of rattle-trap conveyance to take him to the castle. Arrived at the lodge, the vehicle was refused admittance, and to the Prince's despair he was obliged to get out and show himself before they would open the gates, chafing the while at the waste of precious minutes. In spite of his strenuous efforts, when he finally reached the castle he found the family already seated at table. There was no remedy, and so, making the best of a bad job, he walked quietly into the dining-room, just as he was in his rough yachting clothes, and made his apologies to his royal mother-in-law so simply, and was so bright about it, that he was able to carry off what would have been an absolutely unpardonable offense in another. The Queen seems very fond of him.

The Empress told us also about Mme. de Arcos fainting that night at the Queen's table. Her Majesty, in great distress, and attributing it of course to her bugbear, the heat, turned to the Princess and said, "You see, Beatrice, you will keep the rooms so warm!" So, though a chilly wind was already blowing in on Mme. de Arcos's back, more windows had to be opened.

During yesterday's yachting expedition Mme. Le Breton, the Duke and I went for a drive. The road they chose being blocked, we drove straight on and presently came in sight of the town of Ryde, so I immediately expressed the wish to go and call on the Alexanders. Mrs. Alexander had written to me only the other day, asking if I could come over some day to lunch or dinner, and make their acquaintance. As the Empress was dining out at the castle, I thought I could easily arrange my temporary absence through Mme. Le Breton. Unfortunately I found the family all away for the day. A pity to have missed such an excellent opportunity, as another may not present itself. We never know here from one hour to another, what the arrangements are going to be, or whether or no we shall be free, so it is extremely difficult to arrange a private expedition. Yesterday, while we were all out walking, Mr. Gladstone called and wrote his name in the Visitors' Book. I should like to have seen the G. O. M. He had been to the castle and had a long interview with the Queen, who, the Empress told us, looked much relieved at dinner time, and brightened up noticeably in the evening, having, as the Empress expressed it, adjusted a disagreeable matter. Gladstone, it appears, expects though to get into office again, for he told some of the gentlemen at the castle that he hoped to see them again in a few months. Let us hope he won't.

Saturday, July 31. Today the Prince of Wales and family are to arrive for the regatta week. *Tout ce qui est élégant* in Cowes will be on the Green at 7 p.m. to see H. M. S. *Osborne* come in. All the yachts and steamers are dressed awaiting the royal arrival. We heard the cannon firing a salute on the arrival of the yacht, and later saw the Prince and Princess of Wales landing in the steam launch.

From a letter:

Osborne Cottage,
Sunday, August 1, 1886.

We witnessed the actual arrival from a distance only, as we were obliged to wait about indoors with the Empress, who was expecting a visit from Sir William Jenner, especially sent to see her professionally by the Queen. We had not time to get down to the green by seven o'clock. This was a pity, for though we belong to the royal cottage, owing to etiquette, we see comparatively little of the royal visitors, and we should like at least not to be less au fait than the public at large.

We had tea at Lady Burgoyne's, where we met numbers of interesting people, among others Miss Law, Mrs. Grant, Mrs. Foster, Lady Stapleton, and Mr. and Mrs. Rolls.

P. S. The mignonette I inclose is some I took with the Empress's permission, from a huge basketful sent in yesterday by Princess Beatrice to her imperial friend, for whom I arranged it.

Monday August 2. Admiral Woodhouse lunched here. We met the Duke and Duchess of Bedford coming to call. A. and I went for a long walk with the Empress in the evening from 5:30 to 8:30 in Osborne grounds, as usual along the seawall and sands, where we again picked up some lovely delicate shells. The Empress gave me all she collected, and I shall keep them carefully as souvenirs of the Queen's seashore and of the Empress who picked them up for me.

From a letter:
Osborne Cottage,
August 4, 1886.

I have only sent you postal cards the last few days, but there are a few minutes of leisure now, while the girls are trying on a number of very pretty yachting dresses their aunt is having made for them at Redfern's (the original Redfern, who started in a modest little shop here in East Cowes).

All the girls' summer hats were trimmed by the imperial aunt's fingers. This the nieces did not at all approve of, for although trimmed with much taste, it was absolutely regardless of the prevailing fashion. Prettily made bows and nice fresh flowers could hardly make up in their eyes for this failing, and I quite sympathized with them. But they could not refuse to wear them, nevertheless, and it was always a struggle of politeness to enjoy and be unconscious about these homemade creations, so little in keeping with the many stylish Redfern gowns provided for them. One evening about this time the Empress trimmed a garden hat for me.

The Empress and party were invited through Lady Burgoyne for a little cruise on the steam yacht *Santa Maria*, belonging to friends of hers, Mr. and Mrs. Henry Rolls. Partly on account of not caring for yachting, and partly because she wanted to keep herself disengaged for the Queen that afternoon, the Empress declined for herself but accepted for us. We joined Lady Burgoyne and the other guests, about eighteen in all, at the Royal Yacht Squadron Club, and then started off in a steam launch for the *Santa Maria*, which was moored some distance out. After being shown over everything, we steamed off in the direction of Ryde to see how the eight racing yachts were getting on. We soon overhauled them, and having had a good look at them went down to luncheon, for which we were more than ready.

When we got to the furthest extremity of the island, and had passed the forts guarding the entrance of the channel, we turned back, going full speed past Cowes again, and in a very short time were down at The Needles, which looked very picturesque. We had beautiful weather all day, and were home about 6:30, just in time to see the winning yacht come in, and hear the cannon announcing the victory.

We found that the Empress and the rest of the party had been for a cruise with the Queen, the Battenbergs and Connaughts, in the *Victoria and Albert*, and Mme. de Arcos and the Empress dined out with Her Majesty. Tomorrow the Empress, her two nieces and Mme. de Arcos are invited aboard the *Osborne* as guests of the Prince of Wales, to go around the island. Mme. Le Breton, the Duc de Bassano, and I are not included in the party, and I think, if possible, of accepting Mrs. Alexander's invitation to lunch.

From a letter:

Osborne Cottage,
August 6, 1886.

The card I sent you this morning will tell you that I enjoyed my visit to Ryde very much yesterday, and now that I have some few minutes to spare while M. and her sister are writing to their uncle, a few further details may give you pleasure.

Well, you know already that the Empress, the girls and Mme. de Arcos, went around the island on the royal yacht *Osborne*, and that they, with about fifty other guests, met the Prince and Princess of Wales and their three daughters, also Princess Louise, Marchioness of Lorne, Prince Henry of Battenberg and the Prince of Hesse. The girls do not seem to have enjoyed themselves very wildly; they spent their time principally with the little Princesses – Victoria, Maud and Louise, – who they say are painfully shy. It seems that their conversation concerned itself particularly with cameras, photographs and bicycles, which seem to be their main interest in life at present, and they showed M. and A. *con amore* the many photographs of celebrities and actresses hanging in little collapsible wire frames over the berths in their cabins. But still it was interesting for these Spanish girls to be in such unusual surroundings. The yachting party included also the Marquesa de Santurce and her two daughters, and the Muriettas. They returned home about 7 p.m.

But now about myself, who, with Mme. Le Breton and the Duc de Bassano, were left out of the cruise. I finally succeeded in lunching with Mrs. Alexander. During my visit she told me an interesting anecdote and an appropriate one to my stay at Osborne Cottage. When she was still a baby, a carriage broke down one night near her father's home in the country. All possible assistance and hospitality were given to the stranded travelers, who turned out to be the Duchess of Kent and the infant Victoria. I left Ryde on the 7:30 boat and was back here in time for dinner at 8:30, though we were somewhat delayed by the many yachts around the landing.

During dinner, after her return from the trip on the *Osborne*, the Empress gave us a full account of the day and her reflections concerning the Prince of Wales. She says he is a very good fellow in many ways, *bon camarade*, naturally good-hearted, and has shown himself on many occasions most generous and courageous, but though he knows better he is often lacking in proper courtesy.

After dinner the whole of our party went down to the seashore, where we saw the fireworks over at West Cowes and from the warship *Northampton*, and the royal yacht *Osborne*. All the ships were beautifully illuminated and it was a very pretty sight, with hundreds of lights reflected in the water. We walked home and did not reach the house till nearly midnight; very tired with our day. I am equally so again now, Friday night at 11:45, and can just scribble this that it may go off early by the Queen's messenger and reach you tomorrow, Saturday evening.

Friday, August 6. The King of Portugal arrived on a visit to the Queen. He crossed from Southampton in the *Victoria and Albert*. Paid a long visit to the Empress. After Redfern, and bathing in the morning, we went to call on Lady Burgoyne and the Marquesa de Santurce. Mr. Ward and M. de Pourtales, of the French embassy, were introduced to us, and also the two Murietta girls. In the late afternoon we went down to the Royal Yacht Squadron Club gardens, and sat there a little while. Saw the Murietta party and the Prince of Wales arriving in the launch at the club steps.

Saturday, August 7. All went out at ten to bathe and afterward to see the King of Portugal start in the *Alberta*. Coming home met Maud and Beatrice W., who called on me in the afternoon. After tea, the Empress, the girls, Mme. de Arcos and I went out in the Queen's largest steam launch.

We started from Trinity Pier and went up the river Medina to Newport and back, out in the bay past the Royal Yacht Squadron Club and twice around most of the pretty yachts. Saw Prince Henry on the *Leander* and the Duke of Connaught in the *Alberta's* steam launch. Reached shore at the same time as they did.

While out on the water the Empress was speaking of the probable marriage between Princess May and Prince Victor, the eldest son of the Prince of Wales, and the slight jealousy that exists between the Duke of Teck and the Battenbergs. She also quoted the Queen relative to the Duke of Albany and his delicate health, he having died two years previously.

Sunday, August 8. In the afternoon we went to Egypt House to a reception and tea. Mr. and Mrs. Ward were the hosts. Among the guests were the Duke and Duchess of Connaught, the Marquesa de Santurce and her daughters, Lieutenant Carr, Comte de Montalembert, Captain Hamilton, Miss Stoner and her brother, Miss Agar Ellis, and many others we knew. They danced after we left at 6:30.

From a letter:

Santa Maria, English Channel,
August 9, 1886.

I had not time to write before starting, but I am sure you will like to have a few lines from aboard the yacht on which we are passing the afternoon. At a quarter to ten we arrived at the Royal Yacht Squadron Club, where we were met by the party going with us to cruise in the *Santa Maria*, moored close to H. M. S. *Osborne*. You will probably read in the newspapers tomorrow all about the festive day at Cowes, and will see that the yachts went in procession a good way out to sea, the Prince of Wales leading the line of sailing yachts in the *Aline*, and we leading the eight steam yachts. Lady Brassey's *Sunbeam*, about which she wrote such an interesting book, was the last in the procession of sailing vessels. She passed quite close to us, when we were getting into line, so we had a good view of her. Just finished an excellent lunch, served on deck. It is most interesting to watch the running up of the signals. The Prince of Wales is constantly signaling messages over to us, to pass along to the other yachts. We are having a most enjoyable time, but I find it difficult to write much, as some one is constantly coming in and out of the deck house now. So, I must say goodby for the present.

From a letter:

Osborne Cottage,
August 9, 1886.

Later. We reached the harbor at 7:15 p.m., being the first of the yachts to get in, and were home here at eight, just in time to say good evening to the Empress before she went to dress for her dinner at the castle. Her nieces have kept all the news of their interesting day to tell her tomorrow.

I will give you the names of a few of the people who were on board, as you are sure to know something about some of them. First there were Mr. and Mrs. Rolls, owners of the *Santa Maria*, and their three boys and one girl; Lord Ormond, Vice-Commodore of the Royal Yacht Squadron; Sir John and Lady Burgoyne; Mrs. Foster; Mr. Grant, secretary of the Royal Yacht Squadron Club; Mrs. and Miss Grant; Mr. Fitzgerald, son of Lord Otho; Lady William Lenox; Lady Barbara Stapleton and Miss Stapleton. When you receive this the *Santa Maria* will be well on her way to Oban in Scotland. The Rolls are going to spend the winter cruising in the Mediterranean, visiting all the countries in the South. How delightful for them!

From a letter:

Osborne Cottage,
August 11, 1886.

There are various plans afloat for this afternoon's amusement. While they are waiting around to see if the weather means to clear, I have slipped off to my room to write you a few lines. You will not have many more letters from here, as we shall surely leave next Saturday morning, and which we shall all regret for many reasons. During the latter part of our stay we have had many delightful yachting expeditions, which make up in some degree for the restrictions.

Yesterday morning we stayed prosaically at home, but in the afternoon we had a most amusing time. A nephew of the Empress, Count Joseph Primoli, whose mother was granddaughter of Joseph Bonaparte (Napoleon I's brother), came on a few days' stay and we took him after lunch to see West Cowes. He is very clever, is quite a poet with the most wonderful fund of spirits, and made us laugh so much that we were quite ashamed of ourselves. He would insist upon our all having our photographs taken by a traveling tintype man, and we had the greatest fun possible on the green, a public walk near the sea. Fortunately there were no society people about, that early hour of the afternoon, or we would have shocked them terribly, – and would probably have been reported to and had a reprimand from the Empress – but of excursionists there was no lack, and they gathered around and were as much diverted as we. We tried to make Count Primoli stop his flow of nonsense, but it was no use. He thoroughly enjoyed seeing us doubled up with laughter, and apparently did not mind a bit whether we got into a scrape later or not.

We were just home in time for afternoon tea, and later went for a long drive to Ryde and back. As the Empress and the Duc de Bassano had the victoria, and we all went with Mme. de Arcos in the open wagonette, our party had much the same fun as before. We laughed the whole way there and back. Count Primoli, much to our regret, left for London early this morning, after breakfasting with us at 8:30. He quite enlivens the house, and goes on with his absurdities quite unabashed by the presence of his imperial aunt.

From a letter:

Osborne Cottage,
August 11, 1886.

11 p.m. Before going to bed I must just finish this letter, of which I sent you the first sheet early this morning, not having had time to complete the whole. We had a most enjoyable little cruise in the Queen's largest launch this afternoon. The party consisted of seven, the Empress, M. and A., Mme. Le Breton, Lady Burgoyne, the Duc de Bassano and myself. We went across the Solent, and up to Southampton Water and the Hamble River, nearly as far as the point of the same name, getting home about 8:30 p.m.. In the meantime the Duc d'Aumale and Princess Clementine had arrived on the *Alberta* for a short visit to the Queen. Of course during their stay the Empress will not dine with the Queen as the meeting would be awkward for them all. Au revoir for the present.

Their arrival reminds me of the following: After the passing of the law which expelled French princes last June from French soil, some of the Orleans family asked permission to visit the Queen at Windsor, and the Empress, always very delicate in her feeling for others, immediately wrote to put off her own expected visit at that same date, thinking it might be awkward for both the Queen and them. Her Majesty answered through Princess Beatrice, – "No, by no means put off the visit. If any one postpones it, it had better be *they*. The Orleanists are my relations, but the Empress is my friend and that is much more sacred to me."

From a letter:

Osborne Cottage,
August 12, 1886.

We leave here on Saturday without fail, so I shall just be bidding adieu to the sea as you reach it at Brighton. The Prince and Princess of Wales, and family, left yesterday on the *Osborne* after having been here to call and take leave of the

Surgeon-Major Frederick B. Scott

Empress. They put the *Aline* at her disposal for the few days which remain. Unfortunately, I do not think it will be much use to us, as there are yachting engagements made already for every remaining day. Pity we did not get the boat sooner, as the Empress does so enjoy a sail; it puts new life into her. The Duke and Duchess of Connaught also leave here today, and as I see one of the royal carriages at the door in front of my window, I suppose they are taking their leave now, so I do not know when we shall get our luncheon. It is already a quarter to two and we are all famished. From the fourteenth to the seventeenth, on which latter date the Queen starts for Edinburgh, she will have Osborne Castle all to herself, for all the other royalties will have departed by then.

Thursday, August 12. We remained in all the morning. Lady Ely, the Queen's old and trusted friend, made a long call. She has also been a friend to the Empress ever since the latter's girlhood and the Empress expresses the greatest affection for her. She is a dear old lady; sweet, and dignified old age personified.

In the afternoon Dr. Tyler with a party of thirty came to see the Empress; there were Hindoos, Greeks, Malays, etc. The Oriental salutations and the bright, rich, varied costumes made a very unusual sight. At 5 p.m. Mme. Le Breton, the girls and I drove to the Parkhurst athletic sports and met Prince and Princess Henry of Battenberg returning. Nearly 400 people had lunched there. General Nightingale and Captain Worral of the 93d Highlanders were among the officers introduced to us.

Friday, August 13. Stayed in again all the morning, waiting to see if we were expected to go on an expedition or not. All of the party, except us three girls, went to call on the Queen. In the afternoon we visited H. M. S. Northampton in the Queen's steam launch. The ship was beautifully decorated with flowers, flags, etc., just like a huge ballroom. There were from 300 to 400 people there, among others Lord Brassey and his family, three admirals, some Spanish naval officers from a ship in the harbor, but strange to say, no royalty whatever. We danced and enjoyed ourselves immensely.

From a letter:

Farnborough Hill,
Saturday, August 14, 1886.

I am very glad I followed my instinct, born of my knowledge of the Empress's methods, and did not stay up writing last night, but packed nearly everything instead, for this morning came a hasty message to our rooms. We were asked to get up, to finish our preparations as quickly as possible; and to take a donation from the Empress to the little church here, which is very poor, and then to meet her at the Queen's private landing place punctually at 10:45. So we had hardly time, though we hurried. We were not late, however, and even had a few minutes to spare at Trinity Pier, talking to Major Bigg, Lady Burgoyne and some gentlemen, who had come to see us off. When the Empress's carriage arrived, we all went aboard the *Alberta* whose officers, as well as those of the *Victoria and Albert*, were in attendance. We found Prince Henry, too, on deck, and he remained talking to the Empress till the moment for starting had nearly come, then bowed to her, said a few words to us, shook hands all round, and went ashore. I regret deeply that we were not at Osborne Cottage at the general departure, as the Queen and Princess Beatrice and several maids of honor came to take final leave of the Empress. After a little conversation between the two Majesties and the Princess in the drawing-room, the Queen passed into the hall, where she shook hands with the Duc de Bassano and the ladies, and kissed the latter, herself handing them into the carriage. She asked with astonishment where we three were, and expressed regret at our absence. The Empress acknowledged that as only one of her carriages was still at Osborne, she had sent us ahead on foot.

Major Bigg accompanied us to Southampton, where a special saloon carriage attached to the main train carried us rapidly to our destination. At two o'clock we were home at Farnborough, finding it all looking very pretty, after an absence of a month. We were not sorry to have our luncheon. The Empress and her nieces have gone now for a walk around the grounds, but I preferred to remain at home. Unfortunately, the servants must have missed their boat or train, as neither they nor the luggage have yet turned up (6:30 p.m.), and we shall not be able to dress for dinner tonight unless they make haste. It is delightful to feel we can go about with more freedom again. There are some restrictions here, it is true, but nothing like those involved by living under Queen Victoria's roof.

Sunday, August 15. Dr. Scott with Major and Mrs. Scott came to tea, and to welcome us back to Farnborough.

PART IV

Later Events at Farnborough Hill

PART IV

From a letter:

Farnborough Hill,
August 17, 1886.

On Monday morning the Empress sent word she was going
shopping in London, and I was to accompany her. We lunched
at 11:30 and an hour later started from home, to which we
returned again at 7 p.m., having spent the intervening time
hovering about from silversmiths to glass and china shops,
choosing different things for the dinner table, and all this in
honor of visitors who arrived from France that very evening.
They were: Prince Joachim Murat,* grandson of King Murat

---

* Joachim Joseph Napoleon, Prince Murat, born in Bordentown, N.
J., February 21, 1824; son of Lucien, Prince of Naples.

of Naples who married Napoleon's sister Caroline; Joachim's daughter, Princess Eugénie Murat; his sister, Duchesse de Mouchy;* and M. Protais, an ald artist, accompanied by M. Pietri, who was returning from a business trip to Paris.

From a letter:

Farnborough Hill,
August 18, 1886.

I have not had time to send my letter off today, for directly after luncheon the Empress asked me to write some English letters for her, so thanks to a communication to a Parsee in Central India called Nosherwanjee Cowasjee, and another to a gentleman at the Cape of Good Hope, I was unable to get my own correspondence done.

Yesterday Count Sormani, an Italian senator, arrived. He is tall and gaunt, with a long shaggy gray beard, not very lively, and makes no great addition to the party. We now sit down twelve every day to luncheon and dinner, and tomorrow the Duquesa de Ossuna arrives, so until some one of the party departs, the superstitious ones will have a hard time of it, if they notice the number.

Friday, August 20. Lieutenant Carr, one of the young naval officers we saw a good deal of at Osborne, arrived to make a call and stayed to lunch, making thirteen, so A., being the youngest of the party, had on account of some foolish superstition, to lunch at a small table alone. General the Hon. W. Fielding came to call at tea time.

Tuesday, August 24. The girls went for a drive with Mrs. Byrne. Princess Eugénie and I took a long walk together and were joined by Dr. Scott. Colonels Wood and Williams called at tea time.

---

* Formerly Princess Anna Murat, born in Bordentown, N. J., February 3, 1841; married in Paris, 1865, Antoine de Noailles, Duc de Mouchy.

From a letter:

Farnborough Hill,
August 25 1886.

I cannot by any means say it is dull here, as the house is full. Still there does not seem to be much news to write; as every one more or less remains quietly at home, the girls are busy with their English and music and *le monde* does not appear till lunch time, except when Princess Eugénie comes out for a walk with us at twelve o'clock, which is nearly daily the case.

Lunch is a merry meal, and soon afterward we three go off to our *petit salon*, or the tent if it be fine weather, and we are neither seen nor heard of until tea time at five. After this we are free to take part in whatever is going on. Some of the twelve drive, others prefer walking, but we three generally like tennis best, and are usually joined by Princess Eugénie Murat and her father, or some of the other gentlemen. The other day when we played it was Princess Eugénie and A. against Prince Murat and myself. Yesterday, besides our own party of twelve, General and Mrs. Byrne came to tea and also Dr. Scott, his brother the Major, and the latter's wife, so we were eighteen in all, – and there was plenty to do I assure you, pouring out tea and providing all kinds of delicious cakes for that number of hungry and thirsty individuals. Tonight at dinner we shall be a formidable party. The poor Empress is quite tired out and annoyed that her visitors should all want to come at the same time. For months past their dates have been conveniently fixed, and now, what with one thing and another, and our extra fortnight on the Isle of Wight, they have all arrived together – and this afternoon three more are coming.

Princess Murat* is a delightful girl, over six feet in height, broad generous proportions to match, beautiful hair and skin,

---

* Eugénie Louise Caroline Zenaide Murat, born in Paris, 1855; married June 18, 1887, Paris, to Giuseppe Caracciolo, Duca di Lavello.

and a fine intellectual brow. She is a great deal with us. We have just been in her room, – the two girls and myself, – where she has been showing us her jewels, etc., which are magnificent. She owns some splendid diamonds and emeralds, which come from her mother, who was a Princesse de Wagram.

From a letter:

Farnborough Hill,
August 27, 1886.

Our household keeps on increasing daily. We sat down fifteen to dinner last night – an Empress, a Prince, a Princess, two Duchesses, two Dukes, and a Count – pretty well for one family dinner party. The Duc de Mouchy and the Duquesa de Ossuna arrived two days ago, and the girls' uncle, Don Antonio de Vejarano, last night at 8:30 from Madrid. He will prolong his visit to the very last possible extremity, but must be in Madrid by the fifteenth of September. This morning I have retired into my room to write to you and give the girls absolute freedom with their uncle. After a year's separation they must have much to talk over with him.

From a letter:

Farnborough Hill,
August 28, 1886.

I have only a very few minutes free, so I must hurry. Since I began this I have had some letters to write for the Empress, and so the post went out with only a card instead of a long epistle. I hope the heat of these last few days has not tried you too much. Here even it has been very oppressive.

Yesterday the girls and I went to London. We were sent off to get us out of the way, for besides our own very large party there were six other people. Among them the Duque de Alva, the Empress's nephew, and his wife, the de Rivières and Mgr. Goddard, and the latter I was very sorry to miss. They all came to lunch, and as it was really too much of a good thing to have twenty-one at table besides ourselves, the girls benefited by it, to get off on a sight-seeing trip to the metropolis. We visited the Tower, St. Paul's, and South Kensington Museum, where we lunched. Then we went to the Oratory, and back to Waterloo Station, taking in Westminster Abbey on our way, where we specially enjoyed the old cloisters and their adjoining picturesque court yards.

At Waterloo Station we met the Duc and Duchesse de Mouchy and Princess Eugénie, who were returning from lunching with Lady Holland at Holland House, and we all traveled homeward together. We did not lose a minute of that day, and the girls enjoyed all they saw very much, but we were terribly tired, and pleasant and bright though the evenings now are, we could hardly keep our eyes open till eleven o'clock, when the Empress retired and we three also. On leaving the room this evening the Empress made a most wonderful courtesy, which we had never seen before, but had heard about in connection with Tuileries days. It was half a bow and half a courtesy, full of ease, and graceful in the extreme, and though addressed to the whole room, had the quality of seeming to take in personally each individual.

The Duc de Mouchy is a born musician, and plays by ear with very good chords and harmonies anything in the operatic line, and almost every other well-known air, and all this without having learnt one note of music. Besides the Duc's playing and mine, there are all sorts of *parties de cartes* going on, everybody being scattered about in groups, doing what they each like best. No one seems willing to leave Farnborough; those who came for a few days only are staying on, and on!

The Duquesa de Ossuna belongs to Queen Christina's royal household in Madrid. She has been a great beauty and is still young, elegant and amiable. If alone, we should probably be enraptured with her, but surrounded as she is by such a gathering of exceptionally interesting people as the others are, her own charm pales somewhat. Before the Duquesa arrived, the Empress told us, in speaking of her, about the origin of the family name, *Giron*, which in Spanish means *rag*. It came from an ancestor who in the melée of battle saved the king's life and gave him his own horse to replace the fallen one. In the scuffle he accidentally tore off a piece of the king's cloak. Instead of throwing it away, he carefully kept it. The next day there were a hundred claimants to the honor of having saved the king's life. Whereupon, our astute hero begged leave to inquire of the king if his cloak was intact, and if not he suggested they should settle the conflicting claims by trying to find the man who possessed the missing piece. Both his valor and quick mind were in consequence, I understand, amply rewarded, and honors showered upon him.

Talking at luncheon one day about the little King of Spain, the Duquesa told us that the day of his birth the Infanta, his sister, asked what the baby's name was to be. When they answered that perhaps it would be *Fernando* she said quickly: "Oh no, if papa really sent him he must be named *Alfonso*."

The Duquesa told us, also, that by good luck it was her turn the particular week of his birth to be *de service* at the palace, and as such had by law to be a witness of the royal child's arrival, so she was the first of his subjects to see him, an honor which she much appreciated. She told us it was a Spanish custom, when the royal infant was twenty-four hours old, to put him in a kind of silver basket warmly wadded, which, carried out by one of the dignitaries to some high steps (either of the palace or cathedral), was raised up in the sight of all the people, and the covering lifted for a moment. She continued, with many interesting traits about his peasant wet-nurse, the fuss and ceremony involved in choosing her from among so many aspirants to the honor, and what a great personage she thinks herself now. We also heard about her trousseau and her life, with its privileges and restrictions in the royal nursery of Spain.

The Duchesse de Mouchy is simply perfect, and so pretty, graceful and witty, – and so young looking though she has a grown-up son. She has quite won our hearts and so too has the Princess Eugénie Murat, her niece. The trefle which the Duchesse de Mouchy always wears now, no matter what the dress or the hour, was one which had been the first gift of the Emperor Napoleon III to the Empress. She got it before they were engaged, at a little lottery for the guests of a house party staying at St. Cloud. Louis Napoleon was at the time already desperately in love with her, and the Empress herself says that with his connivance they rather helped her to win the beautiful prize, a handsome trefoil of emeralds and diamonds, which she always regarded as her engagement gift and as a kind of mascot. Invariably during her years of sovereignty she wore it somewhere about her clothing, and up till June, 1879, it never left her person, even at night. When the news of her son's death reached her she took off the jewel, put it away and later on gave it to her favorite niece, with the request that she wear it for her sake as long as she lived. This wish Mme. de Mouchy was carrying out when she came to Farnborough, and the Empress herself pointed the trefle out to me one evening, and requested the Duchess to unfasten it and to put it in my hand for examination while telling me its history.

The men of the party are such thorough gentlemen, – all so friendly and at ease together. I must say I prefer foreign to stiff English society.

When the Empress presented me the first evening to the Murats she did it very nicely. After naming me, she said, "Joachim, this is the grand-daughter of Colonel Macirone who served your grandfather so faithfully." This fact seemed to strike him very much, and may possibly have influenced them in the interest they took in me. Nothing could have been kinder than they were the whole of their stay in Farnborough, and later on in Paris, I counted both father and daughter among my best friends there.

My maternal grandfather, Colonel Francis Macirone, was born in Manchester in 1788, of an English mother and Italian father. His mother died in 1800, and in 1803 he was sent to Rome with letters of credit on Paris, Genoa and Florence, at the early age of fifteen, to live with his uncle George, then postmaster-general to Pius VI. I now continue in my grandfather's own words:

"Soon after the occupation of Naples by the French in 1805, I was preparing to return to England and had actually obtained my passport, when in consequence of the noted decree of Berlin, I was constituted a prisoner of war, and detained as such in that country nearly seven years (on parole)."

During those years he became acquainted with members of the Neapolitan court and the royal family, and in King Joachim's hour of need became one of his staunch friends. Already he had been on an embassy to the Emperor of Austria to beg an asylum in his country for the hunted and dethroned Joachim and his family, and was actually on his way to England to seek further help from the Prince Regent of England, when he was arrested at the instigation of the infamous Marquis de Riviere at Marseilles. After several weeks in a Marseilles dungeon and much mental and physical suffering, he was escorted to Paris, the Marquis' secretary having first brutally announced to him the assassination of the brave King Murat.*

Arrived at the capital, he was immediately re-arrested by Des Cazes and confined *au secret* in the Conciergerie and at the Abbaye prisons. All his diplomatic papers and valuables, including a bill from King Joachim for 40,000 francs on a Paris bank, his personal effects, arms, etc., were confiscated, and only his carriage was returned to him later. Except for his ingenious expedient of letting his faithful valet in Paris know

---

* Shot at Chateau de Pizzo in Calabria, October 13, 1815.

his whereabouts, he might never have got out alive. His servant informed Sir Charles Stuart, the English ambassador, of his master's plight, and soon after the Colonel was released.

His own account of the part he took in the capitulation of Paris in 1815, his hair-breadth escapes, and his interviews with Murat, Napoleon, Wellington, Blücher, Metternich, Fouché, Talleyrand, Carnot and many other celebrities, being all told in a book published by him in 1817,* are well worth reading by all lovers of history, and ought to be especially interesting to his descendants. These incidents of several generations back made my meeting with descendants of King Murat of additional interest to me.

From a letter:

Farnborough Hill,
Saturday, August 28, 1886.

M. de Varu, a French military attaché, lunched here. After dinner, when we were sitting in the drawing-room, the Empress read us a long interesting letter addressed by Prince Alexander of Battenberg to the Queen, giving her the details of the shameful way he had been treated. Prince Alexander (the King of Bulgaria) describes very graphically in this account how soldiers with fixed bayonets forced him at night out of his bedroom and down the back stairs. They tried by threats to make him sign an abdication, which they hastily wrote out for him in pencil on a leaf torn out of the Visitors' Book in the hall. They roughly took away his uniform and gave him peasant's clothes. They were glad to do anything that could make him look ridiculous and humiliate him. Prince Alexander wrote that afterward on the Russian frontier he was left alone locked in his railway carriage for many hours without any food, and as a refinement of cruelty they obliged him to

* "Interesting Facts Relating to the Fall and Death of Joachim Murat, King of Naples."

The Emperor and Empress in 1865

194

keep a light burning brightly in the carriage and the blinds up, so that all might see him. For two hours he remained thus in the station with a seething mob hooting and jeering at him. He was not allowed to protect himself by pulling down the blinds, and so securing privacy for himself.

The Empress asked us not speak of his letter for the present outside the Farnborough circle, the Queen having sent it to her for private perusal, and she was not authorized to make it public, though she felt justified in reading it aloud to the guests in her house.

Sunday, August 29. Added to the usual Sunday party at tea was a young Catholic officer named Staunton, who had been one of those deputed to receive the Empress at the church door in the morning.

The Empress, who dislikes to see people wearing showy jewels (or those using perfumes) said one day at lunch to her niece, Mme. de Mouchy, who always wore large handsome pearls in each ear, that she thought it very foolish of her not to take them off in traveling and on long walks alone in the mountains of Switzerland, and added that she thought it was inviting robbery, and that some day she would be attacked for the sake of the jewels.

Mme. de Mouchy laughed at her aunt's fears. Soon after she returned to Paris. Before she had been gone more than three weeks, she wrote saying that her aunt's words had actually come true. During a drive in the Bois de Boulogne in Paris she had got out to walk a little, her carriage following, and in a by-path two men had sprung out on her, snatched at her earrings and would have succeeded in tearing them from her ears, had not a passing friend by good luck seen the assault and with his uplifted stick put the robbers to flight.

From a letter:

Farnborough Hill,
August 30, 1886.

The visitors remain the same and do not seem at all in a hurry to leave, and as I have said a few words about each of them, there is no more at present. They are all amiable and pleasant to get on with, and I shall be very sorry indeed when the party breaks up.

Talking of robbers and burglars one day with Mme. de Mouchy, here are two stories she related. The first was about an acquaintance of hers in Paris, a young woman who was suffering from an attack of rheumatism, which kept her in bed and unable to move. She was under good doctors, but had no regular trained nurse, and therefore advertised for a ladies' maid, – "a strong healthy woman capable of lifting a rather heavy invalid." A few days after a very buxom maiden appeared, neat, cheerful, healthy-looking and rosy, to whom she took a great fancy and who lifted her with the greatest ease, adding much to her comfort. One day she rang her bell, and on inquiry found her invaluable maid had gone out, – a most unusual thing. A few minutes afterward, there was loud knocking at her front door and a police agent asked to see the mistress of the house, and told her he had come there to arrest a man. She protested there was no man, but he was equally sure there was, and informed her that an escaped convict, had been traced to her house, and that the clue ceased there. It appears that the prisoner, on getting out of jail, saw the invalid's advertisement, disguised himself and obtained the position, which he kept six weeks, living in the meantime in perfect security from detection. At last some slight imprudence on his part put the police on the scent, and he was traced to the invalid's house, much to her consternation. He had, however, departed for good.

The other story was about Marchandon, the Parisian, who murdered in a most barbarous way the aged lady he was serving as butler. Attracted by the renown of her jewels, he had tried, the Duchess said, to get into the house as footman, and only a certain instinct against him prevented her engaging him, – for he came well recommended, – when he presented himself to fill the vacancy in her household. She had reason to congratulate herself on the escape, for soon after the terrible murder with its gruesome details took place, and made all Paris shudder. She herself would probably have been the victim instead of the old lady, had she taken Marchandon into her service.

Tuesday, August 31. After dinner Princess Eugénie, the girls and myself went for a walk on the terrace. I had a very unexpected fall and spent a sleepless night in consequence, my head, foot and back hurt me so.

From a letter:

Farnborough Hill,
September 3, 1886.

I have your letter this morning and have hardly more news to send you than you have to give me. Till Tuesday morning everything went as usual, and then there was a change in our party. On Wednesday, the first, while several of the gentlemen were starting out for their first partridge shooting, Count Sormani was taking his leave of Farnborough to return home to Venice, and this morning very early, to our great regret, Prince Murat left with his daughter and M. Protais. She is so very nice, has been such a companion to us, and has been so kind to me especially, that I shall miss her very much. She would not say adieu but only au revoir.

The girls and their uncle will most likely be leaving for Madrid about the twelfth, and are already beginning to think about packing. I can hardly believe it. How these months have flown! I shall remember them all my life through, and what interest I shall now take in people and places which until my stay here would have been unknown to me! The girls will be very sorry to leave, though M. thinks there is no place half so nice in the world as Madrid. A. on the other hand, who hates society and loves the freedom of country life, says that, once the joy of seeing her friends in Madrid is over, she cannot think what will become of her, shut up closely in the town nearly all the year round. They wish very much that I were going home with them, and so do I.

From a letter:

Farnborough Hill,
September 4, 1886.

It has been so much cooler here these last two days, and I hope it has been the same with you, as the heat tries you both so much. I have not felt it at all, as I have been very quiet indeed these last three days. Do not be alarmed; it is nothing at all, – a slight sprain. Only as a measure of precaution, Dr. Scott, who is constantly at Farnborough and now comes in very handy, thought I had better keep my foot quiet and not walk up and down stairs for a few days. It does not pain me now, and I can move about my room a little, though feeling rather stiff from the bruises I got, and also from lack of my usual exercise. I will tell you how it happened:

Could you have seen me without being startled, – as I was, – you would have laughed with me at the commotion I caused in the house. It might have been very serious, but as it turned out it was nothing, though I got a great deal of sympathy and attention; so much so, that I really felt quite ashamed of myself for falling down as I did. Princess Eugénie, the girls and I, had gone out on Tuesday the 31st at the Empress's suggestion, it being a lovely moonlight night, for a little walk on the terrace which runs around the house. The other ladies were mostly in the drawing-room and the gentlemen in the billiard room, the lights and open windows of which attracted us. We went up to the window to see what was going on. We were all in a frolicking mood and ready for a joke, and thought it would be fun to call out all together from the different windows at which we had stationed ourselves while looking in. Under the window which I had chosen was the opening into the cellar, of which we knew nothing. I rested my hands on the window sill and before I had time even to scream, my feet were in space and I had disappeared down into this hole. It was done in the twinkling of an eye, and still I had time to reason out that I was falling, – as I thought, – into some disused well and that in a moment I should strike the water, make a splash and be drowned. Many years of my life, and thoughts about those I was leaving behind, were able to crowd into my mind in that incredibly short number of seconds.

I was dragged out by main force by the Princess and one of the men-servants, who was first to arrive on the scene, all three girls calling out lustily and concluding from my absolute silence that I must be dead. By the time I was landed on the terrace, had somewhat resumed my scattered wits and grasped the idea that I had had a bad fall, all the gentlemen had run out of the house and were standing around. Without asking "by your leave" I was picked off my feet like a baby and carried the nearest way into the house by Prince Murat, where all the servants were assembled. Then the ladies came flocking out of the drawing-room to inquire, condole, sympathize and report the exact state of things to the Empress.

When I had been made to swallow a glass of brandy and water by practical Mme. Le Breton, had had a cut on my wrist attended to, and dozens of handkerchiefs and much advice offered, I was escorted by the whole troop back to the drawing-room, where the Empress was anxiously waiting with a face that rivaled all the others in interest and alarm. After she was satisfied that I was more frightened than hurt, I was escorted to bed, the girls coming with me and helping me up the stairs, with Princess Eugénie following. When in bed, she insisted upon bathing and bandaging my poor foot with improvised bandages, for it had doubled under me when I fell, and later swelled up. It was half-past twelve before my room was quiet, for every minute maids and visitors were coming to my door to inquire and offer services. The next morning before ten o'clock I had visits from nearly the whole household, including the Empress, who brought Dr. Scott with her.

The following day of my imprisonment the Princess, thinking it too hot on my side of the house, very simply, and with her gigantic height and strength, and perfect good nature, gathered me up in her arms as if I had been a feather weight, and carried me down to her room. There she read to me, showed me her jewels and did everything she could think of to distract and amuse me. The Empress came later to make a little call, after which Prince Murat came in and told me he was *à mes ordres* when I wanted to be carried back again. Instead, I was carried downstairs by him to dinner.

P. S. The Empress and the whole party have just been under my window calling up to ask news of me, and inquiring if I am going to be allowed downstairs this afternoon.

Monday, September 6. The Duquesa de Ossulla left for Spain. The girls went on General Byrne's coach to the ruins of Waverley; so sorry I could not go with them. The Duque and Duquesa de Alva dined here.

Tuesday, September 7. The Archduke of Austria and his aid-de-camp came to pay a visit to the Empress. I saw them several times from my sofa by the window.

From a letter :

Farnborough Hill,
September 7, 1886.

There is really very little news to give you, except that Dr. Scott has promised me I may go down this afternoon. Should he, however, think it more prudent for me still to wait one more day before walking down three flights of stairs, the Empress, who paid me a nice little visit this morning, will have me carried down, for feeling as well as I do, it must be, she says, in spite of visitors too dull in my room. Yesterday morning I already had a most delightful and affectionate letter from Princess Eugénie.

From a letter:

Farnborough Hill,
September 9, 1886.

Post time went by while chatting with Mme. de Arcos, who lunched here today, and so I have, I am afraid, lost all chance of letting you have your usual letter tomorrow. Before dressing for dinner (I am glad to say I am going down) I must write you a few lines to welcome you back to London.

The Empress met me on the stairs as I was hopping down, leaning on the banisters, and though Dr. Scott said it would not hurt me in the least to walk down carefully, she insisted upon my finishing the rest of the journey seated in a hall chair, carried by M. Pietri, who was unceremoniously pressed into service assisted by one of the valets standing by. Quite an ovation was given me when I got to the table and they drank my health in champagne, a very unusual beverage here. Really, every one is wonderfully kind, and I cannot help being grateful for it all, including the pleasant months I have spent here.

I cannot believe the girls are really going on Saturday. I shall feel so lost without them, and they seem almost as reluctant as I to say goodby, but I hope we shall meet again some day. If ever I go to Spain, there is a warm invitation awaiting me to stay at Calle Sacremento in Madrid. How I should enjoy it. I have written to H., asking if you can arrange to let her spend the afternoon of Saturday with the girls in London. Their uncle has promised me not to let her get over-tired and to see that she is sent safely home long before they themselves start on the evening train for Paris.

Friday, September 10. The girls' last expedition on General Byrne's coach. They went to Aldershot, where they bought presents and souvenirs to take home. Dr. Scott came to dinner and spent the evening.

Saturday, September 11. At 10:30 M. and A., and their uncle, went to the station accompanied by the Empress and Mme. Le Breton. Dr. Scott was to meet them at Woking Junction, and H. at the Charing Cross Hotel at 3 p.m. Quite a sad parting. The Empress was most kind, and especially affectionate to me all day and at dinner, but it did not prevent our spending a rather quiet and dull evening, and I was glad when bed time arrived.

From a letter:

Farnborough Hill,
September 14, 1886.

Very glad H. was able to see M. and A., as it was a mutual pleasure; a pity though it was Saturday, for when everything is shut up, London looks so dismal. As they seem to have amused themselves all the same, it does not matter. I had an account of the afternoon from Dr. Scott on Sunday, when he came to give the Empress the last news of her nieces, and at the same time to see if my foot was gaining in strength.

Tuesday, September 14. Dr. Scott turned up very late, – at seven o'clock, having been until that hour at a field day. The Empress asked him to stay to dinner, which he did. His efforts at French are most amusing, and he is quite unembarrassed at the choice of the wrong word, and pleasantly uses any one which happens to come into his head.

From a letter:

Farnborough Hill,
September 17, 1886.

The Empress spent Wednesday in London. She had promised to meet her niece, Mme. de Mouchy, now staying with Lady Holland, and go with her to the Colonial Exhibition. There, the Empress's party, – the Duc and Duchesse de Mouchy, the Duc de Bassano, Mme. Le Breton and M. Pietri, – were met by chance by the Duchess of Teck, who was lionizing her sister the Grand-Duchess of Mecklenburg-Strelitz and her children, – so the party was a large one. On leaving the Exhibition they all went to Lady Holland's, where those who did not already know the old historic house were shown over it, and were delighted at its quaintness, its dignity, and the treasures it contains. Before leaving, the Grand-Duchess said to the Empress, "You are going, of course, to see my mother, are you not?" So the Empress felt obliged after this leading question, tired as she was, to drag herself off to Kensington Palace to see the old Duchess of Cambridge (she was ninety her last birthday). They were home here at 8 p.m., the Empress quite done up.

I certainly should not have failed to be one of the party, had it not been for my wretched sprain. Dr. Scott came to see me and after painting my foot with iodine, had tea and spent the rest of the afternoon with me.

Yesterday evening M. Rainbeaux, who was here previously in June and took so many photographs, arrived on a second visit, this time with his wife* and Felix, a son of about nineteen, – and tonight a M. and Mme. Duruy, and Victor, their little boy of twelve, reached Farnborough. Today the dear Duchesse de Mouchy and her husband came to take final leave of the Empress, and to accompany the Grand-Duchess who lunched here. They leave Lady Holland's for Paris tomorrow morning. It seems strange to have had granddaughters of George III under the same roof as myself. A very close link with the far off past.

I have already had a long affectionate letter in Spanish from M., which gave me great pleasure.

---

* Daughter of M. Mocquart, banker, and secretary to Napoleon III.

From a letter:

Farnborough Hill,
September 22, 1886.

As strangers are coming to lunch, among others a brother of Count Joseph Primoli, our Cowes friend, and I shall very likely not be able to write before post time, I send you now these few lines scribbled hastily, that you may not be disappointed in case I have not time for more. Our party continues the same, serious and interesting, but not so full of *entrain* as when Mme. de Mouchy was here. The King of Portugal was to have lunched with us on Monday, but unfortunately, the Duchess of Teck had invited the Empress to go and pay a visit at White Lodge, Richmond; and since on a previous occasion it had been necessary for H. I. M. to decline some invitation of the Duchess's, and there had been a misunderstanding and some offense taken in consequence, the Empress felt obliged to sacrifice the King this time. It was a very awkward affair all around, and I personally was extremely sorry, for I should have liked to meet his Portuguese Majesty, although according to the Empress he is exceptionally plain.

Yesterday Sir James Lacaita, another savant, took his midday meal here, so the conversation at table was of a very serious nature. I send you Princess Eugénie's nice letter of yesterday. Please return it when read.

From a letter:

Farnborough Hill,
September 25, 1886.

I am hurrying to finish this before going down for lunch, to which the Prince de Wagram, maternal uncle of Princess Eugénie Murat, is coming. The Duruys left this morning; they are a very gifted family. He is an *ancien ministre d'instruction sous l'Empire*, belongs to the Académie Française, and is a member of l'Institut de France and of the Académie des Beaux Arts, – in fact a very distinguished man all round, who is now

The Duchess of Alva and her children

Marshall Macmahon
President of the French Republic, 1873-1879

completing an illustrated history of ancient Greece he has been working on for these last twenty years. He is well known already by his history of France. His wife was formerly Mlle. Redel, governess to the daughters of the Duchesse d'Albe, and in that capacity well known to the Empress. She helps her husband with his writing and so do his two grown up sons, one of whom, Georges, has quite a reputation as a novelist. The Duruys will be a nice addition to the Parisian friends I have made. I have invitations from all the visitors here, to go and see them whenever I can.

Dr. Scott who came to see us yesterday, pleased with the wonderful improvement in my foot during the last few days, has given me leave to do anything in moderation now, provided I guard against fresh sprains by keeping on the bandages for some time to come. I do hope I may be able to get to the Colonial Exhibition some day now, as I think the Rainbeaux will go again before the closing day.

Sunday, September 19. The regular Sunday party for afternoon tea, with the addition of Sir Algernon and Lady Bothwick and daughter.

Conversation after dinner, as was quite usual, drifted to the past, and included eventually the Orsini *attentat* of January, 1858. The Empress told us that they (the imperial party) were one night on their way to the Opera House, then in Rue Lepelletier, when all at once there was a terrific rending noise, and the carriage suddenly halted with a jerk that threw the occupants out of their seats, while injuring the coachman and killing the horses. Then came a second terrifying report. After the third bomb exploded they were left in absolute darkness, which added very much to the horror of the experience. The concussion had been so great it had put out all the lights in the street. The cries of the frightened people and the wounded, the rearing and neighing of frantic horses, was succeeded by a *silence de mort*. They all held their breath, expecting another explosion, and thinking their end had surely come. The first terrible shock over, a man stepped forward to open the carriage door, and the Emperor following his first impulse, and thinking him probably an assassin, dealt him a terrible blow on the head which felled him to the ground. The suspect later proved to be an anxious and friendly official come to the rescue, and the Emperor fully made it up to him afterward for the very natural but awkward mistake. As there were no more explosions the imperial couple thought they had better keep to their original plan, and go into the Opera House, and by showing themselves reassure the public, then in danger of a panic. To do so they had to step over the wounded and dead bodies strewn about. When the Empress finally entered her box and stood there bowing, and feeling more dead than alive, everybody rose and gave her a warm ovation. Noticing the glances of the people fastened persistently on her, she looked down and saw the front of her satin gown covered with blood, the result of a tiny cut on her cheek which in the excitement she had not even felt, but which was responsible for the stain. To quiet the people's anxiety for their sovereign an announcement had to be made from the stage, stating that she was not seriously injured. Then, till messengers were despatched and had returned, came the hardest part of the evening to bear, – to sit through the play in suspense, dreading lest some attack might have been attempted against her little two year old son at home in the Tuileries. At the end of her narrative the Empress added: "Je ne nie pas que j'avais très peur; le bruit, l'obscuritè, l'incertitude, les cris et les gémissements des blessés; la vue des cadavres tout autour; la voiture traversée; et le chapeau de l'Empereur criblé de trous, – tout cela était épouvantable. L'Empereur a montré un sang-froid admirable, et moi, tout en ayant affreusement peur, j'ai passé (comme du rests je l'ai fait toute ma vie), pour avoir un courage extraordinaire! En apparence, j'avais la peur la plus digne qu'il fut possible d'avoir, car j'avais trop peur pour crier, et trop peur pour bouger, – j'étais paralisée, – et alors on croyait que j'étais complètement indifferente et que cela ne me faisait absolument rien!" *

She only reached home and her son after midnight, and then had to hold a reception for grateful subjects.

Saturday, September 25. General Fielding, Earl Denbigh's brother, came to take his final leave of the Empress before his departure from Aldershot. He had tea with us on the terrace.

From a letter:

> Farnborough Hill,
> September 28, 1886.

I hope you will not expect me today, as I have been persuaded, much against my inclination, not to join the Exhibition party. On account of the departing Indians the crowd will be very great, and though I can now walk quite well on level ground with a stick, everyone thinks it would be foolish for me to attempt the expedition. Dr. Tyler wrote, very kindly offering to have a bath chair at the main entrance for me, but I don't like to accept and take up his time on this, his last day in England. They sail for Bombay Thursday. So I have decided to give up the trip altogether, great also as is my disappointment in not seeing you.

But my visit to you need only be postponed a little, I hope. I have a plan for next week. When Mme. de Mouchy

---

* "I do not deny that I was very frightened; the noise, the darkness, the uncertainty, the cries and groans of the wounded, the sight of the corpses strewn around; the carriage and the Emperor's hat riddled with holes - all that was terrifying. The Emperor was admirably calm, and I, though fearfully frightened, appeared (as indeed I have done all my life) to have wonderful courage. I had on the surface the most dignified fear it is possible to have, for I was too frightened to scream, too frightened to move, – I was paralyzed, – and so people thought I was completely indifferent and that the affair had absolutely no effect upon me."

was here and they all went with the Empress to visit Lady Holland, I told the former how sorry I was to have missed my opportunity of seeing the old historic house. She agreed to speak to Mr. Lane, the steward, and get me permission to visit it when in London. The place will not be dismantled for another fortnight, he writes, and I have only to name the day and hour, and he will be ready to show me over everything. Now, this is what I propose: when the visitors have left, I hope to go to London and take H. and some other friend to visit Holland House, and then spend the remainder of the day with you. M. Rainbeaux has given me two photographs of this house; that is all he has to spare at present but he has plenty in Paris, and has promised me a copy of each one in which I appear.

The other day, the Empress who never would, so far, allow herself to be included in any of the groups, gave her consent, and in a moment M. Rainbeaux had taken two instantaneous pictures before she could change her mind. Unfortunately, I was not on the spot at the time, so I shall have no claim on these, but I think one may be given me all the same, as our amateur photographer is generous and good natured, as well as clever.

Yesterday we had his excellency the Portuguese minister, M. D'Antas, and M. le Baron de Varu to lunch, and in the afternoon arrived the Duque de Alva, whom I missed a fortnight ago, and also his wife, because of my sprain. I cannot say much for his personal appearance; small and thin and with a nervous *tic*, he is not at all what one would imagine a Spanish grandee of the first class, and a descendant of so great a man as the famous warrior, would be like. But he is kindly and sociable, and during a drive we took together this afternoon in the dogcart (the Empress and others being in the landau and victoria) we got along splendidly. He told me many interesting incidents of his childhood during the war, besides a good deal about people in Madrid I know by name through

M. and A., so the drive was quite a pleasant one. In the interest of our conversation he forgot his nervous eccentricities for the time being.

He has all sorts of queer tricks and mannerisms which he practises when he thinks himself unobserved, and at which the Empress laughs unmercifully, hoping thereby to shame him out of them. I noticed one day that he dropped his napkin at table and stooped to pick it up; this happened not only once, but several times during the meal. After dinner, the Empress talking to us about her guest, explained this queer habit. He feels that he must during the meal touch his knee at least once to the ground. If he is prevented from doing it, he seems miserably preoccupied and will not eat, so he makes a regular practice now of dropping his napkin at once, and in picking it up slips his knee to the floor, and is thus contented. He always tries also to touch with the soles of his feet the lintels of any door he passes through.

I noticed how cleverly when going into dinner he made conversation, or slight pauses in the doorway, until he could accomplish his end and properly step on the lintel. The Empress, whose arm he had, hurried him along, and said laughingly, "Now, Carlos, I know what you are doing, – come along, we can't wait for you."

Talking one day of plucky and courageous acts, the Empress told us several anecdotes and among others one about her sister, the Duquesa de Alva, – anecdotes which I think come in appropriately here. She and her husband were living in Madrid, in the Palacio Alva, then one of the most beautiful of the old palaces, and now, since its skilful and artistic restoration, quite the *most* beautiful, the Empress says.

In the evenings, following the Spanish custom, they often went to the different *Tertulias*. It happened one night, when they had been playing cards, that the Duchess went home with her maid at a somewhat earlier hour than usual, leaving the Duke behind. She entered the palace with her woman, crossed the numerous uninhabited suites of rooms in the huge building, and entered her bedroom, locking in herself and her maid as she always did at night, if her husband had not returned with her. While undressing she accidentally dropped something and stooped to pick it up. In so doing she thought she noticed something unusual under the bed, but paid little attention at first. She felt impelled, however, to look again and this time she distinctly saw two eyes glistening. The fact suddenly dawned upon her that some one was there, but her presence of mind made her realize at once that she must not appear to have seen anything. So with extraordinary self-control she quietly went on undressing. Her first aim was to prevent her maid's suspecting that there was anything wrong; the girl would, she argued to herself, in all probability scream, and disaster might follow. Her second aim was to obtain aid, and that immediately. She thought hard for a minute as to what she could do, undressing leisurely all the time, and soon her plan of action was evolved. She began casually telling her maid about the evening she had spent, and how pleasant it had been. She explained also that she had played cards and been in luck, and won quite a large sum of money. Then seeming suddenly to remember that she had left her purse behind, and simulating great concern about it, said to her maid, "You must go and get it tonight, for the *frotteurs* and cleaners will be there early in the morning, it will be pocketed, and I shall probably never see the money again." She instructed the maid to go in person to the house of the Duke of — —, to deliver into his own hands a note she would write telling him about the money, and then bring back the purse when found. The note was written and sealed, and the maid quite unconcernedly went on her errand, leaving the Duchess alone in the room with the "somebody" under her bed.

Then began, the Empress told us, the hardest time for her plucky sister, who tried to eke out the minutes and invent things to do without exciting suspicion. At last she realized she could delay no longer, and that she must get into bed or the man would be suspicious of her dawdling, so she took her courage à deux mains and unflinchingly walked over to her bed, and very slowly and deliberately stepped in.

Later on she congratulated herself on having had the forethought and nerve to do this, for it will appear later it actually saved her life. She then spent ten or fifteen terrible minutes of suspense, wondering whether the intruder would now creep out and stab her, – first feeling impelled to bound out of bed and rush from the room, then resisting the temptation so as to protect her property. However, these few trying minutes, which seemed like hours, passed at last, – she heard to her infinite relief the tramp of footsteps coming down the long corridor, and knew she was safe. The note to her recent host had briefly acquainted him with the trying situation she was in, and urged him to come as quickly as possible, with her husband and the police. Another minute's delay, the door was burst open and the police made straight for the bed, then secured and dragged out the would-be burglar.

When brought to justice, he was asked at the trial what his intentions had been and he confessed that he had come to steal the Duchess's jewels, tempted by the knowledge that she possessed some of the most beautiful and renowned pearls in Europe. He intended at first to secure these only, but hearing her tell her maid of her winnings at the card-table, he thought he would keep quiet a little longer and so get the purse of gold besides.

In the first few moments, he said, he imagined the Duchess had seen him, and he felt inclined to jump out at once and seize the jewels, and owned he was quite prepared to take her life, too, if she resisted. When she wrote the note his suspicions were again aroused, he said, and he watched closely for tell-tale signs of fear on her part; but after the deliberately calm way she got into bed, his mind was quite at ease, and he decided within himself that it was not possible she could know of his presence. He could not believe any woman could get into bed so quietly under such untoward circumstances. But here he had reckoned without his host, - her pluck was superior to his reasoning, and he paid in prison the penalty of his would-be theft, and of his lack of judgment in the character of an exceptionally fine woman.

From a letter:

Farnborough Hill,
October 1, 1886.

The Empress has invited me to stay on here, as she is not leaving for Italy just yet.

I look forward to spending Tuesday or Wednesday with you, and I hope I shall find you well and H.'s cold quite gone. She has a *compagne de malheur* in the Empress, who has a violent influenza cold, too, in spite of the lovely weather. On Tuesday, the twenty-eighth, Mme. and Felix Rainbeaux, whose first visit to England this is, went to see Windsor Castle, and the whole party (the Rainbeaux and the Duruys) left this morning for Paris, so we are now very quiet. The Marquis de Bassano came to lunch and to say goodby to the Empress; he is starting on a shooting trip to Algeria, spending a few days first with his family at Folkstone, and the Duke, his father, has gone to see him off.

From a letter:

Farnborough Hill,
October 2, 1886.

At present the Empress, Mme. Le Breton, M. Pietri and myself are quite alone - rather a difference now in the size of the table at meals. Next week a few people are coming to enliven us again, - Mme. de Arcos and her sister, and a young Frenchman who has already been here, M. Urbain Chevreau.

After the lovely day of yesterday we had a most violent storm at night. I hardly ever remember seeing such lightning, but it did not last long, – only from about 7:15 to the end of our dinner at nine, and then the stars came out. I wish the Empress would think of inviting H. down for a day now, – everything was so cold and bare when she was here in March, – but of course, it is rather too much to hope that she will think of it, and the Empress never could imagine I'm sure the pleasure strangers get out of what she is not only accustomed to, but thoroughly tired of.

This evening at table our party was further reduced to only Mme. Le Breton, M. Pietri and myself, and we spent the rest of the evening in the Empress's *salon de travail*, her cold being too bad for her to come to the dining-room.

From a letter:

Farnborough Hill,
October 6, 1886.

It seems absurd of me to say I have not had a minute all day to write to you, but such is really the case. Now, at 7 p.m., I am sitting down in my room for the first time today for a few minutes' leisure. On getting up this morning I set to work till 11:30 on the dress I am arranging. Then I went to the Empress's room and helped her with her embroidery till one o'clock lunch, after which, it being rainy, we set to work again with our silks and needles till tea time at five; and now I have only just come up to my room, the conversation lasting all this time. The Empress was tired of embroidering and was glad to chat, but I, in a less calm state of mind, was steadily watching the clock, hoping to come up and write to you, knowing how disappointed you would be if you did not hear from me at least tomorrow morning.

I hope to see H. the day after tomorrow, as the Empress has asked me to invite her to spend the day here. Strange that the invitation should have so soon followed the expression of my wish, – thought transference perhaps. Let us hope it will be fine. There is a train at 9:45 reaching here at 11:10, which would give her a nice long day.

I have only seven and a half minutes to dress and get downstairs for dinner, so goodby hastily.

The Empress told us at tea time certain funny incidents, which might belong to the *Punch* series of things "better left unsaid." Mme. la Marquise de la Bédoyère, when at the Tuileries, heard some one in a group in the drawing-room ask, as a lady entered the room, "Qui est ce petit pruneau là qui entre?" An angry but ceremonious voice answered, "Madame, c'est ma femme!" Thoroughly disconcerted and much excited, the lady moved off to another group to tell the occurrence, and had just said the words: "Et je disais: 'Qui est ce petit pruneau là?'" when the same voice behind her answered again:– "Et je repondis: 'Madame c'est ma femme!'" *

We also had a pleasant account of the little plays given at Compiègne on the Empress's fête by her ladies, and all the fun and merriment they occasioned. Prosper Merimée (her childhood friend) often wrote the plays and the charades, and Princess Metternich was one of the principal actors, and led matters with a high hand. She was plain to ugliness, but full of intelligence and ready wit, as the following will show. A lady who was anxiously pressing forward to see this renowned woman, exclaimed under her breath on seeing her, "Oh, quel singe [Oh, what a monkey]!" She was overheard by the Princess, who, bowing politely, turned to her and said without a moment's hesitation, "Oui, madame, le singe à la mode [Yes, Madame, the fashionable monkey]."

Sunday, October 8. General and Mrs. Byrne and Reggie came to tea, also Dr. Scott. The Duc de Bassano returned from Folkstone at 10 p.m.

---

* "Who is that little black thing coming in?" "Madame, it is my wife." "And I was just saying, 'Who is that little black thing?'" "And I answered: 'Madame, it is my wife!'"

Monday, October 4. In the afternoon went for a drive with M. Pietri, who talked interestingly about the Franco-Prussian War and the Prince Imperial. We called on Mrs. Scott, who was out.

Wednesday, October 6. Worked all day with the Empress, helping her with her embroidery, which she is finishing for Lady Revelstoke (Lady Baring that was). It is going to be made up into a screen, and the Empress showed me how to do parts of it, – just tedious filling in, – which greatly helps her.

Friday, October 8. Embroidery again with the Empress most of the day. Dr. Scott called to inquire after her cold. Went for a long drive in the afternoon with the Duc de Bassano, who told me many interesting things about his childhood and recollections of his youth. His father, first Duc de Bassano, was one of Napoleon I's ministers, and had apartments at the court, so as a child the Duke was often in a position to see his godfather and godmother, Napoleon and Josephine, and later on the little *Roi de Rome*, who indeed became his constant playfellow. He told me of the great awe with which Napoleon inspired him even as a very young child, though the stern soldier-emperor was always kindness and tenderness itself to this little fellow, and all children.

One day in the midst of a very amusing game that the two boys were playing in the Emperor's room, his footsteps were unexpectedly heard approaching. The little *Roi de Rome* got an affectionate greeting from his father, and then ran away elsewhere, forgetting his playmate. Bassano was so startled that he darted instinctively behind a curtain and hid. The Emperor, who had forgotten something, came in and began to write, and was so deep in his work that several hours passed before he finished and went away again. Every minute the little boy stayed hidden it became more difficult for him to make up his mind to come out, so he finally resigned himself to

*Memorial to the Prince Imperial on Chislehurst Common
from a drawing by B.B. Long*

217

indefinite imprisonment behind his curtain, much dreading that the Emperor might come to the window it covered and wondering what he could say for himself if he did. After his long life, eighty odd years, the Duke said he remembered now perfectly his infinite relief when Napoleon finally departed and he crept out of his hiding place.

The Duke also told me about Queen Victoria's coronation (1837), at which he was present as a young attaché of the French embassy in London. He described the entrance of this young girl in a simple white dress into Westminster Abbey, and the unforgettable impression made on him by the glitter of uniforms and the dazzling gorgeousness of the jewels and the coronets of the peeresses and the court.

The Duke also remembered well riding (with one of the Bonapartes) in the steam coach invented and run by my grandfather, Colonel Macirone, in the New Road (now Marylebone Road), till an act of Parliament at a great monetary loss to the inventor put a stop to it, on a plea of its frightening the horses.

Saturday, October 9. H. arrived at 11 o'clock. We showed her the state carriages before lunch and afterward went for a drive all through Aldershot, both North and South Camps. She left at 7:27, having very much enjoyed our day and the Empress's kindness.

From a letter:

Farnborough Hill,
October 12, 1886.

A few visitors are beginning to arrive here again, Mrs. Edmund Vaughan yesterday afternoon, M. Urbain Chevreau today, and Mme. de Arcos on Thursday next – a change from the monotony, which was beginning to pall. Yesterday we had some people to lunch: Prince Roland Bonaparte and his aid-de-camp, Mr. Bonot. Prince Roland is a grandson of Napoleon I's brother, Lucien. Today old Prince Louis Lucien Bonaparte, who lives in London, is coming to lunch. I have seen him already here once before. He is uncle to Roland, who came yesterday. Now I must say goodby. I hear the Empress going into her salon de travail and I must follow her. I am sorry H. did not see the embroidery; it is like a most lovely painting of flowers, and it will certainly go down to posterity with honor.

Wednesday, October 13. After dinner the Empress, under much protest, took the very first lesson of her life in whist; she had strenuously resisted learning, she said, till then, but was urged to try by Mrs. Vaughan who taught us. It was my first lesson, too. The Empress played with the Duc de Bassano against Mrs. Vaughan and myself.

Thursday, October 14. Went for a drive with Mme. Le Breton, Mrs. Vaughan and the Duc de Bassano; M. Chevreau following alone in the dogcart, driving Umgenie.

Before his arrival the Empress spoke a good deal about Urbain Chevreau's father, who was Ministre d'Intérieur, the last minister under the Empire appointed by her. Among many other schemes, which interested her in behalf of her different subjects, the Empress took special thought about a project for shortening, and thereby softening, the ceremonial preceding the execution of criminals. It was arranged that they should enter by a door nearer the scaffold, should wear no strait-jacket, and that their hair should be cut off beforehand in the prison. M. Chevreau and she worked together over these and other reforms for a long time. One day the Minister came to announce that all was settled and in working order. The Empress expressed her pleasure to him, and as he was leaving her presence she said, "Eh bien, c'est une bonne affaire de faite;– qui sait si nous n'en profiterons pas nous aussi.

Peutêtre aurons nous un jour à nous feliciter personellement de ce travail."* M. Urbain Chevreau is a frequent visitor at Monza, the country place of the King and Queen of Italy, just out side Milan. He told us a good deal about Queen Margharita one evening; how charming she is, both in public and private life, and especially the latter; how bright and interesting her conversation, as she sits of an evening knitting warm things for some of her poor subjects, all of whom worship her.

Friday, October 15. Blowing a heavy gale of wind and rain ever since last night. No possibility of our going out, but in spite of it all arrived Mme. la Marquise de Gallifet, who had arranged to come and make a call on her former sovereign. The Empress had not seen her for a good many years and was painfully impressed by the change which had taken place in this once beautiful woman, who is now through illness, contracted during her devoted nursing of cholera and over patients, more than plain of feature though she still retains her distinguished air.

Saturday, October 16. At 1 p.m. Stag, the Prince Imperial's favorite horse, over thirty years old, died. Uhlmann, who came in to inform his mistress, had tears in his eyes. This brought back many sad memories of course. The Empress gave orders to have one of Stag's hoofs kept and made into an inkstand. The faithful beast had been with the Prince Imperial in Zululand, and took part in the funeral procession at Chislehurst when, draped with a black net, he followed his master's body from the station to its temporary resting place in the little Catholic church. Everybody who saw the poor horse, said he really seemed to understand that something sad was going on.

---

* "Ah well this is a good thing achieved, – who knows if we will not profit by it ourselves some day. Perhaps we shall some day personally rejoice over this day's work!"

The day of the Prince Imperial's funeral London seemed empty. Some thirty or forty thousand sympathizing people had gone to Chislehurst from the metropolis, and reports later said that a number of French had assisted at the interment, besides many thousands of people of other nationalities. The Queen immediately came to Camden Place and stayed with her bereaved friend during those sad hours, when the poor mother's grief was so great and uncontrollable that as I have heard here from her entourage, she repeatedly swooned away and was hardly conscious of what was happening during that day.

It had been the faithful Duc de Bassano who, when the fatal news reached England some weeks before, had had to break it to her. He told me in speaking of this, one day, that it was the very hardest task he had ever had to accomplish in his life. She had only that day received one of the Prince's many cheerful letters, - and she would not, could not understand or believe he was dead. Only the Duke's great love of the dead boy, and his devotion to the stricken mother, helped him through the ordeal.

At 4 p.m. the Duc de Bassano left for France, and at six Mme. de Arcos arrived on a visit.

From a letter:

Farnborough Hill,
October 17, 1886.

We are just home from the camp church, and so before lunch I will write you a few lines in case I should be prevented later in the afternoon, for if you do not hear from me early tomorrow you will be disappointed, especially as I was unable yesterday to let you have your usual Saturday evening letter. This is the reason: Before I was dressed yesterday Mme. Pelletier came up to my room to say that as soon as I was ready the Empress begged me to go down to her *salon de travail*. This I did, and I remained the whole day with Her Majesty, helping her in her annual clearing up of old papers. You have no idea of the quantity of documents, letters and pamphlets which came out of the drawers of her desk, and which, after putting aside those to be saved, I burned for her (the Empress allows nothing to go into the waste-paper basket for housemaids' perusal). After luncheon we finished with the papers, and then I went with the Empress into the inner room, – she calls it her *cabinet de travail*, – and to my astonishment saw her touch a spring in the side of a huge looking-glass reaching from floor to ceiling. It slowly revolved back on hinges like a door, showing behind it a huge iron safe. A small key from the Empress's pocket opened this, and revealed a number of drawers on one side and pigeonholes on the other, dividing the safe down the middle, the compartments bearing a letter of the alphabet, or the names of bankers, Spanish estates, etc. Here the appropriate letters, papers and documents of all kinds are arranged in packets and labeled alphabetically for greater convenience. Each of these drawers was opened in turn, the packets carefully looked through, and the papers of value accumulated this year were put in their proper places. Letters from sovereigns she has kept separately in a special leather case of her own invention. "N" and "I" contained by far the largest bundles, for included under "N" were all sorts of things concerning Napoleon I and III, and under "I" interesting material relating to the Prince Imperial. The Empress showed me several newspaper cuttings about his death. Some were very beautiful and touching, but the majority (nearly all from French newspapers) most cruel and cowardly libels on the brave young Prince. I could not have kept such horrid things if I had been the Empress and I told her so, but she seemed to think it a necessity. I also saw letters from MacMahon and others; and written out with her own hand some copies of political letters she had penned in times gone by. Also the list of invitations to and the order of ceremonial of the Prince's baptism, besides a list of his *layette* and many other interesting things. The Empress had all these and other priceless documents of the Tuileries sent on board a ship of the squadron for safety, as soon as things seemed to be going badly in the Franco-Prussian War, and the future loomed up ominously.

She let me read many letters from different people (who afterward turned against her and betrayed their trust) expressing the writers' devotion and eternal gratitude. Of this nature were letters from Bazaine and Trochu, and the Empress said they would be mortally ashamed if these were made known, and she added, "People would be very much embarrassed in the light of subsequent events, if I were to bring out these papers and confront the writers with their own words now." She said, too, that her experience had been such that, with very few exceptions, she did not believe in or even tolerate the word "gratitude." It angers her, it is usually so false. She believes there is very little, – hardly any such thing as genuine self-sacrificing gratitude left in the world.

I was given to read some very queer letters from crazy people. These last were not among the papers preserved, but among the class of daily letters, which are usually destroyed as soon as answered or attended to. Out of one from America came a large lock of black hair, labeled "from your son by the Comte de Chambord." The letter said, "I am writing to papa by the same post," and ended by begging money to come over to see her. Another claimant writes every week, "Chère Mademoiselle: I will meet you at Charing Cross at the train to arrange about our marriage." The writer continues that he thinks it better to write to the Pope or perhaps the Prince of Wales to arrange matters and signs it "Roger Doughty Tichborne." His latest epistle of six pages ends as follows: "I need only say, Mademoiselle, that I am ready to marry you any day or at any hour. You have only to write *when*, for we ought to have been married twenty years ago. F. P. D. G. L. Roger Doughty Tichborne."

A number of begging letters, too, were destroyed by us. H. I. M. said people behaved just like vultures, swooping down on her during the first month after the Prince Imperial's death. She had the letters put aside at the time and alphabetically arranged, and on examination found that she had been asked for more than a million francs in those four weeks.

Here are two examples of the extraordinary addresses on some of the letters doomed to the flames: *A Sa Majesté l'Impératrice Eugénie, London Bridge, Museum, Angleterre, A l'ex-Impératrice, à Montengo, Chist-le-Rousse* (Chislehurst), *Angleterre.*

I would not have missed my interesting day's work for anything, though it certainly was tiresome sitting all day, steadily tearing up and burning papers handed to me, especially as the Empress hardly spoke at all; she is obliged with her bad cold to be as silent as possible to avoid bringing on a fit of coughing.

Monday, October 18. All morning again arranging papers with the Empress. Dr. Scott dropped in at afternoon tea time. Dr. Chepmell came to make the Empress a professional visit and dined here, leaving by a ten o'clock train. I was shown today a letter from Paul de Cassagnac. Talking afterward of his officious devotion, the Empress said, "Son dévoument est une vraie affliction et ne vaut pas grand chose [His devotion is a veritable infliction and is not worth much]." Writing from Germany in 1870, he had said of Napoleon III and the Prince Imperial: "Nous ne voulons ni d'un vieillard ni d'un enfant [We will have neither an old man nor a child]."

In the evening and under the influence of the letters read during the day, ingratitude became the topic uppermost. We were told incidentally that Don Meurice de Bourbon wanted to marry the Empress when she was a girl, and then the real ingratitude of the Duke of S. was brought to our notice. Both he and his brother were paid for at college by the Emperor, and spent their holidays at the Tuileries. "Apres les événements il n'a jamais dit un seul mot de sympathie, et il ne s'est même pas fait inscrire à Madrid."* Lately he has had the audacity after first sending a visiting card, to write and ask the Empress for money. The letter was not answered.

Here is another instance of ingratitude. The Emperor and Empress once visited incognito the booths at the Foire de St. Cloud, and next day sent one hundred francs to each of the itinerant performers. One was unintentionally forgotten, so H. I. M. sent a gentleman back the following day with the extra money. The recipient was the *géant* of the Foire, a fine big fellow, the son of a gentleman of the court of Charles X, who had had reverses of fortune and was penniless. The Empress when she heard the story bought him out for the remainder of his two years' engagement, clothed him and gave him an appointment at her court. She has never had a single word from him since 1870.

Then the Empress told us of the strong attachment of a little girl for the Emperor and herself at Biarritz. The child was taken ill with diphtheria and would accept no remedies from anybody but the Empress, in whom she had great confidence. The sovereign nursed the child through the crisis of her sickness and operation, and she recovered. No expressions of gratitude were sufficient for the father, – he would never in his life forget her devotion, he said. Nevertheless in 1870 he unmercifully abused the Imperial party, and, added the Empress, "A la mort de mon fils, il a eu la cruauté de dire, – 'C'est bien fait' [At my son's death he had the cruelty to say, – 'It is well done']!"

---

* "He has never said a single word of sympathy since the event, and he did not even have his name written down in Madrid," – that is, in the book provided at a royal court or an embassy for the entering of names of formal callers who come to express sympathy or offer congratulations; the equivalent of a call in private life.

From a letter :

Farnborough Hill,
October 19, 1886.

All day yesterday I spent with the Empress arranging and classifying more papers. This time they were mostly letters of condolence received after the Prince Imperial's death, besides poems, elegies, books and consolatory pamphlets of all sorts, received at the same time. There is another large safe in the upper gallery near the Empress's bedroom, and into this the more bulky and less precious documents are all put alphabetically like the others downstairs. I should say there must be thousands of them in the pigeon holes. The poor Empress arranged them all with seeming indifference, but at the last when Mme. Le Breton was passing by and remarked that she looked tired and pale, and begged her to leave off, she broke down completely, put her elbows on the flat glass cabinet before her and burst out crying. Poor thing!

In looking through the documents this morning, we came across one relating to the Chateau de Marseilles, and this is what was told about it by H. I. M. The town gave the site and the Emperor built the residence himself. After the Emperor's death in 1873, Marseilles requested *citoyenne Bonaparte* to give it back, saying that it was not inhabited as it ought to have been according to agreement. Asked for it in this peremptory way, the *citoyenne* refused to give it up and a lawsuit followed which the Empress gained. Having won, she then handed the chateau immediately over to the town as a gift from *Marie Eugénie Guzman, veuve de l'Empereur Napoleon III*, and stipulated that it was to be used as a hospital. The gift was rejected, but soon after cholera broke out and then the civil authorities were glad enough to accept the chateau. The Empress added that her partisans were as angry with her for doing this as the Duc d'Aumale's now are at the gift of "Chantilly" to his country, which has since exiled him.

Tuesday, October 19. My first real walk since my accident, – from three to four p.m. Went as far as the Memorial Chapel, which is advancing rapidly and is almost finished.

Wednesday, October 20. No message has come to my room as yet, so I suppose the Empress doesn't intend doing any more till the afternoon or tomorrow. I wrote to Princess Eugénie yesterday and hope soon to hear from her. Mrs. Vaughan leaves today, and Mme. de Arcos (or Zizi, as the Empress always calls her) remains till next week. Count Minszech, an Austrian, who came here once before in the summer and who divides his life between Paris, Vienna and England, is coming to lunch tomorrow.

From a letter:

Farnborough Hill,
October 21, 1886.

I cannot say much about the Turkish ambassador, Rustem Pasha, for he did not come to lunch after all, but only to pay his respects to the Empress in the afternoon, and on arriving was received at once in her private apartments. Mme. Le Breton and I only saw him passing down the gallery on his way to and from the carriage. He is a small sallow man, wearing a fez of course. The Empress told us he had years ago become a Christian and was at one time Governor of Syria. She made his acquaintance on a visit to Constantinople, which preceded the opening of the Suez Canal. She is charmed with him now, says he is full of intelligence, and had a most interesting conversation with him, about affairs in the East. Among other things, he said that formerly it was the French and the English merchants who divided trade between them, – now the Germans have the principal business. They first tempted the natives by cheapness, under-bidding other nationalities, and have now become the leading dealers.

During our walk after dinner and following our talk about

The Empress, about 1870

Rustem Pasha, our hostess gave us a whole string of Eastern experiences, one after the other, and here are the notes I made before going to bed, and which I have just filled out as such, adding only a word here and there to make the narrative intelligible:

First she told us about the opening of the Suez Canal. The Empress went alone to the opening of this important waterway. Affairs in France being in an unsettled state, the sovereigns did not both dare to absent themselves together for any length of time, so it was decided that the Empress should be the one to go. All the fleets of Europe were represented, and among the sovereigns there were present the Emperor of Austria, the Crown Prince of Prussia, and the Prince and Princess of the Netherlands. The roar of cannon was deafening. In recognition of the gigantic engineering feat having been undertaken and carried through by a French engineer and under French auspices, the Empress was given precedence everywhere. All the royalties came and paid visits to the Empress on her yacht, *L'Aigle*, which led the procession of yachts, and was the first to enter and go through the Suez Canal.

This is the telegram the Empress told us she sent to the Emperor on arriving, November 17, 1869: "Arrivée à Port Said - réception magique - la chose la plus magnifique que j'ai jamais vue [Arrived at Port Said - a magical reception - the most magnificent thing I have ever witnessed]." After the opening of the canal, a regular triumphal program commenced and all the following things happened during this wonderful and delightful trip:

For the opening religious ceremonies, a magnificent tribune was erected, where the sovereigns sat. One side was devoted to the Catholic services of thanksgiving, and the other to the Mohammedan ceremony of the same, and the whole was very solemn. A splendid ball was given next night at Ismailia. The Empress of the French presided at the supper; she was seated between Emperor Francis Joseph I and the Crown Prince of Prussia. The Khedive Ismael Pasha sat opposite. During the supper the Khedive suddenly left the party, locking the sovereigns and their suites in the banquet room. All wondered what was happening, and the Emperor of Austria went to reconnoiter. He discovered that the Khedive was uneasy about his guests. M. de Lesseps had brought in such a number of *reds*, the Empress said, that Ismael feared there might be an outbreak or some attempt on their lives. After supper all the sovereigns went to the public ballroom to look on at the multitude of merry-makers. It was very amusing. The *Republicans* were all dancing with their fezzes on in that fearful heat, because they would not uncover themselves before royalty for anything. So they danced on in a fearful state, like a Turkish bath, the perspiration pouring down their faces, while royalty looked on and enjoyed their unnecessary discomfiture.

The party arrived next day at the town of Suez, and the Empress, the other sovereigns and their suites, signed their names to an entry in the yacht's log-book, which stated that the journey through the Suez Canal had been actually and successfully achieved.

The Empress then told us about the Khedive's wonderful munificence, and the number of boats, on the Nile put at their disposal for the journey with her numerous suite. The Empress had a good sized sitting-room for herself and her nieces in one dahabeah; there was a dining-room in another. One was exclusively taken up by a laundry for themselves and suite. Another was filled with preserves and stores of all kinds. Still others contained live cattle and poultry and stores of vegetables and fruit. Perishable food was preserved in ice and the whole party had a plentiful supply of this, as of all else through the entire journey. A dahabeah was also the traveling home of the camels and mules, and the tents and baggage, for excursions into the desert. There were numbers of other boats to supply minor wants of the numerous suite and the servants, and one exclusively reserved for a barber's shop. A relay of dahabeahs was left behind at each of the three cataracts and a fresh relay as fully equipped found ready. It was, the Empress said, exactly like one of the *Arabian Nights'* fairy tales, and the whole of this outlay was at the Khedive's expense.

The same evening, the Empress told us about her cousin de Lesseps. She described at some length his tremendous imagination and indomitable energy, his life in Paris and his great prodigality and open-hearted hospitality. Their house, she said, must have been a very difficult one to run, for he sometimes came home of an evening bringing in his wake and unannounced a collection of twenty to twenty-five friends with him, picked up in odd corners at different intervals in the day, and invited with the greatest cordiality. His wife was often at her wits' end, but had to do the best she could. Their children were well known in Paris for the way they rode their ponies in a furious wild Indian fashion through the Bois de Boulogne. Mme. de Lesseps told the Empress that she had first fallen in love with her husband through her great admiration for his genius, – a genius which would probably have saved her mother's life if his *chef d'oeuvre*, the Suez Canal, had existed sooner. It seems that as her mother was returning from a visit to some island, she was so terribly seasick that she had to be carried ashore at the Cape, and died there of exhaustion soon after. Had the journey been shortened, as it could have been by the existence of the Suez Canal, the fatality to her mother might not have occurred.

The Empress told us about her interesting visit to the harem of the Sultan of Turkey, Abdul-Aziz, during this royal progress through the East. The women, she said, were *très ordinaires*, in spite of their very lovely eyes, and were entirely without education. They did nothing all day long and lived almost entirely on bonbons. They had absolutely no privacy, no sleeping-rooms of their own, but reclined on their divans day and night and held the position of slaves. Only the mother of a male child was honored and treated as a wife of the Sultan. She also told us about the return visit of the Sultan's women to her, a most extraordinary innovation to rule and a wonderful event for them. They had never before been outside of their harem, till they were taken to Beylerbey Palace on the other side of the Bosporus, put at the Empress's disposal by the Sultan. Before they were allowed to go, however, an attendant was sent by the Sultan to visit every nook and corner of the palace, to see that no man was anywhere concealed. All the gentlemen of the Empress's suite and her men-servants had been previously obliged to leave the premises and go and wait aboard the imperial yacht. By some oversight the Empress's small negro page, Mustapha, given the Empress by some barbaric ruler, was forgotten. He was her personal attendant, and had in the eyes of many much the position of a pet dog, so that in making a list of the men to be ousted he was not remembered. The harem women arrived like a buzzing swarm of bees, – thirty or forty of them. They poured in with unmannered haste, so delighted with their new found liberty that they ransacked every corner and turned everything topsy-turvy to examine it, even spilling her work basket and trying on her thimble. The Empress began to fear for her jewels when she saw their utter lack of control. At last, in the course of their investigation, the ladies of the harem came accidentally upon Mustapha, hidden away in a corner behind a door. Great astonishment and pretended horror on their part, – mingled with wonderful curiosity and excitement at the extraordinary event. The poor page's fright was terrible and genuine. He feared the Sultan's knowing that he had seen his wives, for he knew the usual penalty of such audacity was death. Nothing the Empress or anybody could say would comfort him or allay his fears. He begged so insistently and piteously to be sent immediately on board *L'Aigle* for safety, that at last he had to be yielded to.

The Empress had a long talk with two of the Sultan's daughters; one was being brought up in the English style and only spoke English. She had an English governess and spent her days riding round and round in a small courtyard of the palace, trying to be what she imagined English girls to be like. The other daughter was brought up as a French girl and only spoke French. Her attendants were French and all her books were French. The Empress took up some of them and discovered most of them were by Paul de Koch. This girl said in course of conversation: "We two are much more to be pitied than the other daughters of the Sultan, – they do not know their loss, but the Sultan has by education opened for us a window to look into the outer world, which, however, is denied us, and he has made us very unhappy! We both hope we shall be allowed to marry Christians, and so escape from this terrible existence."

H. I. M. ended up this much prolonged talk about the Orient, by telling us of a very strange experience she had on the Bosporus. It was during this same official visit to Constantinople, during which she was the guest of the Sultan, and being entertained with princely magnificence. The Empress described her costume that day, and said she was decked out in all her most gorgeous finery, – a robe of scarlet cashmere embroidered with gold, – and she wore some of the crown jewels, among others a diadem having in the center the famous "Regent" (which Napoleon had bought for 14,000,000 francs). For the first time on record the Sultan allowed a woman to cross the Bosporus in his private caique. This was an unheard-of honor, but no honor was deemed too great to be paid to his guest, the Empress of the French. She was being rowed by six splendid *caigi*, whose beautiful and strange dress of diaphanous materials she described. They are lightly clad because they have to row with all their might. The boats go like the wind, and never under any consideration whatever are they allowed to stop an instant. If anything gets in the way, they run it down as a matter of course. The men never take any precautions against the dreadful heat of the Bosporus, and get alternately so overheated and then so chilled, that nearly all ultimately die of consumption, in spite of being such magnificent men and having such splendid physique to start with.

Well, the Empress, then, was in this caique, going along with lightning speed, when all of a sudden she saw, right across their bows, a small rowboat with one man in it. It came upon her in a flash that in a few seconds more he would be run down. She knew it would be no use to beg the *caigi* to stop, – such an idea would be unheard of. Even if she had they could not have understood her language, and would not have obeyed in any case because of the fearful penalty this breach of discipline would bring. In this terrible moment, the Empress said, in default of all else, nature came to her assistance and made her do the one spontaneous thing which really saved the man's life. A little shriek of alarm so astonished the *caigi*, that for an instant they turned to look and forgot their duty. In that incredibly short space of time the man in the small boat had time to swiftly move aside. He then stood up in his boat and waving his hat called out in English, "Long live the Empress!"

Amid so many others equally thrilling she completely forgot this incident. It never crossed her mind again, she said, till driving down the rue de Rivoli during her memorable flight from Paris, Dr. Evans asked her if she remembered the occurrence, and said, "I was that man! Your Majesty saved my life once; I am delighted to be of some service in my turn." The Empress said in finishing this story, "Il m'a vue aux deux points les plus opposés de ma vie, – au plus haut! – au plus bas [He saw me at the two greatest extremes of my life – at the highest and the lowest]!" Soon after the various events in the East, the Empress was summoned home rather suddenly for the opening of the "Chambre."

From a letter :

Farnborough Hill,
October 21, 1886.

The Empress had a letter from Princess Beatrice yesterday, which she partly read to us. She was writing to ask the Empress "from Mamma," to postpone her departure for Italy till the Queen's return from Balmoral, which will be about the fifth or sixth of the month, as the Queen wishes very much to see her friend. Of course the Empress cannot refuse to wait. So much the better for me, for this will probably lengthen my stay here. The Empress says she cannot go to Windsor till at least the seventh or eighth, and she will probably not return here afterward. Princess Beatrice writes that Prince Joseph of Battenberg, who, with the Prince of Hesse and his daughter Irene, is staying with them at Balmoral, tells them most interesting and terrible things about poor Prince Alexander's treatment and imprisonment in Bulgaria. She adds that she herself will be very glad to get settled down at Windsor, as she is not feeling at all well.* The gong will be sounding in a few minutes, so I must stop. My foot still swells at night and will for a long time to come, the doctor says, but it does not pain me in the least now. Yesterday we walked all around "Compiègne," a part of the Farnborough property with a picturesque pond in it, then through the *jardin potager* where the Napoleon I willows grow, and back through the park.

I have only a few minutes before lunch to write. Dr. Scott is invited, and later the Empress is likely to ask me to help again, as I did yesterday, and arrange papers with her till tea time, after which conversation is prolonged sometimes until it is nearly time to dress for dinner, and no one can leave the room till the Empress does.

I had a charming letter from Princess Eugénie Murat yesterday; she and her father are staying with the Prince

---

* Her eldest boy, Alexander Albert, was born shortly after this.

de Wagram, his father-in-law, and will be back in Paris in a month.

In the evening at the usual walking and talking time, the Empress was speaking about an official journey through Brittany in August, 1858. She told us how very tired she was with the constant strain of speeches and people being presented, for the train kept continually stopping. At a small wayside station a poor little dressed up, frightened child was popped into the carriage with an enormous bouquet. The Empress in her usual affable way, trying to help the child, asked her, "Mon enfant, comment te nommes-tu?" General Fleury, who was always fond of a joke, could not resist the temptation of whispering behind the child, "Dites: J'ai nom Eliacin,"* much to the general amusement and the poor child's confusion, who could not understand what it was all about.

From a letter:

Farnborough Hill,
October 26, 1886.

Monseigneur Goddard is expected to lunch, so I must begin and finish my letter now, as I shall not be able to do so afterwards. I spent yesterday afternoon in London with the Empress, who went up to consult Dr. Chepmell. He came to see her as usual at Mme. de Arcos's house in Wilton Crescent. The visit over, the Empress went to several shops to get a certain kind of portfolio for keeping old letters, and not succeeding, finally ordered one of her own invention at Jenner & Newstubbs. We then drove back to the station.

Wednesday, October 27. Dull day, – nothing happened, – but there was a most interesting conversation after tea, the Empress telling all sorts of anecdotes about Napoleon I and

---

* Celebrated answer in Athalie.

her own reminiscences. "Napoleon I était un vrai genie; lui seul pouvait tenir tête à tant d'esprits réunis contre lui."*¹ She was remarking how strange it was that some of her family in the past should have been against Napoleon I. In one of Napoleon's letters (that she has read) he writes to his brother Joseph: "Beware of Montijo. Keep an eye on him, – he is dangerous." This Montijo was her own father's brother. He has been called the "Spanish Mirabeau," was an inveterate enemy to France, and a revolutionary leader at home. Eugénie's father, Don Cipriano Guzman de Palafox y Portocarrero, on the contrary, was always an ardent admirer of Napoleon and distinguished himself as a colonel in his army.

The Empress had found among her Napoleonic documents a letter addressed to an ancestor of the present Duke of Fernan Nunez, now her relative by marriage. The letter had been intercepted 89 years ago. She has just forwarded it to the descendant of the Duke it was originally addressed to. H. I. M. also found one day in the Tuileries, behind a looking-glass, a piece of paper which proved on examination to be a list of the *gardes nationaux* who entered to sack it in 1830.

Napoleon I when a young man about to leave l'Ecole de Brienne, where he was educated at the expense of the French king, was passing the place de la Grève at the time of the *émeute* at the Tuileries. Napoleon's first movement was to draw his sword and go to the defense of the king, but at that moment Louis XVI appeared at a window with a *bonnet Phrygien* on his head, and the young Napoleon was so disgusted at his ill-judged complaisancy to please the people, that he returned his sword to his scabbard and went his way.

Here is an instance of the usual good luck*² of

---

*¹ "Napoleon I was a real genius; he alone had the capacity to hold good against so many minds united against him."

*² Napoleon III had this same belief in his "star" and fate that his uncle had.

Prince Napoleon

Princess Clotilde

Napoleon I: He was himself visiting the outposts in a post chaise on the eve of a battle. Suddenly the postilion stopped; it was a pitch dark night, a fierce storm was raging and the frightened horses were prancing madly, and had become quite unmanageable. A tremendous flash of lightning showed a tree fallen across the road. But for this object the post chaise would have dashed headlong into the river, as the bridge a few steps farther on had been destroyed by the enemy.

Here is an instance of adverse fate when his "star" was beginning to wane: Once, and once only, the Emperor departing from his custom wrote his plans to the Empress Louise, and that time the courier was taken prisoner and the correspondence intercepted.

Speaking of army reserves, the Empress said: "C'est Stern, Ministre de la guerre, l'homme qui avait le plus de talent en Prusse à cette époque qui imagina le système d'armée allemande à cause des conditions que lui avait imposées Napoléon après la bataille de Jena (1806), leur permettant seulement d'avoir 40,000 soldats." [1]

Here is a *mot du Premier Consul* in which the lady in question certainly got the best of it: "Peu de temps après la Terreur, il dit brusquement un jour à une dame, qui s'exprimait très franchement aux Tuileries: 'Madame, les femmes ne devraient pas s'occuper de politique.' – 'Dans un pays où l'on coupe le tête aux femmes, cela doit leur être permis de savoir au moins pourquoi,' repondit-elle." [2]

---

[1] "It was Stern, Minister of War, the most able man in Prussia at that period, who evolved the German army system through the conditions imposed on him by Napoleon after the battle of Jena (1806), allowing them to have only 40,000 soldiers."

[2] "Soon after the *Reign of Terror* he said one day sharply to a lady, who was expressing herself very frankly at the Tuileries, 'Madam, women ought not to meddle in politics.' – 'In a country where they cut women's heads off, it ought to be permitted them to know at least the why and wherefore,' she responded."

The following is an interesting side light on a debatable historical enigma. The Emperor when helpless from long and depressing illness and fiercely attacked on all sides, had the weakness, the Empress told us, to own to responsibility for the death of the Duc d'Enghien. She asserted, though, that in spite of this there were positive proofs to her mind that he was not responsible for his death, that the accusation was false, and that several historians now agree with her. She has read a letter of Joseph's to one of his sisters, telling how terribly grieved Napoleon had been about it. The Empress is convinced the death was brought about without the knowledge of Napoleon. The Duc d'Enghien had been warned, but did not heed the warning and was seized on French territory. It was to Talleyrand's interest to act quickly. He had him tried late at night on his own responsibility, and had him hurriedly shot in the early dawn. The Duke had begged to be allowed to see the *premier Consul* but this boon was refused him. The *juge d'instruction*, who was the lawful person to condemn him, was waked in the morning and was given an urgent letter from Napoleon, sent by special messenger, telling him to stop the proceedings against d'Enghien. It was then only 4 a.m.; the judge rose at once, and hastened to where the Duc d'Enghien was imprisoned at Vincennes, but it was too late. The execution was already over. As the judge arrived at the fortress, he met the squad of soldiers returning from their deadly work.

The Empress has lately been reading Mme. de Stael's *Letters*, and finds what she thinks is a clue to this author's and her father's inveterate hatred of Napoleon I. M. de Necker had prepared, it appears, a reception for the young General Bonaparte and invited him to come to his house on the Lake of Geneva, at Fernay, which had formerly belonged to Voltaire. Ignoring M. de Necker's important position and polite invitation, Napoleon answered flippantly: "A Fernay? – Mais je croyais Voltaire mort [To Fernay? – But, I thought

240

Voltaire was dead]." M. de Necker never forgave this slight. "Mais," the Empress added, "Mme. de Stael aurait volontiers pardonné plus tard, si Napoléon l'avait voulu [But, Mme. de Stael would have willingly forgiven him later, if Napoleon had wished it]."

This is what the Empress told us about the Duc de Reichstadt: History says he was not liked by his grandfather, the Emperor of Austria, but this was not the case. On the contrary, Franz Joseph was extremely fond and proud of his grandson. The Empress told us of the surveillance exercised over him, because of the plots to rescue him from Austria and put him on his captive father's throne. She told us about his cousin Napoléone (Countess Camerata, daughter of Eliza Bonaparte) and how she waited about Vienna for a month trying to manage an interview with him. At last, in desperation, she bribed the servants of a professor to whose house young "Franz" was permitted to go alone, and she was allowed to stand on a turn of the staircase. Many times she waited there in vain, but at last one evening her opportunity came. The Duc started up the stairs, coming face to face with her, but when she tried to stop him and explain who she was, misunderstanding her motives he darted up the stairs, and his one chance was lost forever. On arriving home at the Castle of Schönbrun he found a heart-broken letter from Napoléone explaining all, and begging him to accept the chance of escape from Austria. He vacillated, refused his opportunity and never got another.

This young Duc begged so hard to have a regiment of his own, that his grandfather finally gave him one. Then the young soldier could be seen morning and night drilling his regiment, and when he finally got it so that he was proud of it, he asked his grandfather one day to assist at a review. At first Franz Joseph refused the request for fear of what *Congrès* would say, but at last he yielded. The Duc de Reichstadt delightedly brought up his regiment, saluted his grandfather in a very gallant way and then galloped off. There was a large fosse close by; this he jumped fully accoutred and the whole regiment followed after him, crying in their excited enthusiasm: "Vive Napoléon!" Next day there was a note from Congrès and the regiment was taken away from poor Franz. He died of consumption in 1882 at Schönbrun, at the age of twenty-one, and is buried near the Emperor and his four wives. This was all told the Empress by Count Prokesch-Osten, the Duc de Reichstadt's only intimate friend, whom the Empress met when he was a very old man.

Thursday, October 28, 1886. We learn that Mrs. Standish's house, "Le Berystyde," was burned to the ground on Tuesday night. The Empress telegraphed at once and sent over M. Pietri and M. Chevreau to offer her condolence, to inquire concerning Mrs. Standish, who was terribly burned, and offer assistance in any shape. The gentlemen returned at 2 p.m. with a sad account of the occurrence. At three the Empress, Mme. Le Breton and the two gentlemen started off to pay a farewell visit to Lady Holland at St. Ann's.

From a letter:

Farnborough Hill,
October 29, 1886.

This morning early, as soon as the Empress was down, there was much commotion in the house, – orders and counter-orders, and as much fuss as if it were the very first time anyone of note had been received at Farnborough. The servants in gala dress, – knickerbockers and silk stockings, – running about, putting up the awnings over the porch and laying the royal red carpet at the entrance. The Empress is in a very nervous state.

At last, at 12:50 the royal party arrived in the two carriages sent to meet them, accompanied by M. Pietri, who, in the absence of the Duc de Bassano, does the honors. Grand salutations and royal kisses, and when the Duchess and her children had taken off their things in the Empress's room and had chatted a little with her, the door opened and all appeared together, making their way up the gallery. When they reached the spot where Mme. Le Breton, the two gentlemen and myself were waiting, the Empress presented us each in turn to the Duchess of Teck, behind whom followed Princess Victoria Mary of Teck, a pretty girl of eighteen, Prince Adolphus, about nineteen or twenty, and the youngest boy of twelve, Prince Alexander George. Such a size as he is, - and such fat rosy cheeks, and such an appetite! The lunch went off very comfortably and pleasantly, our guests being simple and natural, and Prince Alexander not a little astonished at being called *Votre Altesse* by the Empress, for at Mr. Morton's near here, where he is at school at present, he is only "Alex," or "Teck" to his comrades. Each and all have wonderful appetites, - no wonder the good-natured Duchess is so stout. Her daughter "May," as she is called by her family, however, has a lithe charming figure and is a sweet looking girl, rather shy and retiring. I took her all over the house after luncheon and showed her the interesting things in the glass cases, but not even the wonderful Charlemagne "talisman" in the chapel elicited from her any expression of pleasure, surprise or interest. All she said was "very nice" to anything I showed her. Only once all day I remember her making a spontaneous remark of her own, and that was in perceiving high up over a doorway a rather common-place picture of a Swiss mountain. The Princess recognized some old favorite of hers, her face lighted up, and she really did seem pleased for the time. Mme. de Arcos, who stays often with the family at "White Lodge," Richmond, and sees them in the most intimate way, said that Princess May hardly ever speaks except when spoken to, but sits quietly in the drawing room of an evening, sewing away, making various flannel petticoats and garments for the poor. The Duchess is at the head of some large organization work for poor people and her daughter helps her tremendously. What a handsome man the Duke must have been a few years ago. He was most polite to me and while we were all dispersed through the reception rooms, looking at the different pictures, etc., I heard some one behind me saying to M. Pietri: "But please present me to Mademoiselle W.," and before I had time to turn around the speaker came up to me, as he might have done to an old friend he had not seen for years, saying, "Mademoiselle, l'Impératrice a passé si vite à table, qu'elle ne m'a pas presenté. Aussi vous m'excuserez de ne vous avoir pas parlé avant, car [and here he laughed] je suis un homme si bien élevé, que je n'ai pas osé le faire avant la présentation."*

At 3:30 the whole party went for a drive with the Empress, and at five their special saloon carriage was hooked on to the express train which took them back to "White Lodge," Richmond. After seeing his family off, Prince Alexander returned here in the carriage with the Empress, who gave him a good solid supper, - cold meat, sandwiches, and all sorts of things, to which he did full justice before returning to school. It was amusing to see how his eyes lighted up with schoolboy gratitude and expectation when supper was mooted by his hostess.

In the evening while talking about our visitors, we happened to get on the subject of nicknames and the Empress expressed her general dislike of them. She told us, what we already knew, that Princess Victoria of Teck is called "May" in her family, while Prince Albert Victor of Wales is called "Eddie," - *Collar and Cuffs* is his vulgar and popular name. The Prince Imperial was called "Lulu" until his seventh birthday, when the Emperor interfered, saying, "It is impossible in

---

* "Mademoiselle, the Empress went to table so quickly that she did not present me to you. So you must excuse my not speaking to you before this, for, I am such a well brought up man, I did not dare to do so before the presentation."

France for a man to make himself eminent having a ridiculous nickname." The name *Plon-Plon*, the Empress thought, did Prince Napoleon* more harm than any other thing outside of his own character. He gave it to himself as a child.

Apropos of nicknames, the Empress continued with an amusing little scene she witnessed once at some races. It was a dialogue between the Princess Royal of England (Empress Frederick of Germany) and the Duchess of Edinburgh (daughter of the Czar).

Duchess (very excitedly): "Vicky! Vicky! the opera glasses, quickly." Receiving no answer: "Vicky, don't you hear?"

Princess Royal: "I hear perfectly, but I am only 'Vicky' for Mama and my brothers."

Duchess, with much emphasis and pique: "Oh, very well I will call you 'Royal Highness' with pleasure, but you will be kind enough to call me 'Imperial Highness'!"

Saturday, October 30. The Duc de Morny and his bride (Senorita Guzman-Blanco) came to lunch. She is a perfectly lovely little creature and her father, who is president of Venezuela, is fabulously rich. M. le Baron de Varu accompanied them, also a Mme. Serre, sister of Mme. de Saulcy, who visited here earlier in the season.

The conversation today partly concerned Clotilde, Princesse de Savoie. She is the wife of *Plon-Plon*, daughter of Victor Emanuel, sister of King Humbert of Italy and the Queen of Portugal. The Empress considers that Princess Clotilde missed her vocation, – she lives in the world the life of a nun and dresses like one. She gets up at five, and goes

---

* Born 1822; died 1891. Son of Jérome, youngest brother of Napoleon I.

alone to church, carrying in winter a little lantern; visits the poor and is very charitable; but with all that, she has a great deal of pride for the *Maison de Savoie* and is very particular about *questions d'etiquette*. The Empress thinks that had she dressed better, kept herself less apart, and been more a *femme du monde* she might have influenced *Plon-Plon*, her husband, a little for the good. Clotilde's hair is quite white, though she is only forty-three years old. It is thought probable that as soon as their daughter, Princess Letitia, marries, the mother will go into a convent. Princess Letitia is quite unlike her mother, very gay and bright, and they dote on her at the Italian court; she is often at Monza, near Milan, where the royal family spends a great deal of its time.

Prince Napoleon, the Empress added, strongly resembles the type of Napoleon I, but has not a good expression, – a man who is full of hatred, as he is, must show it in his face she thinks. He gives to Princess Letitia all the affection he fails to give his son, Prince Victor. *Plon-Plon*, the Empress says, with his republican ideas would willingly marry her to *le premier venu*, but her particular, aristocratic mother would not allow it.*

M. Chevreau told us about some of Letitia's pranks. She is a fine looking girl, tall and strong and full of life and mischief, and recently took away the breath of the King and Queen of Italy by appearing in the midst of a very ceremonious occasion at the races, bestriding a bicycle. This was in the early bicycle days before ladies had begun to use them freely. She had quietly procured one, learned to ride it, sworn the courtiers to secrecy, and enjoyed the fun of shocking the court by her daring and unexpected proceeding.

Monday, November 1. All Saints day. Went up to London with the Empress, M. Chevreau and M. Pietri. I left them all at Waterloo Station en route for Chislehurst, and went

---

* Princess Letitia since married (1888) the Duke of Aosta.

myself to see G. Got back to the station in the late afternoon fifteen minutes too soon, but found the Empress and the two gentlemen already waiting there, the former very much tired out, not being at all well now.

Tuesday, November 2. All Souls day. Went to mass and Holy Communion with the Empress. I have not seen H. I. M. really alone for some days, and I must talk over my coming departure for Paris. Very nice letter from Mlle. Henriette Conneau from Paris. Dr. Chepmell arrived to see the Empress again and dined here, leaving at 9:30 p.m.

From a letter:

Farnborough Hill,
November 3, 1886.

All the time we were walking up and down this evening after dinner, the Empress was impressing upon me the necessity of making a "budget," as she calls it, for the year, fixing the approximate sums I propose to spend for different needs and keeping scrupulously to them, putting the balance away regularly. H. I. M. says she is always anxious for young people to learn to plan according to their income and to save, be it ever so little, for a rainy day. She has given me one of her own sheets of special foolscap, ruled for the months of the year, for receipts and expenditures, and has begged me to use it for her sake, which I certainly shall. She also means to give me *un petit mot de sa part* for her own *homme d'affaires* in Paris that I may not fail, as she says, to invest my *petites économies* safely and advantageously. M. Langlois is a clever and conscientious man, and will gladly advise me well and willingly for her sake. Is it not good of her to take such personal interest? She has advised me to take one or two small shares in the "Crédit Foncier," which pays three and one half per cent., besides dividing the yearly surplus into a certain number of prizes. The *gros lot* is, I think, one hundred thousand francs and the

Empress says, now that I am *en bonne veine* she has a strong presentiment I shall have good luck and gain something. She repeats and persists in saying this. How nice if I should. She has explained to me at great length the absolute security of the "Crédit Foncier"; how wars even would only temporarily affect it, and then only the interest, not the capital.

Wednesday, November 3. Dr. Scott called in the morning, and I sat and talked with him until the Empress came down to see him. The early afternoon slipped by while I was helping the Empress to take a pattern of some magnificent church work, - splendid old Spanish vestments. Later on that day, while driving with her alone and talking among other things about the outbreak of cholera in Paris, in 1865, the Empress gave me an interesting account of her public visitation to the hospitals in the different cities that were most stricken. She usually went with a large retinue, but actually visited the patients by herself. The visiting was done not so much for the benefit of the poor sick patients, but to impress rather the minds of the timid people at large, and to give them courage. Her own courage did much good in that way and made them take heart. In fact the Empress considered it was an absolute necessity to prevent the public, - the nation, - from getting thoroughly demoralized with fear. The following is what happened during a certain visit to Amiens, one of the worst cholera centers that year:

The imperial party was met in the morning at the station by a deputation of priests and civil dignitaries and conducted in carriages to the Cathedral, where there was first a solemn service imploring God to remove the scourge. The Empress then visited each of the hospitals, and after a little refreshment, started to return to Paris in the late afternoon. When she got back to the station she happened to ask where a certain very nice looking young priest was, with whom she had talked in the morning, and who had particularly interested her by his zeal and intelligence. She saw they hesitated to answer her, and renewed her question. After vainly trying to spare her the knowledge, they had to admit at last that he was dead. He had succumbed to the epidemic soon after the interview with his sovereign, and from perfect health had been gathered in by death in that short interval. This was naturally rather a shock.

While visiting a ward of the principal hospital that day, her attention was directed in the midst of all the terrible groans and screams to one man who was outdoing them all in noise. She went up to him and bending over the poor fellow, said: "What is the matter?" "Oh, Madame, I am suffering so terribly!" She saw by the placard over his bed that he was a soldier and she reproached him, saying, "You a soldier, you ought to be able to bear pain better than that! Allons, du courage! ne mourrez pas! Cramponnez-vous à la vie!"*[1] She forgot the incident entirely, as it was only one of a great many other similar cases. Some months later, walking across the place du Carousel, a soldier came rather sheepishly forward. He saluted and then standing in front of her he hesitated, evidently deeply embarrassed, and not knowing how to begin his little speech. Thinking he wished some favor granted, she tried to help him out. At last, making a great effort, the soldier blurted out these words: "Madame, je me suis cramponné à la vie, et me voici. – Merci!"*[2] – and then he fled. He was her noisy soldier of the cholera hospital at Amiens.

The cholera reminiscences reminded the Empress of another interesting case. In going through some other hospital at another time she saw a very strange phenomenon. The doctors showed her a woman who had imprinted on the iris of her eye, a very clear and exact representation of a coin bearing the profile of Napoleon I. Much interested in this case, on

---

*[1] "Come, have courage, do not die! Cling on to me!"

*[2] "Madame, I did cling on to life, and here I am. Thank you."

questioning the woman, they found that shortly before her birth her father and mother had sustained great financial losses, which had distressed and greatly preoccupied the mother. When the baby was born, this strange phenomenon was noticed and has remained in evidence all her life.

Thursday, November 4. I am writing this in the train on my way up to London, where I am going to pilot Mme. Le Breton about. At three o'clock we are going to the Muriettas' (Marques Santurce) bank in the city, where Mme. Le Breton has money matters to attend to. She has volunteered to broach the subject of my departure to the Empress this evening, if possible, so that I hope my plans may be definitely made by tomorrow. The train is going so fast and shaking so dreadfully I cannot write any more.

Thursday, November 4. At 6 p.m., M. Pietri and M. Chevreau returned from London, bringing with them the Duque de Alva, who is coming to spend the night at Farnborough Hill. M. Chevreau's presence here brought out in the evening many reminiscences, while sitting around the big table in the *grand salon* playing *jeux de patience*. The Empress was telling about travels in Switzerland and reminded M. Chevreau about the story of a Greek gentleman, Mr. Carnelgie, whom they met and who used to join them in their walks. One day they came to a brook with stepping-stones. M. Chevreau's father was behind the Empress, Carnelgie in front. The latter offered her his hand to help her across. "When they were in the very middle of the brook with the water rushing on both sides, he surprised her with a formal declaration. He said to her: "Je t'adore." Between her fear that Chevreau would overhear the nonsense, and her dread of letting go Carnelgie's hand and falling into the water, she was in a very unpleasant position. She had already invited Carnelgie to dinner, so there was nothing to do but let him come, and he arrived jauntily bringing a guitar. After the meal he got out his instrument and began singing love-songs, and at night he walked up and down in front of her windows. The next day Chevreau told him he must go away, and he went obediently. He turned up again in Paris, however, struck up a great intimacy with one of the grooms, who let him know privately concerning matters at the Tuileries. The groom informed him of the fact that there were painters in the house, so Carnelgie disguised himself as a painter and got in. He was soon discovered and dismissed again, but was not at all discouraged in his efforts. Nothing daunted, he next went to Pépita, the Empress's Spanish maid, and talked her over to his side, by telling her he had a letter from a condemned man which was very urgent, and that he must see the Empress. Pépita, quite convinced, carried the letter and gave it to the Empress, who on opening it found it was a love-letter with a picture of two doves cooing. After this last amatory effort, he was taken home to an asylum in Greece. The poor man is now dead.

The Empress and M. Chevreau told each other a lot of funny incidents and anecdotes about a Countess Ratazzi, and then came this strange story about Comtesse Potocka.

A lady presented herself one day at the Tuileries and begged and implored to see *la dame de service*. That week it happened to be the turn of Mme. de la Poësse, who went down to the salon set apart for interviews and found a strange looking but very beautiful woman robed in a long black velvet dress reaching almost to her feet. She was in a very excited state. She told her story to Mme. de la Poësse and begged very hard to see the Emperor. This was refused. She said she thought the Emperor had it in his power to force Comte Potocki (who held a position in the imperial household) to keep his promise of marriage with her. She was a *Parisienne* by birth but of no family, and had set her heart on marrying

Interior of Memorial Church, Farnborough

Comte Potocki, who was a mere acquaintance of hers. She had proposed the match to him, but he refused, saying his Polish pride could not allow him to marry her.

"But if I were of a family like yourself, then would you marry me?" she asked. He answered in jest, "Certainly, – then," thinking that would give a quietus to the matter. The beautiful suppliant then went away and disappeared altogether from Paris for some years. Comte Potocki had quite forgotten her existence, when one day she returned, went to see him and claimed his promise, saying that she was now "Comtesse Potocka." He professed his incredulity and again refused to marry her, and hence her visit to the Tuileries to plead her cause with the Emperor and induce him to force the Comte to keep the letter of his word.

This is what had happened during the intervening years. Having heard by chance of the existence of an old Comte Potocki, an invalid, and paralyzed, living in Dresden, she determined to make use of him to gain her end. She got herself introduced, said she had heard of his sad case and was much interested in it as she had wonderful natural powers of curing paralysis. She explained that in her long hair there was a quantity of electricity that she could apply to his cure; and she felt sure she should be successful. She induced him to let her take up her abode in the house and made herself so indispensable in every way, that he became much attached to her and finally adopted her in due legal form. She became in this way a "Potocki," and at the old man's death two years later, she inherited from him with a fortune the title also of Comtesse. Armed with this she returned to France to claim a husband earned by her cleverness, though not by her straightforward dealing. The sequel of this strange story is not known.

From a letter:

Farnborough Hill,
November 6, 1886.

I shall very likely leave here Monday, but as yet I do not know definitely. As I told you I spent the whole day yesterday in the Empress's sitting-room, so I had no time to think about my packing. Now I must finish this hurriedly and get some of it done before lunch, as afterward the Empress will probably want me to be with her again, – and besides the Marquis de Bassano and his wife are coming to lunch.

I will tell you all about the Duque de Alva's visit of yesterday when we meet, which I hope will now be soon. The Empress's visit to Windsor is put off, as she is not well, and fears the cold and drafts which the Queen so dearly loves, and which are almost death to everyone less strong. Her doctor has forbidden her going out until the fifteenth, so that simplifies matters between her and the Queen. All this will change the plans for Italy, which vexes her very much.

Talking of the cold at Windsor the Empress dilated at some length concerning the Queen's love of it and the low temperature that she could stand, being entirely comfortable while others were freezing. When together in Scotland at Balmoral, or Abergeldie, they used to go out to drive in the afternoons, and it was an ordinary practice to take a tea-basket out in the carriage with them. At a certain hour the carriage was halted, John Brown or some other attendant made the tea, and the grooms stood at the horses' heads while the tea was drunk. The Empress said she not infrequently saw flakes of snow falling into her cup. She did not enjoy it, but the Queen did. Her Majesty evidently believes in the survival of the fittest.

Balmoral Castle being small, the Queen provides a little feudal lodge at Abergeldie for her guests. It is connected by telephone with the main castle building. The Empress said that one day on a former visit in accordance with the usual habit of the royal family, arrangements were constantly being changed, and they were telephoning over to inquire whether she would come over to the castle or whether the Queen should call on her. The telephone was a novelty at that time, and people were unaccustomed to its use. The Empress in her sitting-room, not far from the telephone, was discussing freely with Mme. de Arcos the pros and cons of the visit, saying, "Oh no, I don't think I want to go, – I don't feel quite well," when to her surprise she heard a laughing voice: "I hear you auntie, I hear all you say!" It was the Princess Beatrice at the other end. After that they were more circumspect in their remarks.

Sunday, November 7. Dr. Scott called at afternoon tea time and the Empress asked him to stay to dinner as it was to be my last evening here, and he did.

Monday, November 8. M. Destailleur arrived in the morning to see how the building of the monastery was progressing. After lunch I went with much regret to the Empress's room to say goodby to her. She was most gracious and affectionate to me, as indeed she always has been and especially in these last intimate months. After talking a little while, she went to a drawer of her writing-table and took out some photographs. She chose one among a good many, saying, "Je vous en donnerai une du temps ou j'étais mieux qu'à présent [I will give you one of a period when I was better looking than at present]." She then sat down at her desk and put her autograph to it, and also at my request wrote her name in my birthday-book. This was a very great thing for her to do, as she has a horror of giving her signature, especially on a photograph. After the experiences she told me about, and the wicked abuse that had resulted in a similar case, I quite understood her general reluctance.

I sat with her there some time while she held my hand in hers and talked very intimately and affectionately. Then, when the relentless clock showed me it was really time to make a move, I arose and thanked her again for all her kindness to me. I said goodby once more, bending over her hand and raising it to my lips in the usual manner, but she folded me right into her arms, held me there as though reluctant to let me go, and kissed me warmly on both cheeks. She wished me all good luck and happiness in Paris, and she pressingly invited me to return to Farnborough on my very first opportunity, telling me with one of her winning smiles that I should always be welcome wherever she was. The carriage was waiting at the door to take me and Mme. Le Breton, who accompanied me to the station, and at 3:30 I left the house, deeply regretting that these intensely interesting months were over.

In regard to my stay with her, I can state about the Empress with all sincerity and appropriateness, exactly what, after painting a portrait of Her Majesty, Mme. Vigée-Lebrun wrote in her *Memoirs* of Queen Marie Antoinette:

"Je ne crois pas, que la Reine Marie Antoinette ait jamais manqué l'occasion de dire une chose agreable à ceux qui avaient l'honneur de l'approcher, et la bonté qu'elle m'a toujours temoignée est un de mes plus doux souvenirs."*

---

* "I do not think that Queen Marie Antoinette ever once missed an opportunity of saying an agreeable thing to those who had the honor of approaching her, and the kindness she always showed me is one of my tenderest recollections."

PART V

Reminiscences of Empress Eugénie:
Her Characteristics and Idiosyncracies

PART V

In the preceding pages I have recorded a personal view of Eugénie, Empress of the French, while in exile, with a background of previous events based on a diary and letters, and much of it in her own words. In the following pages, I draw on my recollections and with the help of my records offer a further intimate picture of the Empress as I now see her in perspective.

When I first really made her acquaintance, in February 1886, three months before her sixtieth birthday, she still retained a great deal of her former beauty.* Her hair at that

---

* The Empress told us that as a child she was not considered at all beautiful as compared to her more brilliant sister. She was even painfully selfconscious of her own supposed mental and physical deficiencies, and was especially ashamed of the color of her hair (that beautiful wealth of reddish gold, that courtiers later on raved about and poets sang,) which she said people called red. Her nieces told me they had heard it repeatedly asserted in Madrid that at that period Eugénie was plain almost to ugliness.

period had turned a lovely gray, – she wore it dressed rather high, and with little soft curls just touching her forehead. Her face was very pale, her eyes drooping and sad, with the slightest suggestion of black under the edge of the lids. Above the average height, she was stately, and had a fine figure; a wellpoised head; a face full of expression; beautiful shoulders and arms; and a shapely tapering hand. She was suffering that winter from rheumatism and limped lightly as a consequence, but when I saw her later (in the summer of 1897) she seemed to have entirely recovered from her lameness, had discarded her stick, and walked into the room as firmly and upright as if she had been ten years younger, rather than eight years older, since our last meeting, and had never known a day's sorrow or sickness.* To me her most striking characteristic was her great personal charm, which she was not at all unwilling to make use of, and this very cordial, winning manner caused any preconceived ideas of an unpleasant nature to fall to the ground immediately. No one could approach the Empress with prejudices and keep them five minutes, – everybody in turn fell a victim.

But with all her sweetness she knew how to hold her own. Any indiscreet pushing forward of an individual particularly angered the ex-sovereign, who, when occasion justified it, could become freezingly cold and distant, making the intruder feel that Eugénie was the wrong person with whom to take liberties. She had, too, a most unmistakable *façon de congedier* which there was no gainsaying. When in her estimation the

---

* Mme. Lefèvre, in a letter to me dated July 26, 1901, said of her former sovereign. "During the two occasions each year in which I see Her Majesty, I remain a long time with her; we talk of the past and of those things that are gone. I saw her in the month of June, and she was extremely well and truly beautiful; it has been a long time since I found her so well. Her carriage is superb, and she has taken on again an air of youth, which her long sickness had effaced; she has even flashes of gaiety."

subject matter of an interview was over, and she wished you to go, – you went, whoever you were. She simply rose, bowed and put out her hand in a charmingly compelling manner. Untutored English strangers grasped it; French people lifted it gently, and bending over kissed it silently before retiring.

Born in a garden in Granada, May 5, 1826, during an earthquake which forced her mother to quit the family dwelling, Eugénie's life of strange ups and downs of fortune, opening thus not inappropriately, remained during its whole course a veritable kaleidoscope of rapid and unforeseen changes.

Her character was impetuous and thoroughly Spanish in numberless ways. I should not call her a great woman, but a most interesting one, full of strange contradictory traits. She seemed by temperament naturally gay and light-hearted, but with a touch of serious earnestness, and an underlying sadness, which came quickly to the surface if anything reminded her of her dead son. She talked frequently to me of her shattered nerves, and the ample notes I took of interesting conversation bring back to me many things the Empress said then about her health. She often repeated in my hearing, that she very certainly could never have withstood all the strain, the shocks, and even hunger and privations of all kinds, during her various hard experiences, had it not been for her early bringing up. The Spartan training of her childhood alone had saved her, she was convinced, from complete physical and mental breakdown both during and after her many troubles.

She told us much at different times about her own and her sister's early days. Count Montijo, their father, was an old soldier who had fought all through the Napoleonic wars, and was at that period military governor of a fortified town in southern Spain, and a regular martinet in his family. He did not allow his daughters the luxury of stockings; summer and winter they went without, wearing boots only. Not wishing to have timid, namby-pamby daughters, he resorted to extreme measures. Sometimes he put Eugénie and her sister Françoise astride of a cannon on the ramparts of the citadel, which was then fired off. If the children cried or winced, they were subjected to the ordeal a second and even a third time. For the same ethical reason of training, though the family possessed numerous horses, and the many gala coaches customary for grandees of Spain, the Empress told me she never once during her whole girlhood entered a carriage, except for traveling purposes. How ever snowy, cold or wet, she and her sister, neither of them very rugged, always trudged everywhere on foot. When the time came for them to make their First Communion (1837), they spent a preparatory month in the convent of the "Sacré Coeur" in Paris, and schoolgirls being the same the world over, their companions teased these newcomers unmercifully for not wearing stockings, such an unusual state of things that their small brains naturally could not fathom it. Eugénie's really simple tastes during her whole life (quite contrary to her reputation), can apparently be explained by her bringing up and frugal way of living as a girl at home. She certainly thought so herself.

At his brother's death in 1834, her father, the Comte de Teba, inherited the title of Montijo,* also much property and a goodly fortune, but the parents of the future Empress nevertheless continued their modest way of living, and brought up their children with the idea of judiciously using but not wasting their means. So when Eugénie and Françoise (afterwards Duchess of Alva) were a little older, the Condesa gave to each of these young daughters a small dress allowance. This is how she early acquired the idea of making a certain

---

* Traveling in Switzerland with her in 1887 and later years, her nieces told me she kept the curious at bay by appearing on the hotel register sometimes as Condesa Montijo or Condesa de Teba; at other times as Marquesa de Moya or Palafox, or again as Comtesse de Pierrefonds. Of these many titles the latter was most generally used by her.

fixed sum do, a habit which she claimed she adhered to rigidly during her entire reign and also afterwards. Without economy and ingenuity there would have been little or no margin for the girls' *menu plaisir*, and so to make their rather inadequate allowance go further, they were forced to do much for themselves. They always, for instance, trimmed their own hats and bonnets, and their busy needles and skilful fingers fashioned a great many of their clothes besides. This was just what the mother wished to achieve.

In spite of the wonderful innate power of adapting herself to changed circumstances, of throwing herself into her surroundings, which the Empress evidently must always have possessed to a remarkable degree, she admitted that she naturally had to live through some trying times on first coming to the throne.

Talking one evening of the early days after her marriage, and her inevitable loneliness, the Empress told us that from the royal box at the opera, while looking wearily down on the sea of heads below, she one night recognized in the audience people known to her in Spain, and last seen only a short time previously. In her impulsive delight at perceiving familiar faces, she entirely forgot who she now was and where, and began waving, kissing her hand to them vigorously in true Spanish fashion. Then suddenly noticing the Emperor's cold eye fixed on her, she remembered and checked herself. On returning to the Tuileries she was gently reprimanded and told (what of course she already thoroughly realized) that she must refrain from that kind of thing hereafter.

"Je me sentais si seule, si isolée," the Empress once said, "en rentrant après ma promenade en voiture journalière, dans ces apartements de Palais énormes et peu meublés. Tous les jours dans les premiers temps je pleurais en secret; Pépita avait souvent les yeux rouges aussi, et bien des fois dans notre abandon, nous nous jettions dans les bras l'une de l'autre, pour pleurer à l'aise loin des regards de tous."*

Pépita was bright and capable in many ways, though ignorant and narrow-minded, but showed an almost oriental devotion to her mistress. She had filled the position of ladies' maid ever since Eugénie's girlhood, when as an uneducated peasant she first entered the household of the Condesa Montijo. This serving-woman, living at the Tuileries, was at this time the one and only link the Empress retained with the past. By the exigencies of her new position Eugénie was of course absolutely isolated from all her friends. She had nobody about her with whom she could unbend, or be in the least familiar. Her courtiers, many of them charming men and women, were however chosen for state reasons, and all were new to her at first, and she herself so hedged round with numerous barriers of etiquette, that even had it been permissible they could not have filled for her the gap made by the absence of her old friends. The bitter had to be accepted with the sweet.

The Empress once told me what an ordeal she found the court reception *du Jour de l'An*, especially at first. After the imperial party returned from assisting at High Mass in the court chapel, each 1st of January, all the members of the Bonaparte family and all the ladies and gentlemen of the imperial household, whether it was their *semaine de service* or not, assembled for solemn New Year greetings. Making her way slowly round the room, she had to shake hands with all the men, speak a friendly nothing to each, kiss the ladies, and say a pleasant appropriate word to them as well. To be

* "A sense of loneliness and isolation used to take possession of me, when after the daily drive I returned to the huge and formally furnished apartments of the Palace. In those first days I used invariably to shed a few secret tears. Pépita I often found with red eyes too, and many a time in our desolation we threw ourselves into each other's arms to weep unrestrainedly, far away from all prying glances."

The Empress and the Prince Imperial

unconscious of the keen relentless criticism of her husband's family was often harder for her at such times than any public criticism might be. The practice of having seasonable little nothings on the tip of her tongue on all occasions for so many years had, I noticed, very evidently borne its fruit, for during the months I spent with her at Farnborough the Empress showed herself a wonderful adept in this particular art, – always knew just the right thing to say, just the proper topic to touch on, or on which to be silent. Her memory and tact in this regard were remarkable.

Though strong physically, enjoying a splendid appetite and the ability often denied a younger woman, of walking hours at a stretch, the Empress in 1886 was still severely feeling the nervous reaction from her sorrows and the terrible events of 1870 and 1879. She passed restless nights, waked constantly with horrid nightmares, and enacted over and again in dreams some of the tragic scenes of her life. The many physicians consulted declared she had a constitution of iron, that her organs were absolutely perfect, and that only her nerves were at fault. Small wonder at this after all she had gone through! But in spite of the doctors' diagnoses she nevertheless continued to fancy herself attacked by every malady under the sun. She did not however dread death itself. "J'ai trop d'êtres aimes qui m'attendant la-bas dans l'autre monde," she often said, "pour que je craigne d'y aller," adding "C'est la foi seule qui donne le courage de mourir."[1]

Eugénie expressed a perfect craving for sunshine and the brightness and warmth of the sunny South. In her depressed state the dull sunless English winters tried her very much.[2]

---

[1] "There are too many loved ones awaiting me there in the other world," she often said, "for me to dread going, " adding, "It is Faith alone that gives one the courage to die."

[2] She later bought land at Cap Martin, Alpes Maritimes, not far from Mentone and Monte Carlo, and built a delightful villa, "Cyrnos," where she spent the winter months.

Concerning her unhappy, restless state of mind and her *projets de voyage* for the immediate future, she once remarked: "Je suis comme un corps sans âme. Aussitôt arrivée j'ai hâte de partir de nouveau. Hélas! comme je suis changée! Autrefois je faisais des itinéraires de voyage, pour le seul plaisir de les faire; j'allais en imagination aux Indes, au Pole Nord, – n'importe ou, tout était indiqué, même les heures, et je savais bien pourtant que jamais je ne pourrais réaliser ces rêves! – Mais, cela m'amusait!"*

Referring one day to nervous fear, the Empress recalled with some amazement that during the twenty years of her reign she had experienced not the least feeling of apprehension, in spite of four *attentats*. On driving daily out of the Tuileries gates, Eugénie never knew if she would reënter them alive, but still she did not dwell on dangers, though so continually surrounded by them. Their very frequency, she observed, seemed at the time to blunt her to the sense of their reality, and though she was often much lauded for her wonderful courage, she considered there was no real merit in being undismayed by danger in those days when she was physically strong. Real fear only came to her after many distressing experiences had weakened her nerves. "At present [1886]," I quote her from my own notes as saying, "on the slightest pretext I always apprehend the worst about everything; conjure up in my imagination terrible scenes of fire, disaster, etc." She told us later about certain foolhardy risks she had formerly taken in her disdain of fear. In one instance in particular, I remember, she had lighted lamps put inside the state carriage with its many windows, thereby unnecessarily courting danger in troublous times.

---

* "I am like a soulless body, – nothing pleases me now. Alas, how I have changed! Formerly I planned itineraries for the sole pleasure of dreaming over such imaginary journeys, – to India, to the North Pole, anywhere in fact, – with hours and practical details all worked out, though I knew perfectly well that I should never be able to realize my dreams. – But it amused me."

In the days of the Empire when her public day's work was done, after going to her bedroom and dismissing her maids, the Empress told me it was her custom every night to read through the reports of the secret police service. This was certainly not very soothing or appropriate to the late hour, but by nightly plodding through these lengthy documents she was enabled several times to avert disaster, notably once when she saved the life of the Czar of Russia when returning from the opera. This was on the eve of a subsequent attempt to shoot him on the way back from the races at Longchamps in the summer of 1869. It had been arranged that the Czar and the imperial party should separate after the performance, each with their suites going direct to their respective dwellings. The Empress, however, through the secret service got wind of a plan to assassinate the Czar that particular night, and made a change in the prearranged program, she herself bravely taking him home to the Elysée Palace in her own brilliantly lighted carriage. When arrested, Berezowski, the Pole, confessed that when he saw a woman accompanying his would-be victim, he decided to postpone his plan until next day.*

The Empress always expressed an utter scorn and no mercy for physical cowardice, but her natural sympathy made her kind and even tender to those who were really suffering. Conversely, she approved of endurance to physical pain, and explained how years ago she often herself suffered much, without being able of course to give way to it. She recalled one special evening, while being dressed for some great court function. Tired out by the effort of many hours' resistance to violent pain, and literally unable to bear it any longer, she finally got down on the floor and rolled in a paroxysm of

---

* Berezowski's design was again frustrated and the Czar again shielded, this time by the courage and devotion of M. Rainbeaux, the Emperor's Master of the Horse.

agony for a minute, – then making a supreme effort at self-control again sat up stoically in her chair, while her maids dressed her hair and adjusted her heavy diadem, all the while feeling more dead than alive. At such times it was that her early training stood her in good stead. She was enabled through it to pull herself together, go smilingly downstairs to the tedious state ceremony, and behave as if nothing were wrong. She offered this experience as an example of what will-power and necessity can do for one.

Real love of music, excepting perhaps a most superficial kind, had been left out of the French Empress, I think, in spite of the drooping eye-lids generally supposed to be indicative of musical temperament and ability, – but, on the other hand, her literary and artistic tastes were strongly developed. She drew, and painted in water colors artistically, and embroidered most beautifully.

Speaking about Sèvres china, while showing us some, she said: "Je m'y connais bien, ayant été marchande, pour ainsi dire, pendant tant d'années, car l'Empereur m'avait donné la permission de surveiller les travaux, de commander les cadeaux, et de faire copier les beaux modèles pour les palais."*
During her régime they alternately employed as director of the celebrated factory an artist and a chemist, to keep up the balance between *art* and *craft*. Just before the Franco-Prussian War a dinner service had been ordered for the Palais de Fontainebleau. The design being copied was from a very fine old set of the reign of Henri II. Unfinished when hostilities broke out, the Germans among other things took possession of this uncompleted set. Years later, when making a visit to

---

* "I understand it well as I have been in the business, so to speak, for many years, for the Emperor had given me permission to supervise the working of the factories, to order the official gifts, and to have the most beautiful specimens copied for the different palaces."

the Duc de Bade, the Empress got quite a turn, at seeing this lovely service placed before her on the dinner table. The Duke of Hamilton,* by the way, bought one piece (and that a broken one) of the same set for the enormous sum of 50,000 francs to add to his collection.

The Empress showed always a tremendous admiration, a veneration even, for the heroes of her native land. Her mind fired by the thrilling tales of Spain told her by Prosper Mérimée, she often fancied herself emulating their chivalrous deeds even from her earliest infancy, and spoke of them with great enthusiasm. She knew the history of Spain most thoroughly and was always indignant and shocked when her compatriots were not equally well posted.

Great care about the cleanliness of her hands was a little idiosyncracy of hers, though not afraid to use them freely, and very dexterous in everything she undertook with them. She laughed at me because I outdid her in this respect and predicted that I would rub my hands to pieces. She was perfectly sure, moreover, that when I went to Purgatory, one of my trials there would be a total deprivation of soap and water.

As I knew the Empress she seemed to have a quick, restless, insatiable mind, welcomed any new interest, and worked very hard (in self-defense, she said) as the best means to guard against sad memories, which would otherwise obtrude themselves. Fond of literature, she kept up with all current French writing, which she talked over and criticized in a clear, analytical manner.

Naturally industrious by habit, she rarely sat with her hands idle before her, but filled up odd moments puzzling out *jeux de patience*, or busily clicking her knitting needles. She was very fond of making simple woolen "charity-jackets," which she often gave to friends, or wore herself on chilly mornings.

---

* Duchess of Hamilton had been Princesse Marie de Bade.

One she knitted for me, and I regret the thoughtless stupidity which allowed me to give it away some months after, when disposing of clothing no longer in actual use.

Many hours every day my hostess usually spent by herself in her *salon de travail*, arranging and classifying her interesting historical documents, or attending to her enormous correspondence. The Empress always opened all letters herself and laid them in different piles according to their nature, throwing away the envelopes. She then read all the communications through carefully, making marginal notes, – "Accept," "Refuse," or "Investigate." Thus sorted, these missives were divided up between her secretary, M. Franceschini Pietri and her faithful friend and companion, Mme. Le Breton. He attended to the business letters, and she answered the social ones and all kinds of personal communications from friends, besides special appeals and begging letters, which poured in daily in great quantities.

Sometimes when there were letters, which for some special reason the Empress had to answer in English, she would ask me to read them over and correct them. This was not an agreeable task, for when I showed her the mistakes she did not relish it, and argued the subject in question from an absolutely foreign point of view. When I found, that in spite of all I could urge, she really held very much to her own opinion, I modified my standard of correction, not attempting to Anglicize more than was absolutely necessary for the plain understanding of the sentences, and purposely overlooking finer points she evidently could not or would not grasp.

To sovereigns she always penned her letters herself, but very few others, so it was a most exceptional honor to receive a letter written in her own hand, and she was always (and with ample cause) very chary of her signature. To Queen Victoria and Princess Beatrice she wrote frequently, and always in French, and the Princess's answers were addressed to *Ma chère*

Tante. French was the tongue usually spoken at Farnborough,* but the Empress sometimes whispered little asides to me in English, or to Mme. Le Breton in Spanish. Eugénie's language was flowing and elegant, and her pronunciation charming, but there were certain French words to which she gave a decidedly harsh Spanish intonation. English she spoke exactly like a foreigner, often using thoroughly French idioms. One would never have dreamed that she had spent so many years of her life since 1870 in England, and had as a girl been at school for a time at Taunton, and had in addition inherited through her mother's father, William Kirkpatrick (1764-1837), much English and Scottish blood.

Her love and habit of being amiable, and saying pleasant things, made her instinctively shirk disagreeable situations. When some unpleasant duty (a refusal or anything of that nature) became necessary, she rarely undertook the task herself; it generally fell to the lot of Mme. Le Breton or M. Pietri. In a word, she hated to be annoyed or coerced, and in order to get out of a difficulty without facing tiresome situations, she often made use of slight subterfuges, which seemed, perhaps, more ingenious than strictly direct.

Eugénie genuinely loved nature, out-of-door life and exercise, and was fond of horses and big dogs in their proper sphere. Fern, the Scotch collie given her by the Queen, was a great favorite; but she disliked spoiled house-pets intensely. In speaking one day with much disapproval of women who devote themselves body and soul to their pets, she told us with evident disgust about Comtesse F.'s white donkey, which its mistress actually kept in her Paris drawing-room in a secluded corner behind a gilded railing, and was cared for unceasingly

---

* In conversation with the Empress we always answered her, "Oui, Madame," or "Non, Madame." In questioning we used the third person, thus: "Sa Majesté désire-t-elle telle ou telle chose?" or "L'Impératrice saltelle que ... ?" – usual forms of speech which I found extremely difficult to remember and to adjust myself to during the first days at Farnborough.

by a brilliantly robed Egyptian attendant.

The Empress, naturally enough, liked to be well thought of, but there was often apparent a queer mixture of strong innate independence of character with what might have seemed a rather weak and meaningless deference to public opinion, had one not realized that she was even in her exile the representative of a great cause, which she might injure by any injudicious act. Obliged as she had been, when on the throne, to respect public opinion, the habit seemed to have clung to her, very much hampering her freedom of action. There were many things she would have enjoyed doing, but although in 1886 French opinion could have been of absolutely no practical importance to her, she still could not bring herself to ignore it. Here is an example: One day passing through the gallery leading to the chapel, we were looking at some pictures on the walls, a series representing different battleships. Beside them was an engraving of the Imperial yacht, *L'Aigle*. In front of this the Empress paused suddenly, and pointing to it said rather sadly, "Voilà, mes enfants, de tous les biens matériels, ce que je regrette le plus. C'est même la seule chose, je puis dire [Of all my lost possessions, this is what I regret most, – indeed, I may say the *only* thing I regret]." She constantly referred to her yacht, and to her great wish to go cruising about from place to place indefinitely. In her restless condition, that would have seemed to her the height of bliss. Some one remarked on one occasion, that it was quite within her power to do this, and asked her why, with such an insatiable longing for that kind of life, she did not buy a yacht. She replied that the French people would never understand a woman's choosing the sea without necessity. They would put her down at once as unbalanced, and though she knew it was foolish to mind what they thought, she could not help being sensitive to it.*

---

* In 1896 she evidently steeled her mind against herself, since M. Pietri wrote me, rejoicing that she had bought the R. Y. S. Thistle, a steam-yacht belonging to the Duke of Hamilton, and that an improvement in her health had resulted immediately.

Then she added thoughtfully, and with a little arch look and almost imperceptible smile: "Quand on a toujours dû penser à l'opinion publique, on ne peut plus s'en émanciper, et on devient à la longue comme une vielle coquette, qui continue jusqu'à la fin à coquetter!"*

When Eugénie went about with us, where the public could see her, she very much disliked being followed and stared at, as was invariably the case. Still I think that in her innermost heart, had people not recognized her, or had they been indifferent to her presence, she would not have relished that either.

The Empress constantly condemned the love of display which young people indulge in nowadays, regardless of their often limited incomes. She hated also extravagance, and eccentricity of all kinds. Her greatest fear was to be thought exaggerated or affected. She so disliked these traits in others that I noticed she herself sometimes gave up doing little kindly acts, which suggested themselves spontaneously, because they might have seemed forced or unreal.

She was very methodical and orderly in all household and business matters, and in fact in everything, and was also most punctual, and naturally liked everybody else to live up to her own standards. An excellent head for arithmetic, and loving on the slightest provocation to work out mental calculations, she kept a quick intelligent interest, too, in all that was going on in the political and scientific world, and through the papers and most up to date literature, followed everything as far as possible. She had evidently, however, no deep scientific knowledge, though at first one might have been misled into thinking so. This was due, I fancy, to her wonderful power of quick assimilation. At the Tuileries she had been long in

---

* "When one always has had to take into consideration public opinion, one can no longer emancipate oneself from it, and one becomes in the end, like the old coquette, who continues to flirt to the end of her days."

contact with the minds of all the great thinkers of France and Europe; she was a good listener with a retentive memory, and being a brilliant talker besides, she unconsciously gave out as her own what she had absorbed from other brains, thus impressing her casual bearers with what seemed to be the result of her own thought. After a time, by close observation and comparison, the superficial nature of her *science* came to light. This judgment of mine was corroborated by Mme. Le Breton, who in twenty-five years of the closest intimacy, had learned to know Her Imperial Mistress through and through.

The Empress had a most agreeable way of telling things, but her statements may possibly have been sometimes a little more picturesque than accurate. A regular daughter of Eve herself, and full of curiosity, she put one entirely at ease by her affectionate familiarity, and in conversation drew one out in spite of everything. She possessed a wonderfully quick eye to notice detail, an instinctive penetration of the characters of people about her, and an almost uncanny perception in reading their secret motives. Woe betide you if you had something that you wished to conceal and she to know, for she would read the conversation with so much politeness, so cleverly, so directly, that she invariably succeeded in her aim.

A love of detail combined with a natural executive ability which constantly demanded an outlet, was another of the Empress's qualities. In former days on the throne, her overflow of energy had taken the form of very estimable charities, such as reformatory farms, trade-schools, asylums, prisons, etc., all of which she organized minutely, and supervised personally, accomplishing thereby a great deal of good. She told us of some experiences she had had with women prisoners, half demented with wickedness, rage and despair, and of their rapid change to gentle, affectionate docility after her visits to the prison and friendly tête-à-tête interviews with these poor outcasts, to whom apparently no one had ever before been kind. This seemingly miraculous success, due probably to her charm and beauty, led up to the reforms instituted by her later on. The statistical history of the imperial reign is teeming with accounts of these reforms, which could be counted by the hundreds, and which apart from the other duties of the state machinery alone prove the activity and working power of the sovereigns. During the time at Farnborough about which I write, this unspent energy, for lack of a wider field, rather forced her into taking much personal interest in the members of her entourage. Always fond of bringing about love matches and busying herself in the minute details of other people's lives, planning and arranging things for them, she was very proud of her achievement whenever a marriage of her making turned out happily, as it often did.

Her phenomenal memory which, through the exigencies of a sovereign's position, she had cultivated and thereby increased to an extraordinary degree, must have been invaluable to her when on the throne. When I knew her in 1886, she remembered the tiniest details, and took an interest in people she had never even seen, retaining minute facts about them that placed them forevermore in her memory. I had occasion to prove this in subsequent visits with her, by inquiries concerning friends of mine, and to realize that in this particular she rivaled her friend Queen Victoria, who possessed a similarly royal gift. Eugénie always spoke in the most glowing terms of the Queen of England and her steadfast friendship, which was thoroughly appreciated, as indeed was any token of genuine affection. She often expressed an immense admiration for Victoria's sterling qualities, quiet strength, and plodding persistence, which made a successful sovereign of a sincere and unaffected woman, while she regretfully admitted that she who had been considered a most brilliant woman had finally through unfortunate circumstances failed to achieve her life's mission.

Never once did I hear Her Imperial Majesty say anything disparaging or resentful about the French nation. In spite of all she had endured at its hands, she remained proudly fond of it, and in 1886 she was continuing most of her former public charities, with the only difference that at this date, of course, her donations came out of her private purse. "Others need not suffer and lose because I have done so," she said to me one day, referring to her still active love for France. She possessed quite a large fortune and was most generous with it in large ways, though not always in small, everyday things of life.[*]

The Empress's religious feeling was warm and real, and came to her both by inheritance and training. I am sure it had been a genuine comfort to her in times of stress, though perhaps a little emotional, and not without a slight poetic tinge of southern superstition. She was almost Oriental in her strong belief in fatality, and certainly *Kismet* did seem to have been, for good or evil, a power in her eventful life.

But the deepest sentiment of all in her whole being had been undoubtedly her love for her son. This was unimpeachable, though her very anxiety for his perfection and the honor of his name had made her over-exacting with him, and had probably caused the affectionate though chivalrous youth to seek a wider horizon of action than his home, that he might show his romantic mother of what he was capable. I gathered these facts from Mme. Le Breton and others, when speaking of the Prince Imperial's departure for Zululand.

The Empress did not in my hearing talk very often about her husband, but whatever she did say always showed a loyalty and respect which did her credit. Whatever his failings toward her had been, she professed a warm admiration for his love of hard work, his pluck, and his great kindness of heart and thoughtfulness for everyone. The Emperor genuinely loved the poor and humble among his subjects, and with no thought of policy. He was too good and generous for his people's understanding. Had he been tyrannical, and made use of

---

[*] I was told at Farnborough, on good authority, that she had at the time about 25,000 pounds a year.

The Emperor Napoleon III

them and trampled them down, like some other sovereigns, they would have behaved better toward him, – so, at least, thought the Empress.

Apropos of the Emperor, she told us on another occasion that he once remarked in a speech: "Mes amis ne sont pas dans les chateaux, – ils sont dans les chaumières [My friends live not in castles, but in cottages]," and that, she added, was an absolute truth. He was a dreamer and devoted much of his time to planning with much sincerity for their benefit and for that of all mankind. His life's ambition was to better their lot. He had great personal magnetism, especially with the laboring classes. Once at a workman's ball the guests were all grumbling and when the Emperor attempted to speak, kept calling out sullenly, "L'Armistice! L'armistice!" and their gestures at last became quite threatening. The Emperor's firmness saved his life. From the platform where he stood, he cried out with a tone of thunder: "Taisez-vous!" It was enough, – at the sound of his voice they dropped their hostile attitude at once, and became amenable and even friendly.

The Empress once mentioned another incident, showing how her husband's personal pluck pleased and impressed the people, and she told it with evident pride in him. I give her own words according to my notes: "Promenade en voiture en temps difficiles, pendant un embarras de voitures, les passants montraient tout le temps le poing dans le visage de l'Empereur, qui ne bronchait pas. Effet morale de son courage qui triomphe;– les mécontents disaient en se retirant penauds et convertis, et en montrant du doigt les Souverains, 'Ceux-ci au moins n'ont pas froid aux yeux!'"*

---

* "A drive in troublous times during a block in the traffic, the passers-by clenched their fists in the face of the Emperor, who remained unmoved. The moral effect of the courage which triumphs. The malcontents while slinking away abashed and converted, pointed to the sovereigns, and said, 'They at least know no fear.'"

The Empress instantaneously charmed every stranger always, but the Emperor, I believe, was really much more personally and deeply loved by his entourage than was his consort. This I gathered, and it was often attested to (indirectly and in a delicate way) by the very evident and genuine enthusiasm shown by Mme. Le Breton and M. Pietri, and even by the faithful old Duc de Bassano, every time there was a chance of speaking of the dead Emperor. Mme. Le Breton's face used to light up as she said to me: "Ah ma petite, vous auriez dû connaître l'Empereur. Ah, en voilà un qui était vraiment bon pour tous!"* – and she never tired of telling of his constant acts of friendliness and courtesy, which, with his hard working perseverance and wonderful faith in his *star*, were according to her, his strongest characteristics.

"On a toujours parle contre moi," the Empress said one day, while I was helping her to arrange and classify her documents, and add the year's accumulation to her already wonderful collection. She let me read some of them, and the sight of well known handwriting brought up all her memories and associations. She exclaimed, "Même avant mon mariage on a dit tout le mal possible sur mon compte. Si j'avais été tout ce qu'on a dit d'horrible de moi ou même la centième partie, j'aurais été une horreur, et je le serai probablement restée plus ou moins en bien des choses encore à l'heure qu'il est. On m'a traitée de 'vieille folle,' d'extravagante, etc. Quant a cette dernière accusation j'étais obligée, vous le comprenez, dans les interêts du commerce, d'acheter constamment ce que personellement je ne désirais pas du tout. Les plaintes et les demandes des fabricants de Lyon et d'autres villes, me priant de mettre tel ou tel velours, telle soie, ou telle dentelle à la mode, étaient continuelles, – et ne pouvaient être ignorées. Ces toilettes commandées par devoir je les appellais mes 'toilettes politiques.'

---

* "Ah, my dear, you ought to have known the Emperor. Ah, there was a man truly kind to all."

"En fait, de toilette particulière, personne n'a été moins gaspilleuse que moi. Je dépensais il est vrai une grande somme mensuelle, mais pas autant que beaucoup de dames de ma cour, qui n'ayant certes pas les mêmes obligations, dépensaient follement sans risques d'être critiquées. Moi du moins j'avais toujours de la méthode et de l'ordre. Je donnais tous les premiers du mois à Pépita, ma tresorière d'alors, une certaine somme d'argent; elle pouvait s'arranger comme elle voulait, mais jamais je ne lui en fournissais davantage. S'il me fallait selon elle acheter une autre toilette ou un objet quelconque, et s'il n'y avait plus d'argent dans la cassette, je me passais de cet objet en dépit de sa mauvais humeur. Par conséquent, malgré ma fuite precipitée, et avec une liste civile de millions de francs, je n'ai laissée pour ainsi dire, presque pas de dettes à Paris, car toute note personelle se réglait le premier du mois de la façon la plus bourgeoise."*

---

* "People have always spoken ill of me." "Even before my marriage they said all possible evil of me. Had I been really all the horrible things they said I was, or even the hundredth part, I should have been a horror then, and I should have remained so probably in many particulars even now. Amongst other things they called me 'vieille folle' and loudly censured my extravagance. Concerning this last accusation you will readily see I was constantly obliged in the interest of trade to buy things I personally did not wish for at all. The complaints and applications from the manufacturers of Lyons and other towns (begging me to set the fashion in a certain velvet or silk, or lace) were constant and could not be ignored. These *duty* dresses I used to call my 'toilettes politiques.' As to my dresses in private life, nobody could have been less wasteful than I. It is true I spent monthly a large sum on dress, but not half as much as some of the ladies of my court, who though they had not the same obligations as to appearance spent recklessly. I at least spent with deliberation and method. I gave on the lst of each month to Pépita (my private treasurer at the time) a certain sum of money. Pépita might do the best she could with it, but never did I add any more. If she wished me to buy some extra garment or any thing else, and there was no more money left, I went without it, in spite of her appeals and subsequent expressions of annoyance. Consequently, notwithstanding my sudden flight and though with a civil list of millions of francs, I hardly left any personal debts in Paris worth mentioning, for every bit of mine was paid regularly the lst of the month in the most bourgeois fashion."

Both from her own statements to me about herself, at different times, and from the testimony of persons who saw her daily at the Palace of the Tuileries when the Empire was at the height of its prosperity and glitter, I believe her reputation for extravagant dressing to be altogether false. Of course at public functions she had to be elegantly and even magnificently dressed, and her radiant beauty enhanced the brilliance of her appearance. These facts taken in connection with the jealousy and envy of less favored persons, seem enough in themselves to have created and confirmed the damning accusations which did her so much harm, and made such a lasting impression on the minds of the French people. Besides which, when defeated and humiliated by Germany, they found it hard to forgive those in power, and vented their wrath on their sovereigns, to whom they attributed all the disasters of war.

My own observations at Farnborough absolutely coincide with what Mme. Carette (who had lived at the Tuileries for several years as *lectrice*, and later as Dame du Palais) says on the subject in her *Souvenirs Intimes de la Cour des Tuileries*. It elucidates the vexed question, I think.

"Chaque jour," she writes (page 165), "chez Elle, aux Tuileries comme dans les autres residences, l'Impératrice était simplement vêtue, avec beaucoup moins de recherche que ne le sont aujourd'hui la plupart des jeunes femmes dans leur maisons. Presque toujours de la faille noire ou du drap peu façonné..

"Pour sortir en voiture a Paris, l'Impératrice ajoutait un manteau très-élégant, un chapeau seyant et très frais, et ceux qui la voyaient passer rapidement dans les beaux équipages de la cour, dans sa daumont menée à quatre chevaux par deux petits jockeys, parfaitement corrects, précédée d'un piqueur à la livrée Impériale, pouvalent croire qu'elle était trèsparée, tandis qu'elle préférait comme toutes les femmes comme-il-faut s'habiller d'une façon pratique et commode. C'est ainsi que je l'ai toujours vue."*

At Farnborough, care in the choosing and handling of her own clothes, and not allowing us, often to our dismay, to wear anything but our oldest garments in bad weather and other occasions, were characteristic traits of the Empress. She wore during the day the most simple black woolen dresses without any trimming, whatever. In the evening for dinner she wore a long plain black silk gown, opened slightly at the neck, and a jet brooch used merely as a fastening, – not a jewel or ornament of any kind, except three plain rings on the fourth finger of her left hand: her own wedding ring, a second gold one (probably the Emperor's) and a platinum guard, – but oh, the infinite grace and dignity of her bearing as she walked into the dining-room! You could not fail to be impressed by her fascinating simplicity, and still she was every inch an Empress.

As a summing up of these characteristics, jotted down just as they come to my mind, or as I have found them scattered through my diary and notes (a record of conversations and events during the ten months spent in closest daily intimacy with the Empress), I think I may say that though she often seemed to share the many little weaknesses of our common

---

* "Every day," she writes (p. 165), "at home, at the Tuileries, as in the other royal residences, the Empress was simply dressed, with much less display than the young women of the present day affect in their own homes. Nearly always black silk or a plainly made cloth gown. To drive out through the streets of Paris the Empress added to this a very elegant mantle, a becoming bonnet always of great freshness, and those who saw her pass rapidly in the beautiful court equipage, in her four-horse *daumont*, driven by two perfectly correct little jockeys and preceded by a *piqueur* in imperial livery, might naturally have imagined her to be overdressed, whereas in reality she preferred, as do all *comme-il-faut* women, to be clothed in a practical and comfortable fashion. It is thus that I always saw her."

The Empress Eugénie about 1880

humanity, yet in times of public calamity, or great personal sorrow, she rose to the heights of a great woman. Her heroic fearlessness during the cholera epidemic in France (1865) was truly worthy of the admiration Europe unstintingly accorded her. Romantic, impulsive, and too proud to do wrong, she nevertheless laid herself innocently open to misunderstanding, and was her own worst enemy. Though in prosperity she may sometimes have seemed rather thoughtless and shallow, she unquestionably improved in this respect under sorrow and anxiety, and attached to herself from then on a coterie of excellent men and women, who by remaining enthusiastically devoted and faithful to her through all these years, have testified to her real inner worth. To me and others, as I said at the beginning of these pages, she was an altogether puzzling mixture of contradictory traits. Not a deep nature, but a sparkling, brilliant and irresistibly fascinating woman.

Toward myself she was invariably thoughtful and kind, even tender at times, always calling me *Petite* when alone in the most intimate and affectionate way. I should have been unimpressionable indeed, even while perfectly aware of her faults, had I not fallen in love with her many charming traits, as I did in point of fact, almost immediately after my arrival at Farnborough.

LATER

Since 1886 I have kept in constant touch with the Empress and her life, through frequent delightful letters from members of her immediate household, her friends, and even from herself. I have enjoyed being able to pay my respects to her, and lunch and dine with her a good many times both at Farnborough and in Paris. The last time we met – in January, 1911 – I found myself by a happy coincidence in rooms contiguous to hers at the Continental Hotel in Paris, and I was glad of the opportunity to see her *sans cerémonie* again. When Madame d'Attainville, her niece, took me in to the Empress, it was toward dusk. She sat in her large room by a blazing fire, buried under an immense fur rug, in a high-backed colonial chair. My first impression was one of disappointinent;– I feared that at last "Time" had laid a heavy hand on her, she looked so small and aged! But when I sat down on a cushion by her side and she began to speak of the past years, her old self reappeared at once. When I dined with her the following evening she came forward to greet me with all her old graciousness. I sat by her side, and she chatted with me with all her former vivaciousness and keen interest in life. I found her absolutely unchanged – as interested as ever in America, and my affairs, and our common friends and acquaintances. She was still the wonderful woman I had admired so much! It was a very happy glimpse – for the very last one!